ABOUT RUNNIN'

" If you are fascinated by recruiting wars, then you will absolutely love Tark's stories. In *Runnin' Rebel*, the Father Flannigan of college hoops, a master at coaching second chance kids into champions, tells about all his successes and failures. "
—*DICK VITALE, ESPN/ABC*

" The way that Barry Switzer laid it all out there in *Bootlegger's Boy*, here comes Tark with the memoir that will make them queasy in the ivory towers of the NCAA. When you're finished with the wildest college basketball story ever told, you'll be left to reconsider what you thought about who the good guys and bad guys are in the sport. "
—*ADRIAN WOJNAROWSKI, AUTHOR OF* THE NEW YORK TIMES *BEST-SELLING* THE MIRACLE OF ST. ANTHONY

" UNLV has been one of the premier programs in college basketball, and one of its most colorful and controversial. Dan Wetzel, one of the brightest and most perceptive basketball writers in the business, captures perfectly the Runnin' Rebels and fleshes out what is perception and what is reality. A great read. "
—*JAY BILAS, ESPN*

" Regardless of your opinion on Tark, he's always been a good quote, and there is no coachspeak in *Runnin' Rebel*. Dan Wetzel was able to elicit the stories to let the public understand one of the more intriguing figures in college basketball history. "
—*ANDY KATZ, ESPN*

" No writer has a greater appreciation for basketball's many characters than Dan Wetzel, and there has been no greater character in the game than Jerry Tarkanian. Whether you come down on the NCAA's side of things or Tark's doesn't matter. There are laughs to be found in every direction. "
—*MIKE DECOURCY, SENIOR WRITER,* THE SPORTING NEWS

" Oh. My. GOSH. Damn what a book. "
—*GREGG DOYEL, SENIOR WRITER, CBS SPORTSLINE*

" Wow! If you thought the NCAA had troubles before, wait'll you read Jerry Tarkanian's *Runnin' Rebel!* Jerry fast breaks his way through a storied career that names names and kicks backsides. We even learn where that towel came from! "
—*JIM BOHANNON, RADIO TALK SHOW HOST OF* THE JIM BOHANNON SHOW, AMERICA IN THE MORNING, AMERICA THIS WEEK, *AND* OFFBEAT

RUNNIN' REBEL

Shark Tales of "Extra Benefits," Frank Sinatra, and Winning It All

JERRY TARKANIAN

with Dan Wetzel

Commentary by
Bob Knight and Greg Anthony

SPORTS
PUBLISHING

Sports Publishing books may be purchased in bulk at special discounts for sales promotion, corporate gifts, fund-raising, or educational purposes. Special editions can also be created to specifications. For details, contact the Special Sales Department, Sports Publishing, 307 West 36th Street, 11th Floor, New York, NY 10018 or sportspubbooks@skyhorsepublishing.com.

Sports Publishing® is a registered trademark of Skyhorse Publishing, Inc.®, a Delaware corporation.

Visit our website at www.sportspubbooks.com.

10 9 8 7 6 5 4 3 2 1

Library of Congress Cataloging-in-Publication Data is available on file.

ISBN: 978-1-61321-214-1

Printed in the United States of America

Contents

Foreword

Basketball is a game that can be played many different ways. There are a wide variety of approaches to defense and all kinds of things a coach can choose to do on the offensive end of the floor. However, there are two things that really stand out in my mind as essential for a coach to get his team to do if it is going to be successful over the long haul of a season.

These two ingredients are getting players to play as hard as they can play each possession of the game at both ends of the floor and doing it as intelligently as possible. I simply try to tell our players that they have to play hard and they have to play smart if we're going to win. I also tell them that my definition of playing hard carries with it a much higher standard than their own definitions would have. Getting players to match my definition of playing hard as a coach is probably the most singular difficult overall skill there is in teaching the game of basketball.

There is no one I have observed in my 40 years of coaching who has been able to do a better job of this consistently than Jerry Tarkanian.

There are three phases of the game where playing hard or not doing so is most noticeable. They are rebounding at both ends of the floor, playing defense, and running the floor to the offensive as well as defensive end. I have always felt that left on their own, players want to play the game as comfortably as they possibly can. That is why to be successful a coach must have much higher standards in regard to playing hard than the players may think possible. Playing hard seems to be a very simple thing, but it is not, and that goes back to the comfort level that the players themselves basically want throughout the game.

Jerry's record at University of Nevada–Las Vegas is one of the outstanding coaching records in the history of college basketball. Let's take a look at how I think he compiled this record through what he taught his teams.

First of all, they exerted great pressure in taking the ball to the offensive end of the floor. They were looking to beat the defense down the floor on every possession, and this was done from the first possession to the last possession of each game they played. Thinking that all kids enjoy the fast break and want to run is a real fallacy in coaching. Again, they want to stay within their comfort level in all that they do on the floor.

The real trick is to get your team to get back.

The key to Tark's success in all that his teams did was his ability to push them way beyond their comfort level, and this was always apparent in the offensive pressure that they placed on the other team. Now the real trick is to get your team to get back on defense with as much energy and concentration as they take the ball to the basket. This is the most difficult thing in basketball for players to learn.

Jerry's teams never failed to make it as difficult as possible for the other team to apply the same kind of pressure as they themselves exerted. Not giving up easy baskets is the direct result of a coach instilling in his players the idea that going to the defensive end of the floor is every bit as important as going to the offensive end of the floor, and Tark was a superb teacher of this concept. So that first ingredient that I think is necessary to success in basketball—running the floor—was taught by Jerry Tarkanian as well as anybody who has ever coached the game.

Second, Tark's teams played both backboards with an energy and a determination that every coach I have ever known would like to see in his own teams. You knew when playing UNLV that if you did not keep them off the offensive boards, you were going to be in for a long night with your defense. At the other end of the floor you were going to really have to work to get good shots. Then not only was your problem in preventing the Rebels from turning a missed shot quickly into a basket at the other end of the floor, but you had to be able to get something off your own offensive board to be in the game.

This was the key to their success, because game after game rarely did the other team get an opportunity at more second-chance baskets than they did. Tark did a great job in teaching his players that the block out and the defensive rebound were keys to limiting the offensive pressure that they consistently exerted in running the floor in the other direction. Just as in running the floor with consistent energy was unmatched by most teams, the same was true of Tark's players' approach to rebounding at both ends of the floor. This was the second of those three ingredients I think is so necessary to basketball success.

That leaves us with the third ingredient, and that is defensive play. Whether on the full court or the halfcourt, Tark's players went at the opponent as though their only objective was to make it impossible for that team to score a basket.

If running the floor to the defensive end is the most difficult thing to teach players, then getting them to play whatever defense you are using with energy and concentration on every possession has to be the second-most difficult thing to teach in basketball, particularly if they are going to have to do this the entire game.

Jerry Tarkanian taught these three ingredients necessary for success in basketball as well as anyone who has ever coached. Tark's teams ran the floor in both directions, rebounded, and played defense as well as any teams I have watched play. In each case it was a direct result of his ability to teach and get them to go to a standard beyond that which they would have set for themselves.

I think that we have covered Tark's teams as far as playing hard is concerned. Now let's look for just a moment at playing smart. When I was a player in high school in Orrville, Ohio, one of our biggest rival games was with Rittman, which was about 10 or 12 miles away. They had an outstanding coach named Ashton Hall, whom I respected enormously. He once told me, while I was still in high school, that basketball was not a game of great plays, it was a game of mistakes, and the team that made the fewest mistakes had the best chance of winning. I have never forgotten this, and it has been an essential part of my approach to coaching from the day I started.

Tark's teams throughout his career have epitomized playing without mistakes and even with the tremendous pressure they exerted on the offensive end of the floor, they did not throw the ball away. They were careful with the basketball. They made sure that they got an opportunity to score rather than giving up the ball without doing so. They were very sound fundamentally at the defensive end of the floor and did not make the kind of mistakes throughout the course of a ballgame that enabled the opponent to get a lot of easy points against them. A team that doesn't make mistakes is a team that has been extremely well prepared and taught by its coach.

I always felt Jerry Tarkanian had a great love for the game of basketball and taught it very effectively as it should be played. This is why in the final analysis, his teams played both very hard and very intelligently while they were playing hard. Too often coaches are afraid to demand the most out of their players. With today's athlete I think being able to demand their best in thought and performance is more important than ever.

The best teachers I have known are intolerant people. Intolerant in many different ways, but one thing is always part of a great teacher's approach and that is getting the students to be better than the students ever thought they could be. I have always said that players will accept and be satisfied with whatever the coach tolerates.

Tark demanded the very best from his players and got it. There is no better recommendation for a coach than that.

Jerry Tarkanian the man has been a person whom I have always enjoyed being around. I'm not sure that I have ever met anyone in all of coaching, regardless of the sport, who has been as successful as he has been and has been as down to earth with an extremely rare sense of humility for what he has accomplished.

As I watched his teams play, I developed a great respect for him as a coach. As I got to know Jerry Tarkanian as a person, I enjoyed him very much as a friend.

—BOB KNIGHT
September 5, 2005
Lubbock, Texas

Acknowledgments

A s with any book, this one could not have reached publication without the work, assistance, help, and support of many people. I want to thank all of the players, coaches, and (most of the) administrators who played for and worked with me throughout the years. There are too many to mention by name, but I cannot thank each of you enough. We had some great times.

I want to give a special thank you to my assistant coaches throughout the years, who were absolutely fabulous. This is especially true for my assistants at Long Beach State, who worked long, long hours for very little pay.

I was blessed with two of the greatest athletic directors a coach could ever work for, Fred Miller and Brad Rothermel. They were both instrumental in my career. There were some tremendous people in Vegas who stood by me during my battle, most memorably Mike Toney, Freddie Glusman, Irwin Molasky, and Chuck Thompson.

In Fresno I had some great friends and supporters during my time with the Bulldogs, including Harry Gaykian, Stan Gajarian, Mike Manouel, Ed Kashian, Mel Renge, Jeff Negeretti, John Shegarian, Jim Tuck, Brian Tahmazian, John Broske, Jim Winton, Carol Reed, Dino Eguilar, and SMI Marketing.

—Jerry Tarkanian

A number of people helped provide background and clarifications, and kept Tark's memory sharp. In particular I want to thank Lois and Danny Tarkanian, Brad Rothermel, Mike Toney, Sonny Vaccaro, and Don Haskins.

Special thanks to Greg Anthony and Bob Knight, who wrote passages for the book despite pressing schedules.

Jonathan Pecarsky at the William Morris Agency helped keep this train moving forward through thick and thin and provided all of the support you can ask of an agent.

At Sports Publishing L.L.C., Elisa Bock Laird is a terrific editor who did a great job with the manuscript and kept the overall tone consistent. Likewise, Kevin King and Scott Rauguth pushed this project from the start.

Craig Stanke, a former editor of mine at CBS Sportsline, proved he could switch over to book editing at any point by making a thorough and detailed effort at a still rough narrative and he made this book infinitely better.

Two books served as incredible resources, *Tark* by Terry Pluto, and *Shark Attack* by my friend Don Yaeger.

Thanks to big-time Tark fan Anton Tielemans of Tielemans Design in Las Vegas, who did a terrific job designing the cover of this book.

Friends and colleagues Adrian Wojnarowski and John Canzano both helped with accuracy and some background information when they gave the manuscript a read through.

Steve Carp, Rob Meich, Steve Cofield, Andy Katz, John Branch, Frank Burlison, David Scott, Mike DeCourcy, Jeff Shelman, Paul Gutierrez, Brian Windhorst, Dick Weiss, Gregg Doyel, Mike Vaccaro, Ian O'Connor, Seth Davis, Michael Rosenberg, Pat Knight, Mike Sheridan, Brian Murphy, Paul and Matt Tryder (the biggest Runnin' Rebel fan in Massachusetts), John Berry, and Pat Mungovan all provided help, inspiration, or a cold beer at one point or the other.

My bosses at Yahoo! Sports Sam Silverstein, Joe Lago, Jeremy Stone, and Greg DeForest never once (out loud at least) wondered if I had developed a gambling problem despite the fact I was always hanging around Vegas.

You can never thank your parents enough, and that is especially true of mine, Paul and Mary Ellen, who have offered so much support through the years.

My wife, Jan, is the greatest friend I could ever have, supportive throughout this process despite having a few important tasks of her own, such as bringing our beautiful daughter, Allie, into the world. She remains the best editor I know and in this case even transcribed most of the interview tapes, which allowed her to perfect one mean Mike Toney imitation.

—Dan Wetzel

Introduction

I have thrown in the towel. In 2002 I retired from coaching after 31 seasons as a NCAA Division I coach, seven as a junior college coach, five as a high school coach in California, and part of one with the NBA's San Antonio Spurs. I won a total of 778 Division I NCAA games, among the 10 most all time for a coach. My .794 winning percentage is among the top five all time. I am probably best remembered for coaching UNLV for 19 seasons, where we reached four Final Fours and captured the 1990 national championship.

I now spend my time visiting with friends and family in Las Vegas and California. I couldn't be happier. Things couldn't be better.

I tell you this as an explanation of why I am writing this book at this time. I will never coach again. *Never.* I'm through. As a result, I have nothing to hide. I have no agenda. I don't have to say things to be politically correct, to paint a good picture for future recruits, or to care about the NCAA getting on my case. The NCAA would probably like to investigate my retirement, but none of that matters to me anymore.

Most of the time when a college basketball or football coach writes a book, he is an active coach, which means he can only say so much. He spends space on the page trying to paint himself in such a good light that none of the stories is even true. It is mostly propaganda. And you can't blame those coaches. If they ever told the truth about what really goes on in college athletics or on their own teams, they'd probably lose their jobs. If they admitted they made mistakes, the press would kill them for it. If they said some high school coach once screwed them on a recruit, they'd know they'd never get another recruit from him again. No one *really* wants to tell the truth.

But I don't care. My reputation is what it is. My days as a coach are over.

During my time as a head coach at the high school, junior college, major college, and NBA levels, I met some of the most incredible people, found myself in some of the most incredible situations, and participated in some of the most incredible basketball games and recruiting chases in history. I fought big schools, big problems, and the NCAA. It was more than a son of Armenian immigrants from Euclid, Ohio, could have ever imagined possible.

And that is the story I want to tell.

Let me start with a basic philosophy of college basketball that you have to understand: What the NCAA says is happening is not necessarily what is happening. The NCAA has the ability to paint people in whatever light they want. They do it by selectively enforcing their rules. They do it by deciding which schools to go after and which to leave alone. And they do it by conducting bogus investigations.

The NCAA would like the American public to believe that only a few schools ever break the rules, and it is never one of their golden programs. But other than making billions off of unpaid kids, has the NCAA ever made you confidently think they know anything about anything?

In major college basketball, nine out of 10 teams break the rules. The other one is in last place. Actually, the way the NCAA rules are written, 99 percent of the schools cheat. But that is because what is humanistic to some is cheating to the NCAA. A coach takes a player to lunch, and it is cheating. If a kid is having some personal issues and he comes to your home to discuss it and you say, "You need to call your mother, here is the phone," that call is cheating.

I don't think that is cheating. That's just being humanistic. The NCAA rules state a player can't receive an "extra benefit." The problem is the NCAA determines what an extra benefit really is, and it depends on how they view your school. At UCLA you could probably buy a kid a car and it wouldn't be considered an "extra benefit." At someplace else, you couldn't buy a kid a gallon of gas.

People always wonder why the NCAA investigated me for almost three decades and spent more money looking into my programs than any other in history. The reason is because they couldn't get me. Usually when the NCAA comes in and puts a school on probation, the coach gets fired. But I survived every time. My program actually got stronger. And that just made them more determined. They investigated my teams like no other team ever. If they had done that to any other school in the country, they would have found all sorts of violations. That's reality.

Once you understand that this is the truth—that this is the way it really, truly is—then what goes on in college basketball will appear in a completely different light. It is not what the NCAA says it is.

Not that I cared what schools or coaches did. I only cared about how the NCAA wouldn't investigate everyone evenly. I only cared that the media ripped one guy for doing the same thing another guy was doing.

What is cheating anyway? Take a step back and consider the big picture. In 99 percent of the cases, it is either having a rich booster give a poor kid money or giving the chance to go to college to a kid who doesn't deserve that chance. That's it. Getting a kid or his family a small amount of cash (compared to the NCAA revenue) or getting a couple more guys into some massive freshman class. They build statues and hold dinners for people who do that in other segments of society. But in college basketball, that is cheating. It is paying kids or academic fraud.

The NCAA doesn't want to consider it like that. But for a long time there, I thought the mob had better morals than those guys. The NCAA is all about the money. In the spring of 2005 they passed legislation that expanded the college football season from 11 games to 12 games for the sole reason of making the kids produce one more week of ticket and parking revenue. Now the best college teams, with conference championship and bowl games, play a 14-game season, which is what the NFL season used to be. The NCAA didn't even pretend why they did it. They admitted it was because of one thing—money.

"These institutions need money for the commitments they've made," said NCAA president Myles Brand. "I think those who voted in favor of a 12th game saw it as a way to increase revenue."

These hypocrites don't care one bit about the kids. Not one single bit. It is just about their salaries going up and their TV revenues increasing. You have to understand that also.

I am not here to write just about the NCAA, though. They don't deserve the attention. I love college basketball, and the great part of college basketball is the players, the games, the fans, the fun, and producing a winning team that gets everyone excited. When we had it rolling at UNLV, it was like nothing else. Las Vegas was the greatest college basketball town in America. We had the glitz and glimmer of The Strip, of our famous Gucci Row, which were the seats on the floor. But mostly we were a blue-collar team for a blue-collar town. Vegas is more about the casino employees, waitresses, cooks, and construction workers than it is the high rollers. They didn't go to UNLV, but they loved us.

The popularity of those teams changed my life. I've been in six major motion pictures, conducted basketball clinics around the globe, and given speeches to packed houses around the country. I one time even had a horse named after me, Tark the Shark. It was great. I didn't know much about horse racing then, but Tark the Shark did okay. Until he was gelded, which I didn't feel too good about.

During my time at Long Beach State (1968-1973), UNLV (1973-1992), and Fresno State (1995-2002), we had fans not just from those communities, but from across America. They liked the way we played. They liked that I gave black kids a chance before almost anyone else. They liked that we were just blue-collar guys. They liked that we fought the big schools and the NCAA hypocrisy. They liked that we won.

I remember recruiting back in New York during the late 1980s, and we would go to a playground or open gym and the guys hanging around the court, real tough street guys, broke up their dice games, stopped hanging out—doing who knows what—and came over and shook my hand. They all knew who I was. They all knew the Runnin' Rebels and how I always gave a chance to kids when others wouldn't. It was unbelievable, really. I was big with those guys.

I guess that's why wherever I go now, people always want me to tell a story. They mostly want to know about the big recruiting battles, and we certainly had some memorable ones. Or the colorful players we had. Or what life in the 1970s in Las Vegas was like, when my friends included Frank Sinatra and Sammy Davis. Or why I chewed on a towel. Or how I fought the NCAA until they had to pay me $2.5 million. Or about our championship team at UNLV, the near-undefeated one the next year, or all of the great players we had out there. Or how three of my players wound up in a hot tub with a sketchy guy. They want to hear about the good, the bad, and everything in between.

So right here, right now, I am going to tell my stories. Not just ones that make me look smart or portray me in a certain light or will please some people, including people who are my friends. This is the truth. The truth about four decades in the middle of some of the wildest games, recruiting battles, and craziest situations that college sports has ever seen.

1

How It Really Goes Down

" Oh, don' t worry, Coach, it' s taken care of. USC sent a dentist out to my house. "

—*Bruce Clark's mother*

Before I start at the beginning, let me tell you about the time I learned how college basketball really works. I coached Long Beach State from 1968 to 1973, and we went 116-27, reached four NCAA Tournaments, and at one point were ranked No. 3 in the entire country. It was incredible. I don't think anyone ever realizes what we did at Long Beach State.

But as good as we were, one day I realized I couldn't stay there. The difficulties in recruiting were just too great. The school didn't have the money, the resources, or the alumni to win over the long haul, and that kept getting hammered home to me. Big schools, especially big state schools, just have a huge advantage over smaller schools in recruiting, not just because of media exposure and fan support, but because of the institutional might of the school. The player who convinced me I needed to go to a school like that was Bruce Clark.

Bruce was a six-foot-eight center from Jefferson High School in Los Angeles. In 1969, he was considered the best player in L.A. We started on him when he was a sophomore. He came to our Long Beach State games, and we introduced him around. He loved us. He absolutely loved us.

He told us he didn't like USC, and he said although UCLA was recruiting him, John Wooden wasn't doing anything. UCLA had won the NCAA title every year, so if Wooden got involved with a recruit, it was usually over. But it was just the assistants who were recruiting him. Other than that, it was out-of-town schools, San Francisco and Arizona State. So I thought we had a heck of a chance. I thought we pretty much had Bruce wrapped up.

But that was when it got crazy. The guy who lived across the street from me in Huntington Beach was someone I grew up with in Pasadena. He worked in the stock market. Bruce was really smart, and he was interested in the stock market. He wanted to learn more about it and maybe be a stockbroker one day. So I got my neighbor to hire Bruce for a summer job even though Bruce was still in high school. I thought this was a perfect idea. Bruce was about to start work for my friend when he backed out of the job.

The USC coaches thought it was a good idea, too, and they got him a job with a brokerage firm making twice the money. That was a big problem for us; everything we did, USC could go and do double. We were a teachers college, so we didn't have any stockbroker alumni; all we had was my neighbor. USC had half of Los Angeles wired.

Then one day I was sitting in my office, and Bruce's mother called us. (When the mother of a top recruit calls a college coach's office, everything stops. She gets patched through immediately, because often it's not the player who makes the final decision on where to attend school. So a mom, you can't afford to get on her bad side.) The call came through.

My assistant Ivan Duncan answered and said, "Hi, how are you? What's happening?"

Small talk. And Bruce's mom said things weren't good because she had a toothache.

A toothache? Like I would normally care if this woman had a toothache? But this was Bruce Clark's mother, and I did care. And she knew I would care. She didn't have to say another word.

Ivan told her, "Oh, that's terrible. Hang tight, and I'll see if we can do something to help."

I immediately got the phonebook out and started to call dentists I knew. I finally found a guy who would take care of the toothache if she came over to his office. Ivan called her back and told her to drive over to see Dr. So-and-So.

"Oh, don't worry, Coach, it's taken care of," she said. "USC sent a dentist out to my house."

See, whatever we could do, USC could do double. I started getting concerned at that point. Bruce kept telling us that he wasn't interested in USC and that he wouldn't go there, but USC had him hooked up with a summer job and gotten his mother's toothache fixed. Then we found out his sister had gotten a job from two USC alums. They were working the periphery well.

We were still in there strong, though, when my wife and I went to the City-CIF All-Star game. They used to have a game with the best players from the City of Los Angeles against the best players in the CIF, which is the high school league for most of the rest of Southern California. Bruce was incredible; he had 31 points and 19 rebounds and played absolutely great. UCLA had barely been recruiting him, but Wooden was at the game, and Bruce got his attention.

After the game, they introduced Bruce to Wooden, who talked to him for about two minutes. UCLA hadn't even been in the picture until then. I had been recruiting him for three years, and USC had been all over him. But Bruce had met Wooden.

"It's a tossup between you and UCLA," he said to me.

"What?"

"I talked to Coach Wooden."

I was like, "Talk? I've been working on you for three years." But that's how strong Wooden was back then.

My wife, Lois, heard about this, though, and she started working over Bruce's mom. And she convinced Bruce's mom that it wouldn't be right for Bruce to go to UCLA because they were just jumping in at the end. And Bruce's mom agreed. I couldn't believe it; Lois wiped out UCLA in one conversation. So we still had a chance.

Later that spring Bruce was set to graduate from Jefferson High School. They held the graduation at the football field on about the hottest June day I can remember. Ivan and I decided to be there. They had these chairs out on the football field; the sun was beating down—hot, hot, hot. We were sweating like crazy.

We were the only two white guys at his graduation, so we stood out like sore thumbs. Everyone was looking at us and wondering what the heck these two white guys were doing at the ceremony.

"No looking bored, no looking hot or tired or disinterested," I told Ivan. "Everyone is looking at us."

Again, you never know who that peripheral person is who will make the decision. So when they announced a graduate, we stood and cheered like it was our own son. Every last kid. They'd say, "Roosevelt Booker," and we'd get up and start clapping. When they got to Bruce, we went wild.

Afterward, his dad had a graduation party, and because we had been to the graduation, his dad invited us. We were the only white guys invited to the party. It was at this condominium, not a very big place, but we were sitting there thinking we were in great shape. We were having the time of our lives. As far as we were concerned, this was the greatest party ever thrown. I really thought we were getting Bruce.

Then about two weeks later, we heard they were having a press conference, and Bruce was going to USC. We couldn't believe it. But they held the thing in the press box of Dodger Stadium, right in front of the media there.

So we wound up losing him, and I was devastated. Then the next day, Bruce showed up on our campus, in our office crying. He broke into tears because he said he had wanted to choose us. When he said that, I broke into tears. Then my assistants broke into tears. Everyone was in tears. We were all hugging each other.

I said, "Bruce, what happened? Why did you commit to USC?"

"Coach, I had to go to USC. I had to go."

He just kept saying it over and over. He wouldn't say anything more than that.

That night I was at home, just devastated over losing Bruce. Then I got this call at about 2 a.m. from Ivan who said he was with Bruce's dad. Ivan had picked up a bottle of whiskey and gone over to the dad's condo, and they were both drunker than hell.

"Coach, we are still going to get Bruce," Ivan said. "Here's his dad."

I started talking to Bruce's dad, but it didn't matter. The deal was done. It was over.

I don't know exactly what happened, but all I know is the whole family moved out of that little condo and got a nice house in Pasadena. And then his dad got a job with Columbia Studios in Hollywood.

When I heard that, I called his dad up and said, "Did USC get you that job?"

And he just said, "No. John Wayne did."

2

One of the Guys

"My upbringing was why I always related so well to kids from tough backgrounds or single-parent homes."

—JERRY TARKANIAN

I am an Armenian. That doesn't mean a lot to a lot of people, but to Armenians, it means everything. And for good reason. For centuries, Armenians were discriminated against and persecuted because we were Christians living in Turkey, which was a Muslim country. In 1915, the Ottoman government in Turkey began slaughtering Armenians, and by 1922, 1.5 million were killed. It was like the Jewish Holocaust, just a terrible genocide, but it never got much attention worldwide. Even today, it's referred to as the "Forgotten Genocide."

It wasn't forgotten in our home, though. I grew up on 200th Street in Euclid, Ohio, just outside Cleveland, where a large Armenian community lived. Both of my parents are Armenian, and just getting to Ohio was an achievement that no Armenian took lightly. And they were quick to teach that to their children.

When my mother, Haighouhie "Rose" Tarkhanian, was still young, the genocide began. Both her father, Mickael, and her brother, Mehran, were decapitated by the Turkish military just for being Armenian. In the town my mother lived in, the Turkish military rounded up a group of women and children, locked them in a church, and set it on fire, killing them all. My mother said she never forgot the screams she heard coming from that blaze. They haunted her for the rest of her life.

Fortunately, my grandmother decided to send her children off before it was too late. She sewed some money into my mother's dress and sent her and her younger brother on horseback out of the country to safety. My mother was just a girl, but she had to fend for herself and her brother. Eventually, a friendly Turkish family took them in and then found them passage to Syria and then on to Lebanon. It was there that my mother met my father, George Tarkanian. They married soon thereafter and immigrated to the United States, eventually setting down roots where a community of Armenians offered some support and familiarity.

In 1927, my older sister, Alice, was born. And in 1930, I came along. My mother tried to name me Gregory, after an Armenian saint. But her English was so bad, the nurses just wrote down Jerry. That is my name, Jerry Tarkanian. Not Gerald. No middle name, either. Just Jerry Tarkanian.

My father started a small neighborhood grocery store in Euclid, and the family all worked in the business. Then to make additional money, my dad worked in a Chrysler plant. He worked two jobs. He worked so hard, but that wasn't unusual, because this was during the Great Depression. Euclid was a tough, mostly Italian area and I remember all of the fathers always carrying lunch pails to work in the factories. But they were the lucky ones who had jobs. It was just tough times.

I can hardly imagine now how difficult it was for them. Everything was so difficult, so new. My mother and father spoke Armenian in the home. But I guess having been toughened up by what they came through, America was paradise. Armenians all work hard and to this day do. It's that forged identity of surviving the genocide. We didn't have any money. But we didn't know we were poor. No one in Euclid had any money. Later when I was about 20, I played on a summer basketball team sponsored by a company, and one night the owner took us all out to a steakhouse. I had prime rib for the first time in my life, and that was the

best piece of meat I'd ever seen. To this day, I can remember it. I had
never had anything like that. I never knew anybody could eat that well,
and I never knew food could taste that good. It was incredible.

But when you don't know what you're missing, you don't miss it. So
when I was a kid, I couldn't have been happier.

Everything changed, though, when I was 10 and a half years old. My
father got tuberculosis and died. All of a sudden, we were alone. We lost
the grocery store, and we had to move from Euclid to 140th Street in
Cleveland. That wasn't a long way, but when you're a kid, it seemed like
another state. Then we moved to Cleveland Heights. I was very unhappy
because I was 14 years old, and I had moved three times in a year and a
half. I no longer had my friends, and I no longer had my father. So I was
actually happy when my mother said we were moving to Pasadena,
California. I knew that was a long way away, but she said once we moved
there, we wouldn't have to move again. Even though I had loved Euclid
and I didn't want to ever leave, we all agreed we just needed a fresh start.
California sounded like a good idea.

The reason we moved to Pasadena was there was a small Armenian
community there. It turned out to be perfect. My mother used to wake
up in the morning and look out the kitchen window and see those
mountains and clear blue sky. Back then there was only one freeway, the
Pasadena Freeway to L.A., so there wasn't much smog. You went just a
mile or two miles out of Pasadena, and you'd run into the orange groves.
And my mother used to say, "God bless Pasadena." She just loved it, and
we all did.

It was so different than Cleveland, and I just couldn't believe how
great it was. At night there would be no mosquitoes or bugs. It would
cool off, and you could sleep. It was just like paradise; it never snowed.

My mother remarried when I was 14 and she and her husband bought
an apartment building right on Colorado Boulevard. Although it wasn't
real big or real fancy, it was enough to keep us going. The Rose Bowl
parade went right by it.

My upbringing was why I always related so well to kids from tough
backgrounds or single-parent homes. Especially black kids. When I first
became a coach, there were still colleges that wouldn't admit black
students, and a lot of basketball coaches were uncomfortable coaching

black kids. Even schools that were integrated wouldn't take more than one or two blacks, and they usually came from suburban schools.

I was always at home with the city kids. I just never cared. I understood what it was like to be raised by one parent, to grow up poor, and to have to move around and scrape to get things. I knew what it was like to be a poor student. I even knew what it was like to be discriminated against. Being Armenian and being black in America are two very different things, but there are some similarities. I think all of that was why, when I went recruiting later in life, I was completely comfortable with people of all backgrounds. Who was I to look down on anyone? I was like them. I *was* them.

I attended Pasadena High School and played basketball. All I did was play ball. And maybe drink some beer. I barely got out of high school. Then I attended Pasadena City College, and it was pretty much the same. I loved sports. I loved hanging around the guys. I didn't care very much for schoolwork. I had a lot of fun. Eventually I graduated from junior college, but I was never a good student.

Pasadena was a great time then. It was the late 1940s, and a lot of guys were getting out of the service and coming back to the junior college. There was a big group of guys there who formed a strong bond that has lasted forever. (Each year we have a big reunion, and even when I was coaching at UNLV, I never missed it. I'd fly in for it every year. One guy picked a local bar, and about 30 of us went in there and had the greatest time. The reunion has kept growing, though, to the point we have it in the press box of the Rose Bowl in Pasadena. And they do it twice a year now.)

One day when I was in junior college, some coaches from Fresno State showed up and offered scholarships to five of us—my friend Dale Arambel and I for basketball and the other three for football. We all jumped at the chance to get an education and go to the same school. Fresno State was perfect for us; it was about a four-hour drive north from Pasadena in the Central Valley. Far enough from home to feel like we were getting away, but not so far we couldn't get back to the old neighborhood if we wanted to.

I lived with six, seven, or eight guys at Fresno State, so our house was the party house. They used to call us the "Fun Guys." They were all football and basketball players, and we had one cheerleader. His name was Sid Craig, and he would go on to marry Jenny Craig, who would go on to start a diet business that has been incredibly successful. They built up that huge business together.

In college I had tunnel vision: basketball and partying. I didn't care at all about school. I just wanted to have a good time. That is probably why it took me six years to get through junior college and Fresno State. I just didn't care. I was having too much fun. I wasn't a great player at Fresno, but I worked hard. I was mostly a practice player, but I was very good on defense. I was kind of a floor burns guy. Even though I wasn't the best player, I was named team captain as a senior.

I met two very important people in my life in Fresno. The first was Clark Van Galder, the football coach. Most of my friends were football players, and to make some extra money, I got a job working for Coach Van Galder. I was his gofer, personal assistant, whatever. He was a great man. He really looked after me, and when it comes to influencing my career as a coach, he had the greatest impact.

Van Galder was a really intense coach, and he demanded that his players match his intensity on the field. There was no lack of toughness there. But then off of the field, he was relaxed; he befriended his players. He believed the best way to motivate players was to forge an emotional bond with them, be their friend, and gain their trust. I had never met a coach like that. Back in the 1950s, everyone was like Vince Lombardi and Bear Bryant. Players and coaches could never be friends. But he felt his way would make his kids care more, and they would play with more intensity than the team that hated its coach. That really struck a cord with me and influenced the way I approached coaching. Just about everything I achieved as a coach I owe to Clark Van Galder.

The most important person I met at Fresno State was my wife, Lois. We may have attended the same school, but we were complete opposites. Lois was smart, pretty, and a very hard worker. She graduated in just three years, and the last year she held a full-time teaching position in the Fresno School System. We were opposites. She got nearly all As. I barely passed. She didn't party. That's about all I did. She didn't like sports. I was obsessed with it. She was serious about the future. I wasn't.

The first time I asked Lois out was when some friends and I got hauled in front of the student court. Back then Fresno was really just a farm town, it wasn't nearly as big as it is now, and most of the kids who went to Fresno State were from rural areas. As a result, they had a square dance club. Remember, this is the early 1950s. Well, the square dance club was putting on this big square dance, and my friends—which included Darryl Rogers, who would go on to coach at Arizona State, Michigan State, and the Detroit Lions—and I didn't think much of square dancing, so we snuck into the dance and pulled the plug on the music. I know it sounds like nothing now, but back then it was this big thing. Everyone was mad at us for ruining the square dance. So we got sent in front of the student court, which had the power to suspend us.

Lois was on the student court. I asked her out before our hearing, but she said no. She thought I was just trying to influence her vote on my punishment and get her to go easy on me. But then after we got our punishment, I kept asking her out. She said no a bunch of times because we didn't have much in common, but finally I wore her down, and she said yes. The problem was I was so poor. I couldn't afford to take her anywhere. I just had no money. My mother had given me this old, old Hudson that barely ran. That was my car. And the only way to get it started was to park it on top of this hill near my house, pop it into neutral, and as the car rolled down the hill, pump the engine alive.

On our first date we went to a diner to have coffee. All of the college kids drank coffee, and it was five cents a cup. I had enough for two cups of coffee, but not much more than that. Only Lois didn't drink coffee. She had to be the only girl at Fresno State who didn't drink coffee. She ordered hot chocolate. But that went for 20 cents a cup. She damn near bankrupted me on our first date.

We started going out my junior year, and she cleaned up my act a little bit. It took a while. I was still into partying more than studying, but Lois was a good influence on me. If it hadn't been for her, I might still be trying to get my degree. I just wasn't the most romantic guy, I guess. The night of our wedding, we didn't have any money for a real honeymoon, so I took her to the Idaho State–Fresno State football game. She still hasn't forgiven me. She still brings that one up. I don't blame her, but it seemed like a good idea at the time.

Even with Lois getting me a little more on the straight and narrow, the summer before my senior year, I wasn't sure if I would graduate. I was behind academically and didn't really care. Then I took a summer job back in Pasadena at National Biscuit. I drove a truck and delivered biscuits in the morning and then worked in the warehouse at night. I carried a lunch pail to work, just like the Armenian fathers back in Euclid.

I just remember thinking, "God, what a miserable job." It wasn't real hard work; it was just no fun. It was the kind of job you punched in and then you could hardly wait until the 10 a.m. coffee break. Then you could hardly wait until the lunch break. Then you could hardly wait until the 2:30 p.m. coffee break. And then you couldn't wait to go home. That motivated me for school, because it made me so happy when the summer was over. When I got back to school, I was determined to not have to go back to the National Biscuit warehouse in Pasadena. I became a dedicated enough student to pass my classes and graduate from college.

I was 26 years old and married. I needed a job. There was only one thing I figured I was qualified to do.

3

Climbin' the Ladder

" And if that high school gym in California had been air-conditioned back in 1960, I probably never would have started sucking on towels. "

—*JERRY TARKANIAN*

I was actually a coach even before I graduated from Fresno State with a teacher's degree. I did my student teaching at Edison High School, a predominantly black school in Fresno, and just before the season, the basketball coach had a nervous breakdown. They named the assistant football coach the basketball coach, but he told me he didn't know anything about basketball. So I became the basketball assistant, and I handled all of the Xs and Os. He did the halftime talks and discipline. It was great. Edison had a lot of talent, and we won the city and county championships. I hadn't been around blacks very much until then, so I learned about that, too. When we played Taft High School, which is down near Bakersfield, for the Valley Championship, we couldn't eat a

13

pregame meal in the town because the restaurants wouldn't serve our black players. Then the crowd there said all sorts of racist things.

Other than that, Edison High was a great experience. And that assistant football coach who didn't know anything about basketball was named Fresno Coach of the Year. This was a confidence boost for me, because if I hadn't turned out to be a basketball coach, I don't know what I could have done. There were not a lot of things I had any skill in. I couldn't fix anything. I couldn't hammer a nail straight. So becoming a high school teacher and coach was perfect for me.

In 1956, I got hired by San Joaquin Memorial, a Catholic school in Fresno. I loved that place and have always been indebted to it for giving me my break. Throughout the years, anytime they called and asked for fundraising help, I would fly up and do whatever I could. We went 18-4 my second year, and after my oldest daughter, Pam, was born, I took a job in Southern California at Antelope Valley High School in Lancaster because it paid more money. But Antelope Valley was a football school, so I was only there one season before jumping to Redlands High School just outside San Bernardino.

I was in Redlands for two seasons, and two important things happened. The first was that I decided to get a master's degree. I figured it would help if I ever wanted to coach at the college level. And if not, you got a jump in pay as a high school teacher if you had a master's. With our second daughter, Jodie, on the way, I needed the money.

So I enrolled at the University of Redlands, which as a school was about five times harder than Fresno State. But I was very determined now. Education was important to me, and I got all As and one B in my master's. That taught me a lesson. Academics is often just about priorities and focus. At Fresno State, I had neither. When I went to Redlands I was married and had two kids. I wanted to get that master's degree, and I knew it was important for my future, so I studied and worked hard.

That helped me in coaching because it helped me realize that a lot of these kids are not bad students—it's just that their priorities aren't in order. They just didn't realize how important an education was. So when I was recruiting, and someone said the kid was a bad student, I related back to my experience. I was a bad student, and I wound up getting near straight As in a master's program. So I always gave kids a chance. And that burned me sometimes, but I always did it.

The second big thing was when my Redlands High team was playing in the 1960 league championship game against Ramona. It was really hot in the gym, and my mouth kept getting dry. I could hardly yell to my team. I kept going to get drinks from the water fountain. Back and forth, back and forth. Finally, I got tired of doing that, so I took a towel, soaked it under the water fountain, and carried it back to the bench. Then when I got thirsty, I sucked on the towel.

We won the game and the league championship. Because I was a superstitious person, I kept sucking on towels the rest of my career. It became my trademark, me sucking on a white towel during the most stressful times of a game. Everywhere I go, people ask me about the towel. People used to mail me them. Fans brought towels to the game and sucked on them, too. It was the big thing. Eventually when I was at UNLV, we got smart and started selling souvenir "Tark the Shark" towels. We sold more than 100,000 of them. It was incredible.

And if that high school gym in California had been air-conditioned back in 1960, I probably never would have started sucking on towels.

Redlands is only eight miles from Riverside, California, so the success we had at Redlands High School caught the attention of Bill Noble, the president of Riverside City College. Before the 1961-1962 season, he was looking for a coach who could win a championship and called me. We talked for a few hours, he offered me the job, and I took it. Just like that, I was a junior college coach. I was really excited.

When I say I had some great teams and coached some great players in junior college, I mean it. At a time when other coaches were wary of juco players, I loved jucos. I was a juco, and I was always proud that I was a juco. There are great players in junior college ball now, guys who didn't qualify for a four-year scholarship or got their game together late. But back then, the talent in juco was even better, because so few schools recruited blacks. Even the ones that did take blacks would only have one or two guys. So a lot of juco players were playing at that level not because of grades but because of race. That was why there was so much talent.

And that was why I got so many great players to play for me at Riverside City College (1961-1966) and Pasadena City College (1966-1968). I didn't care about race. I didn't care at all. I would take someone of any color.

What we did with those players in that era is one of the greatest accomplishments of my life. I am just so proud of what happened, and not just on the basketball court. At Riverside, I took over a program that went 10-18, and in five years we won three California state championships. In my last three seasons there, we went 97-6. We had some great teams, but we had even better people. I look back on the lives that were changed because of junior college, and I can't believe it. In 2004, we had a big reunion of my Riverside teams, and it was just amazing to see what happened to all of those kids.

The first two kids I recruited were from Cleveland—Tommy Crowder and Sam Knight. They rode a bus all of the way from Cleveland to California. They had a stop in Oklahoma, and when they went into this restaurant to eat, they wouldn't serve them because they were black. They didn't refuse to serve them, or say anything specific, they just never waited on them. They just ignored them.

Eventually the guys got the hint, so they got back on a bus and were forced to eat candy bars and potato chips all of the way from Oklahoma to California. That was all they had. It took them three days to get to Riverside. When they arrived, all of their belongings were in big grocery bags. They didn't even have luggage. It was my first year coaching, and I wanted to get them jobs so they had some money, but I didn't know that much about where they could work. I didn't know the community that well and didn't have many connections. All I could get them was a job in our school cafeteria as bus boys. They did such a great job that the lady there called and thanked us. Then she got them summer jobs, so they stayed in California all summer and worked.

Both of those kids graduated from Riverside. Crowder went on to graduate from Hayward State up in the Bay Area. Then he went to USC and got his master's degree. The best part of the story is his kids. He has one son who graduated from West Point, another son who graduated from Harvard, and a daughter who received a full academic scholarship to Cal–Berkeley and graduated. Now she works for Governor Arnold Schwarzenegger in Sacramento. At the Riverside reunion, she hugged me and said over and over, "You know, growing up I knew more about you than I did my grandparents. We owe everything to you."

After graduating from Riverside, Knight stayed in town, and my wife got him a job at the School for the Deaf and he worked as a counselor and then in group homes. He served on the local school board. He had five kids. He had one daughter who graduated from UC–San Diego, which is a great academic school. The other four kids all were major college football players. One of them played at Colorado, and the other three played at USC. One of them, Sammy Jr., is a defensive back for the Miami Dolphins.

That same year we had a kid named Joe Barnes from Detroit. Through some contacts I had gotten in touch with a high school coach in the area, George Gaddy. We hit it off, and he sent me Joe. Before Riverside, Joe had gone to Central State in Ohio, and he had a problem there. He wouldn't tell me what it was, but something had happened, and he had wound up back in Detroit washing dishes in a restaurant. Joe had a real passion for chemistry, and his goal was to earn his master's degree.

This seemed farfetched for a dishwasher from Detroit, but I had a lot of faith in Joe. So I made this deal with the president of Riverside City College: If Joe ever got his degree and his master's, the president had to give Joe a job at Riverside as a teacher. The president of the school thought it was a great story, so he agreed. But then he left, and I wasn't sure the bet would stand. In 1965, Pasadena City College recruited me to become the head coach there. While we were talking over the job, I told the Pasadena president about Joe and said I wouldn't go unless they made the same deal Riverside made. He agreed, and Joe not only graduated from Riverside City College, he went on and got an undergraduate and master's in chemistry from Whittier College. When he graduated, Pasadena City College lived up to its promise and hired him. Joe retired in 2005 after 35 years as a chemistry professor there.

We also had a guy named Lucky Smith. Lucky was in the Air Force, he was about 22 years old and married, and had a kid. I wasn't paid much money when I coached at Riverside, so to make some extra cash I used to run the clock at the basketball games in the City League. Afterward, I would go out with the guys for some beer and pizza. That's when I met Lucky, who was a heck of a player in the City League games.

One day he said to me, "Coach, I'd love to go back to school, but I'm married. I own a home here, and I got a little kid. I can't afford it."

I told him I understood, but getting an education would be a good investment. So he and I talked to his wife and we set up a plan. They sold the house, she went back to work, and Lucky came to Riverside. He got his degree, made first-team all-state, and received a full scholarship to play at Hawaii. He wound up getting drafted by the Milwaukee Bucks and hung around the NBA a little while. With his degree, he went up to the Bay Area and got into computers. He has a deal with Oakland public schools, one of the largest computer deals in the Oakland area. He made a fortune in computers; he's a multimillionaire. The little kid he had now has my old job as the head basketball coach at Riverside City College. It's incredible.

The kids at Riverside spoiled me, because it made me think that all kids were going be like that, and I took a lot of chances as a result. But not all kids are like that. I was lucky. If those kids had been real assholes, I could have gotten fired and never had another job. That would have ended my career then and there. But those three guys from the Midwest and Lucky were great guys. I only wish all of my players were like them.

I have always felt the media and fans miss this point. There are schools that get a lot of credit for educating players and for graduating players. And there are others that don't. But those guys at Riverside are what I point to. For me, it's about rungs on a ladder: How many rungs on the ladder did you help a guy climb? It is about providing an opportunity that they wouldn't otherwise have gotten.

Consider a place like Stanford. I have a lot of respect and admiration for Stanford—it's one of the best schools in the country. If you coach there, you attract some of the best student-athletes in the country, kids who are serious about school. And you would get praised for getting those kids an education, even if you were bringing in a six-foot-eight guy who would have gone to Stanford even if he was five foot eight. The Stanford players would have graduated from college even if basketball never existed. If you coach at a place like Stanford, you bring the kids in, they do great, and everyone celebrates.

But I look at the rungs of the ladder that a school such as Riverside provided for Joe. He went from washing dishes in Detroit to a chemistry professor. To me, that is what college athletics are all about. That is what junior colleges are all about. There are dozens of other kids from my junior college days who had the same success. People would criticize me for bringing in guys with sketchy academic backgrounds. But look at the opportunity we provided them.

It is a heck of a lot more impressive story to take a kid from the projects who had no future and get him a degree than to get a kid from an upper-class background who would have gone to college anyway and gotten a degree. Even if some of my guys didn't graduate or become millionaire computer guys like Lucky Smith, maybe they just got solid middle-class jobs and just learned how to live better lives. Even if they didn't actually graduate, they got into a college setting and learned about a world outside of their neighborhood. They learned to value education, they learned how important college is, and then they stressed it to their children. Even if they didn't become doctors or lawyers, a generation later, their kids might become doctors or lawyers.

I won't apologize for all of the players I brought into college that other schools wouldn't. I won't apologize because some of them never graduated or never got serious about school. I tried. I took a lot of criticism for that, but if you ever came to a reunion like the Riverside one, you would see that those are great stories—kids who make you proud of them, not ashamed.

4

"Bad Apples" and State Champs

❝ Coach, he's my idol. Trapp is the toughest dude in the world. I don't want to mess with that man. ❞

—*CRAZY KHRUSCHEV*

I never went along with the theory that if a kid had a problem with a coach, then the player was a bad kid. I've seen a lot of coaches who are bad guys. I've seen a lot of coaches who couldn't get along with kids or didn't treat kids right. The kid always got the blame, but that didn't mean he deserved it. Why is the coach always right and the player always wrong?

I learned that lesson early during my first year at Riverside City College. I took over a program that went 10-18 overall and 1-13 in its conference. So I needed some players. That first year we went 14-13. That was the worst season I ever had as a college coach. In 38 years (31 in the NCAA), I never had a losing season and won .813 percent of my games. But I didn't know that was coming. When we were going 14-13, I was just worried I would end up back in the National Biscuit plant.

During my first season at Riverside (1961-1962), right there at Riverside Poly High School, there was a kid named Bobby Rule who was six foot eight with long arms and great athletic ability. I wanted him the first time I saw him play. I knew if I could get Bobby, I wouldn't be working in any factories. But Bobby didn't have a good year as a senior. He was lazier than hell, and he and his coach didn't get along. But I still wanted him for junior college. I thought he could be a heck of a player. There was something about him I liked.

I went over and talked to his coach.

"Don't touch that kid," he warned me. "That kid will never play hard for you. You can't win with that kid."

Well, I tried to be nice to the coach, but I wanted Bobby Rule, and I got Bobby Rule. And we went 67-3 with Bobby and won a state junior college title. He might be the best player I ever coached. He is the most dominant player in the history of California junior college basketball. After two years with me, he went to Colorado State and then spent eight years in the NBA and was even an All-Star. He was one of the few guys who could get 30 points on Wilt Chamberlain.

He was a great player and a great kid from a great family. There was nothing wrong with Bobby. It was his coach who couldn't deal with him. Once I figured that out, it was no problem. I even had Lois meet him, and she thought he'd be fine. The key to coaching kids like that is communication and loyalty. You have to communicate with them at all times. You have to get through to them. And you have to express loyalty so they can trust you. Do that, and a kid will play hard for you, even if he didn't play hard for other coaches. So after that, I never accepted that if a kid had a bad experience with one coach, he was automatically trouble. I didn't care. I always felt that I could make it work—that I could get through to a player. Later I got burned by some players and realized that I was probably a little bit naïve.

I had one of the greatest presidents at Riverside, Bill Noble. One time, Bobby got into a fight, and the media wanted him suspended for the year. Noble suspended him for an in-season tournament and he said at the time, "I don't ever want to put a young man so far in a hole that he can't crawl out." I thought that was a great, great statement.

Another example of this was John Trapp who was from Detroit, and he was a problem for every coach he ever played for. He was a problem in high school. Then George Gaddy, who helped a lot of kids in Detroit and had sent me Joe Barnes, sent him out to San Jacinto Junior College. I was friends with the coach there, and John was such a problem the coach offered John to me if I wanted him. I took him, and my last year at Riverside, John sat out to get his grades together. (Eventually I sent him to UNLV, where a friend of mine and a former teammate at Fresno State, Roland Todd, was the coach. John wound up playing five seasons in the NBA.)

One of John's problems was he was such a mean-looking guy that he scared everyone. Let me tell you how tough John was. A few years later I had a six-foot-nine recruit from Chicago we called Crazy Khruschev. All Khruschev wanted to do was fight. He would fight people in pickup games, on the street, wherever. He loved to fight. He heard how tough John was, and he said he wanted to fight John Trapp, just to prove he was tougher.

We had a guesthouse at our home in Arcadia, California, and Khruschev and another kid were staying there because school hadn't started. My family was up in Fresno visiting Lois's parents, and we had this mean German Shepherd named Ace, who guarded the house. One night after a summer league game I went out to drink beer and eat chicken wings with some other coaches, and my assistant coach dropped Crazy Khruschev and the other recruit off at my house. But Ace wouldn't let them in; he growled, barked, and was so mean they couldn't get into the yard.

The neighborhood was all white, so when these two black kids started wandering around at 10:30 p.m., the cops came by and picked them up. My assistant had to go to the police station and get them. But they still needed to figure out how to get by Ace, so my assistant went and got a former player who had stayed at the guesthouse and knew Ace. But Ace growled and still wouldn't let them in. Finally, they went and got John Trapp. Ace was all mad as hell by this point. But John came over and just shouted, "Shut up, Ace," leapt over the fence, grabbed Ace by the throat, and slapped him a few times until the dog cowered and the recruits could get into the guesthouse. He took on the meanest German Shepherd in Southern California like it was nothing.

Crazy Khruschev told me the next day he no longer wanted to fight John.

"Coach, he's my idol. Trapp is the toughest dude in the world. I don't want to mess with that man."

(Crazy Khruschev ended up never playing for me. He wasn't a great student, so I got him into 12 hours of welding classes one semester, and the teacher told me he skipped class. I yelled at Khruschev about it.

"Coach, the teacher is lying," he said. "I've been going to class. I am going to go down there and pull his tongue out of his mouth."

He was going after the teacher! He wanted to fight the teacher. I had to go and get the teacher out of there. I knew I had to get Khruschev out of Riverside before he caused trouble, so I shipped him to Oxnard College.)

My five seasons at Riverside were incredible. We had a 2,000-seat gym, and when I got there, you could have shot a cannon off and not hurt anyone. At first, we had no fans. But once we started winning, the entire city got behind us. At the Riverside reunion in 2004, one of my former players, Lucky Smith, said, "What people don't understand is in the 1960s, Riverside was a segregated community. Tark and the basketball team integrated the community in the 1960s, and everybody fell in love with the team because there's never been a junior college that had a following like we had."

And that's true. All of a sudden, you couldn't get a ticket to our games. We were really good. We had a four-year stretch where we went 129-9, including a 35-0 season. It was unbelievable. Business people would go to road games only because they couldn't get in to the home games—it was hard to get in there because you had to get to the little gym two hours before tipoff.

We won three consecutive California state championships. My final team was the 1965-1966 team that went 31-1 and won its games by an average of 43 points. All of my players were Riverside guys—Jim Gardner, Steve Barber, Larry Bonzomet, Larry Bunce—except for Lucky Smith, who was a military veteran. In the state tournament we won in the quarterfinals by 54 and the semifinals by 43. We played San Francisco City College, which had Willie Wise, who would play in the NBA, and Gene Thompson, who went on to be a great rebounder for Kansas State. We beat them by 30. As far as I am concerned, the 1965-1966 Riverside City College Tigers were the greatest junior college team ever.

We had Riverside rolling like nowhere else, and I thought I could stay there forever. But then I got a call from Dr. Armen Sarafian, the president of Pasadena City College. Armen was an Armenian, and we became lifelong friends; he was like a second father to me. Pasadena was really down; they had just gone 5-23 and hadn't been any good in years and years. It had the oldest gym in junior college ball, no fans, and no good players. One of the guys I grew up with, Huddy Scott, was a basketball coach there, and he told me it was impossible to win at Pasadena.

There was no reason why any sane person would leave Riverside City College, the best program in the state, for Pasadena, maybe the worst. All these years later, I still can't believe I did it. But I kept getting called by my old friends from Pasadena to take the job. They offered me $15,200 a year to coach the team, and that was big money even for a four-year school. It was more than USC was paying its head coach. Finally one day, I just decided to do it.

My first year at Pasadena was the 1966-1967 season, and we were able to completely change the atmosphere surrounding college basketball on the campus, and it wasn't necessarily because of what happened on the court. In 1967, there was a lot of unrest on college campuses because of the Vietnam War. Our athletic director was Tony Linehan, who was a Marine and had played football at USC. He was a tough son-of-a-gun. And I was always conservative when it came to things like the war. I always believed in supporting the troops.

One day our college president came running into the gym. He was a nervous wreck.

"Tony, the students are in an uproar," he said. "They've got a communist flag on the lawn."

"Well, go get it," Tony said.

"No," the president said. "That's the worst thing you could do. That's what they want. They want a confrontation. There are television cameras out there."

So the president was nervous, and the athletic director was nervous. They didn't know what to do.

"Hell, I'll get John Trapp to go get the flag," I suggested finally. John had followed me from Riverside to Pasadena after the coach who replaced me called and asked if I would take him because he couldn't coach John. Anyway John was easily the toughest guy on campus.

"You think John would do it?" Tony asked me.

"Hell, yeah. He'll do anything. He isn't afraid of protestors."

So I got John, and he agreed to go get this communist flag from the rally.

We walked up to the rally in the middle of campus, and there was this big group of people out there raising hell. The TV stations were filming it. The communist flag wasn't very big, but it was staked in the ground, flapping in the wind. John just shoved his way through the crowd, knocked the hippies to the side, picked up the flag, and broke the stake it was hanging on in half over his knee. A couple people tried to interfere, but he just shoved them aside. No one screwed with John. He just walked off with the flag.

And that was the end of the riot. They showed it on TV and everything. The rest of that year, every conservative businessman in town was buying John lunch. Pasadena City College basketball was popular all of a sudden. I went in a restaurant, and people sent drinks over to me, all because of John.

That season we went 35-1 and won the California state championship. It was my fourth consecutive state title. It was incredible; the people in Pasadena couldn't believe it. We went from 5-23 to 35-1 in one season, maybe the greatest turnaround in the history of college basketball. There were times that season we were so good that I wouldn't even be nervous before games. I walked into the gym just knowing we were going to win.

What happened was I came in and immediately got some guys together. During my time at Riverside, I had been obsessed with recruiting, so I had spent just about every day of the year, including the offseason, driving around Southern California attending high school games, recreation leagues, open gyms, and even playgrounds. If I had heard there was a good rec league game going down in Inglewood, I would be there. If there was a playground down by the beach, I went and watched. A great high school kid in Orange County, I scouted him. I knew every player in the area, so once I took the Pasadena job, I just rounded up a bunch of guys, and coached the heck out of them. We had John Trapp and Sam Robinson, but we didn't have any other superstars, just a bunch of kids who played together. Because the four-year schools wouldn't recruit black guys there were just so many great players hanging around Los Angeles that it was almost simple.

My team at Pasadena was almost all black. Our only white player was really a baseball player. At the time, USC, like most schools around the country, didn't recruit many black players. They'd take one or two, but that was it. During the 1967-1968 season, my second at Pasadena, we had a game set up against the USC freshman team. Back then in the NCAA, freshmen weren't eligible to play on the varsity. So four-year schools formed freshman teams, and they'd play other freshman teams or sometimes juco teams. Bob Boyd was the USC coach, and he said he had the best recruiting class in the country. And he might have. He had Dana Padgett, the Player of the Year from California. He also had the Player of the Year from Seattle, Arizona, and Florida. Four players of the year. People were saying the USC freshmen were better than any junior college team ever. But they were all white. The entire USC freshman team—all 11 of them—were white.

Coming into the game, they were 3-0 and had killed everybody. The game was at our place, and Boyd brought the whole USC varsity on a bus to see the game. They knew we were good, so they wanted to watch the freshmen kill us. But because we were almost all black, I had my guys so fired up to play it was ridiculous. I made the game a racial thing.

"You grew up nine miles from the USC campus," I said to one guy, "did anybody from that school ever talk to you?"

"No, those motherfuckers wouldn't talk to me," he said.

Then I went to the next guy. I went right down the line. I finally got to George Trapp, John's younger brother, who was a freshman for us. The year before, his high school team won a CIF championship. He single-handedly beat Padgett's high school team, but Padgett had been named California Player of the Year instead of George. So I threw that at George.

"George, why do you think Dana Padgett was Player of the Year and not you?"

I had that team ready.

When we came out for the warmups, George led the team on the court. He ran out there with one ball in each hand. Instead of passing one of the balls and then going in for an easy layup with the other, like most teams do, he sprinted down the court and dunked both balls in one jump. Then every guy on the team followed and dunked. They were dunking everything, and these were big, violent dunks. It was like a dunk contest. The backboard was rattling back and forth. I'd never seen a place that wild. The USC guys had never seen anything like that. My guys were jumping out of the gym, physically intimidating them. I was just standing on the sideline smiling. The game was over before the layup lines were done.

At one point of the game, we had them down something like 71-34. They couldn't get a shot against my guys—it was incredible. I had never seen guys play defense like that. But this was a racial deal. My black guys had something to prove against those USC white guys. That was junior college basketball at its very best.

5

Hittin' the Beach

" You can' t win any games in the sauna, get your ass home. "

—Ivan Duncan

I was offered the head coaching job at Long Beach State in the middle of the 1967-1968 season at Pasadena City College. I was thrilled with the opportunity to coach an NCAA Division I school, even if it was a place that had more than its share of hurdles. I had won four consecutive California junior college state championships at two different schools, but I wasn't sure I would ever get a Division I job. I didn't play for a big-time coach, like John Wooden or Henry Iba. I had never been an assistant at a big-name school. I wasn't famous. I was just a junior college coach. So when the Long Beach athletic director, Fred Miller, offered me the job over dinner, I took it. We didn't announce it until after the season, but it was done. I never even asked what my salary would be. That's how excited I was.

I should have asked. It turned out to be $13,300, less than I was making at Pasadena City. Then there was my recruiting budget, if you want to call it that. I found out it was $200 annually. Two hundred

28

dollars will get you one plane ticket. How the heck could we recruit with that? The good news was that because we only had eight and two-thirds scholarships—not the full allotment some schools had—maybe we didn't need much of a budget. Besides, any out-of-state player counted as one and two-thirds scholarships, which was good motivation to sign locals.

No one understands what we did at Long Beach State. Even though we had more success at UNLV, reaching four Final Fours and winning the national title, I'm not sure it's more impressive than what we did at Long Beach. There was no reason in the world we should have been as good as we turned out to be. There were just so many obstacles.

Long Beach was a state college founded in 1949. I went there in 1968, so it was just starting. We only had a few students and a few buildings. There were only a couple of dormitories. It was mainly a commuter school. And it was a teachers college, so our alumni weren't going into high-paying jobs. And they were young. Our oldest alums were 37. To be successful, you need the big boosters, guys in their 60s and 70s with cash to burn on facilities and salaries. We just didn't have the real estate developers, lawyers, and bankers who get buildings built and programs funded. We had no tradition, no money, and very few fans.

Our athletic program was Division II until the year before I got there. My two assistant coaches had to teach classes, and I taught basketball theory. We didn't even have our own secretary. We had one for the whole athletic department, so we had to answer our own phone. Do you think John Wooden was doing that up in Westwood?

When we went on the road, I insisted we stayed at a decent hotel, so we always stayed in something like a Ramada Inn. We never stayed in the really good hotels, but we never stayed in a bad one. I made that a standard. But we couldn't eat in the hotel because it cost too much. Our meals were primarily Kentucky Fried Chicken. We never drove by a Kentucky Fried Chicken without my players going nuts.

I tried to make the best of it. Some of my players heard that guys on other teams at bigger schools ate steak the night before games. So I told them all year that the worst thing an athlete could eat was steak. I said it gave you cramps and hurt your ability. I was only saying it because we couldn't afford it. But then one year we won a championship, so we wanted to do something nice for the players. Lois and I had them all over our house, and we saved up for a week and bought everyone a steak. I remember I got the steaks and thought, "Oh boy, this is a big thing. The guys are going to love this." But when they got there, no one would eat the steaks. They were all convinced it was bad for them. Lois and my children ate leftover steak for a week.

(Sometimes as a coach you have to trick the kids. Later in my career when I was at UNLV, we played a game at the University of Wyoming. Laramie, Wyoming, is at an altitude of 7,200 feet so the air is thin. On the side of the gym, there is a welcome sign that lists the altitude. I had this big center once who saw the sign and got nervous.

"Coach," he said, "it is going to be difficult to breathe here."

I said, "Don't worry, son. The game is indoors."

The kid went out and had a hell of a game.)

Even with the lack of funding, I had high hopes for Long Beach. I was excited about moving closer to the ocean, which I thought would be great for my kids. Plus Long Beach was very open to taking junior college players, because most of the regular students were from junior college. After seven years in jucos, I had a lot of contacts and figured I could fill up my team with junior college players. I had also developed extensive recruiting contacts throughout Southern California and felt good about that. I just had a hunch Long Beach could be good.

And I was right. In 1968-1969, the first year Long Beach was Division I, we went 23-3. I don't think anyone in Long Beach could believe it. We just came out of nowhere. The key was the junior college players. My first year, I recruited the entire California junior college all-star team—every player. I didn't really even have to recruit them. They called me to come because they couldn't go anywhere else. It was incredible. I got the players who would put us in the top 10, and I didn't have to beat anyone for them. I just rounded them up and won.

In my five seasons at Long Beach, we went 116-17, a .872 winning percentage. And during that time, I had four freshmen. Every other kid was a transfer from a junior college or four-year school. Most Division I coaches were wary of jucos so it was an untapped recruiting well, and I wasn't ashamed to hit it.

Few coaches understood juco kids like I did. I remember we played Abe Lemons's team at Oklahoma City in my first year, and he came over to me as our teams were warming up.

"Coach, how do you think your team is going to be this year?"

"Well, Abe, I think we are going to be pretty good, I have a lot of junior college kids."

He said, "Well, if you have junior college kids, Coach, let me give you a bit of advice: You have to be very patient with them, because it takes them a long time to adjust to college ball, and it will probably be the middle of the year before you get them playing well."

"You're probably right, Abe."

Well, we beat them by 22. That next year, he was at the junior college tournament in California recruiting players. It was the first time he had ever come to it. And after that, Abe and I became great friends.

One of the best players I brought in was George Trapp of Detroit. His brother, John, had redshirted at Riverside and played for me at Pasadena, and George Trapp had played for me for one year at Pasadena. His father, George Sr., loved me so much he had moved to California so his sons could play junior college ball for me. So I was in tight with the family. But George had become one of the top players in the country, so when he graduated from Pasadena, there were a lot of four-year schools interested in him. So it wasn't a lock for him to follow me to Long Beach State.

George had had a skating accident when he was in fourth grade in Detroit. He had been hit in the head, and it really caused him trouble with academics. He wasn't dumb; he just struggled academically. But he was a great welder, a really talented welder, just a natural. His mother, Vicky, wanted him to be a welder because this was obviously his gift. Long Beach State had an industrial arts program where you could take welding, so George committed to us. Then he went back home to Detroit for the summer.

George Sr. told me that when his son landed at the airport, the mayor of Detroit had a stretch limo waiting for him, and then the University of Detroit started recruiting him real hard. The coach and the college dean came over to visit the family, and George Sr. called me and said we were losing Vicky a little; she started to like U of D.

I called Vicky up and told her U of D didn't offer welding.

"Oh, then George can't go there," she said.

But then U of D set up another meeting, and the coach and the dean came back and said there was a new program they wanted George to know about. It was called on-the-job training, and George could go and weld at different auto factories around Detroit and get 12 credits and a salary, which was a hell of a deal. I got nervous then.

I flew back to Detroit and I stayed about eight or nine days. I stayed with the Trapps, slept right in their house, sat on the porch at night, and went for walks around the neighborhood. When George got up to come to breakfast, I was at the table waiting for him. I poured his milk for the cereal. That was how close I was to that family. Every day we went down to St. Cecilia's, a gym in Detroit where all of the great players played. There were some incredible games. I saw so many great players there that it was unbelievable. I was the only college coach in there and the only white guy a lot of nights. I got to know everyone in Detroit, and for a while there, I had that city almost all to myself. No one recruited in Detroit.

Being in Detroit won Vicky back on my side. I showed her that George could take all of the welding he would need out in Long Beach and everything would be fine. George could take 15 credits a semester, and 12 of them would be in welding. I was able to hold off U of D and its on-the-job training major.

Vicky had only one other request, and we could get George: She wanted George to have his own dorm room.

"OK, we'll work that out," I told her.

I got George a single in the dormitory, and we got him. I was really excited because I knew George could really help us. George moved into the dorm on a Sunday, but I was worried about everything. I thought maybe another school would try to steal him before we officially enrolled him on Monday morning. So I told the dorm manager that if there was any trouble, any problems at all, to call me immediately.

My house was nearby in Huntington Beach, and the dorm manager called. I was all worried as I walked up to the phone.

"What's wrong?" I asked.

"What is it with this Trapp kid?" the dorm manager demanded.

"Why? What happened?"

"He checked into the dorm today, but the first thing he told me was to take the study desk out of the room. I asked him why, and George said, 'Because I won't be using it.'"

(George had a strange habit of not being any good until after Christmas. When he first had gone to Monrovia High School in

California, he had so frustrated his coach the guy would drive around in a daze. But then after Christmas George single-handedly had led them to the state title. The year he had played for me at Pasadena City College, I had told him that I had wished he had gone to Citrus Junior College instead. But after Christmas he led us to a state title. After I left for Long Beach, my successor, Danny Ayala, had started taking classes to sell mutual funds because George had been so frustrating to coach—George would play bad; he wouldn't listen. Then, sure enough after Christmas, he was just a great, great player, and they won a state title. You couldn't explain it. There was no reason for it.

So when he got to Long Beach, I had all our fans send him Christmas cards on Thanksgiving, and he was great for us.)

I was incredibly driven those first years at Long Beach. All I did was work, recruit, work and recruit. Back then the NCAA didn't have restrictions on how much a coach could recruit, so I would be out almost 365 days a year. I never stopped. I was obsessed with getting the program going. For my top assistant, I hired a guy named Ivan Duncan, who had been a reserve player on one of my Riverside City College teams. But he was a straight-A student, a real smart guy. His father was the principal of Corona High School in California. Ivan had been in the service, so he was a bit older.

Ivan wasn't paid much at Long Beach, but he worked his ass off. He just loved recruiting. He was crazy. He didn't even care about coaching. We'd win a game, and he'd be thinking about recruiting. In 1971, we almost beat UCLA, so the Long Beach boosters gave my family and me a trip to Hawaii. It was like a 12-day trip. I didn't get paid much then, so a trip to Hawaii was a huge deal. I had four young kids by then. I worked so much that I didn't get to see them very often. When we got to Maui, I checked into the hotel and there was a message: "Call Ivan." I called Ivan and he said, "You can't win any games in Hawaii, get your ass home."

That was the way he was. He never saw the value in anything but working. The next season we had a good year, and one of our boosters put together a trip for my family and me to go to Palm Springs. I was in the sauna, and my son, Danny, came running down.

"Dad, Ivan's on the phone."

I ran up and said, "Did we lose a player or something?"

"You can't win any games in the sauna," he said, "get your ass home."

One time his wife wanted to go on vacation. She kept complaining he never took her anywhere. So he bought her a fishing pole and took her to the Long Beach pier and said, "This is your vacation." He was nuts. But that was the only way we could make it work. We had to outwork other people.

On Sundays in Los Angeles, they used to have these open gyms with what they called fraternity leagues. There were some good players in those gyms, and every once in a while, you could find one to recruit. Ivan and I used to go all the time. All of the players, all of the people in the gym were black. Ivan and I were the only white guys there. The black guys loved that we were willing to come. No other white coaches dared. So I was so big that when I walked in, they announced my arrival on the P.A. system, "Jerry Tarkanian, Long Beach State, is here." They treated me like a god. Once word got out that Long Beach State was taking black guys, it went crazy.

Ivan never cared much about the game beyond recruiting, so he never became a famous coach. Right before I went to UNLV, he got a junior college job in Scottsdale, Arizona. Scottsdale is a real wealthy area, lots of rich, upper-crust white people, and he brought in all of these players from New York and Philadelphia, so that got screwed up in a hurry. Later he coached in Europe. He became ill and passed away young, in his 40s. He was a great friend and a great recruiter, maybe the greatest college basketball recruiter of all time.

My philosophy was to never hire an assistant with a set of golf clubs, because no one ever recruited a player on a golf course. Ivan made it even stronger.

"Coach," he said, "we have to take it a step further. Don't ever hire an assistant who has a fishing pole or a camper, either."

6

The Greatest Player I Ever Saw

" But you don't have any money. Where did you get the Corvette? "

—*JERRY TARKANIAN*

The greatest player I ever recruited was also the greatest player who ever came out of Los Angeles, Raymond Lewis. Not many basketball fans have ever heard of Raymond, but anyone who knows anything about high school basketball in Southern California will tell you the exact same thing.

Raymond was a six-foot-two point guard out of Watts, a tough neighborhood just south of downtown Los Angeles. He was as fast as Allen Iverson, only taller, bigger, and stronger. I kid you not. He could handle the ball like you couldn't believe, just make the ball disappear. I never saw anyone guard him one on one. I never saw anyone contain him. I never saw anyone stop his dribble penetration. In a college game once, he scored 73 points. I was mesmerized by his ability, and I just couldn't believe it.

Slam Magazine recently did an article on Raymond and said the same things, that he was the greatest player from Los Angeles, ever. *Sports Illustrated* once did a 10-page article on him. Raymond died a few years back, putting an end to a truly sad adult life that saw him on the streets after he pissed away a sure NBA All-Star career through bad management and bad decisions.

When I first saw Raymond, he was a sophomore at Verbum Dei High School in Watts. That was only about 20 minutes from Long Beach State. His high school coach was a good friend of mine, George McQuarn, to whom I got real close during the recruitment, and I eventually hired him as an assistant when I was at UNLV.

Raymond as a sophomore was absolutely phenomenal. Even then, he was the best player I had ever seen in my life. As a junior, he was the California Player of the Year. As a senior, he was the best player in the country. Raymond was a little bit of a different kid, and as a result, I thought we actually might have a chance to sign him at Long Beach State. He wasn't initially interested in going to UCLA, which was the big team back then.

When I say different, I mean it in a number of ways. Even though the California Interscholastic Federation named Raymond California Player of the Year, he never went to the awards dinner. He stiffed them, because he wouldn't eat in front of anybody. He preferred to eat alone, so the idea of a big banquet was out of the question. When he talked, he wouldn't look at you. Not even a glance. He was a very shy guy.

But I got very close to this kid. I used to go to a lot of his games. The NCAA allowed you to call as much as you wanted back then. It was hard to call him because he wouldn't talk much and so I wondered if I was irritating him. But I kept calling. We went to his games, and then he started coming over to Long Beach to watch us or just hang out. We developed a relationship with him. For whatever reason, the kid didn't like USC, so USC was out of the picture. Even though UCLA wasn't recruiting him initially, I always feared it. Denny Crum, who would go on to be a Hall of Fame coach at the University of Louisville, was the assistant then, and he was dangerous. By the time Raymond was a junior, he was so good that UCLA couldn't ignore him.

His junior year, Verbum Dei was in a CIF playoff game at Long Beach City College. The place was packed because everyone had started to hear about Raymond Lewis; he was drawing crowds. All of a sudden, John Wooden showed up. I never thought I would see it. Wooden didn't go to many high school games back then, hardly any. You never saw him around. If he did come, it was only for a senior. He'd make a final appearance to close the deal. Raymond was just a junior, so this was big. Then right after Wooden came Crum. And then another assistant and another. It turned out the whole UCLA staff was there to recruit Raymond. On the other side of the court were Bob Boyd and the whole USC staff.

Raymond had an incredible game, just dominated every aspect. Usually after a game, Wooden would leave, but not this time. He was going to meet Raymond Lewis. All of the coaches were waiting around outside the locker room to say hello. Wooden hung in the background, but Denny Crum was right up front, obviously to grab Raymond and bring him over to Wooden. At this point I was really worried that we were going to lose this kid to UCLA. This was John Wooden. He was a legend, he was famous, and he had all of those NCAA titles and undefeated seasons. John Wooden was like Jesus Christ to high school players. I was just this guy at Long Beach State.

Raymond walked out of the locker room and walked right by USC, walked right by Denny Crum, and grabbed me.

"Coach," he said. "Coach, I want you to meet my mother."

A mother? I had no idea Raymond had a mother, because she had deserted the family a while back, and his father had raised all of the kids. But if there is one thing in recruiting to remember, it's when you get a chance to meet the mother, you meet the mother. Mothers are very important people.

"My mother is out in the lobby; I want you to meet my mother, Ella Mae."

So away I went. All of the other coaches had to just stand there and watch. It turned out the kid loved his mother. It was the darnedest thing. She had bailed on the family, but in Raymond's mind, she could do no wrong. And his mother said, "Oh, this is my son, Raymond." She was all proud of him. She had found out that he was a great player and realized he had a future in pro ball. So she was back.

From that point on, Ivan and I would meet with his mother at least once a week. Once we got the introduction, we called her and called her. We met at a coffee shop or somewhere. I was in my early 30s back then, and she was about our age and pretty attractive. So the story started spreading around Long Beach that Ivan and I had a black girlfriend. At the time Lois said I went to bed at night, and I woke up saying, "Ella

Mae, Ella Mae." She was on my mind 24 hours a day, because this was the best player I had ever seen. I was obsessed with recruiting him.

In 1971, Raymond's senior year, we almost beat UCLA in the NCAA Tournament; we were a hot team. After the game, I called Raymond.

"Coach, I know where I am going to go to school," he said.

Oh, my heart dropped as I expected to hear him say UCLA.

"I'm going with you, Coach. I'm going with you."

"God, Raymond, that's wonderful. They have a sportswriters luncheon on Monday, will you go to the luncheon and announce it? Then it will get in the papers and be official. I'll have our sports information director arrange it."

"Oh, no, I'm not going to any luncheon."

I had forgotten about Raymond not liking to eat in front of anyone.

"You have him make the announcement. I'm playing for you."

So that Monday we announced Raymond Lewis was coming to Long Beach State. It was the damnedest thing. I couldn't have been happier. I figured we could really win it all with this kid. That's how good he was.

But then all of a sudden Southwest Louisiana started recruiting him. The principal of Verbum Dei was from Louisiana, and he had arranged the recruiting deal at the last minute. Southwest Louisiana sent a private plane to pick up Raymond, a couple of teammates, and the high school principal. They were going to fly everyone down to Louisiana to get the deal done. But Raymond never showed up for the flight. Raymond stood up his own principal. That was the kind of kid he was. He didn't care. If he didn't want to see you, he could hide out in Watts and you'd never find him. So the other players and the principal flew to Southwest Louisiana by themselves.

That scared me, though. I knew that until Raymond was enrolled at Long Beach State the next fall, he was still capable of bailing on me. There was no binding National Letter of Intent then. The only way a guy was locked into your school was when he was enrolled in fall classes. Then he was officially on your team.

I started going wherever Raymond was playing, just to keep an eye on him. I will never forget that summer, they had a three-on-three tournament at El Camino Junior College, which is out by the Los Angeles airport. It was a great tournament—all of the best college, junior college, and playground players around the city were in it. One team had three USC players on it, including Dana Padgett and Paul Westphal. Raymond played with his two high school buddies, and they just killed everyone.

Then Raymond started playing in the Los Angeles Pro League. In those days, the Lakers rookies, USC alumni, UCLA alumni, and some AAU groups had teams. Raymond was playing with some of his high school buddies, and in their first game he had 52 points, and they beat the Lakers rookies. And he was a high school kid.

His second game, they played the USC alumni. I didn't go to that one, but because Raymond had gotten so big, the newspapers started staffing the summer league. The USC alumni included Mack Calvin, who was an All-ABA player for Denver at the time. The newspaper said Mack Calvin held Raymond to 33 points. So I saw Raymond the next morning.

"Hey, Raymond, it said in the paper Mack Calvin held you to 33?"

"Coach, he couldn't guard me; he was fouling me all game. They just wouldn't call it because he's a pro and I'm just a high school kid."

That summer we got Raymond moved into our dorm, got him a job on campus, and got him enrolled in our summer school program. That didn't bind Raymond to Long Beach, though; only fall classes did. But it allowed me to keep a closer eye on him. I also took one player from his high school, Randy Eckles, who was a good student and a good player. I even got Raymond's girlfriend into Long Beach State, just one more reason he didn't ever have to leave campus.

That year we got Ernie Douse, who was the New York City Player of the Year and a playground legend back East. He also came out for summer school, and we introduced him to Raymond. Raymond didn't talk much; he wasn't very friendly.

As soon as Ernie left the room, Raymond turned to me and said, "Can he play?"

"Sure he can play, Raymond, he's the New York City Player of the Year."

I'm not sure Raymond knew that was a big deal. I'm not sure he knew what New York City was.

All I know is Raymond had Ivan arrange a one-on-one game between Ernie and him. I was in the office when I heard about this game going on in the gym, so I said to myself, "Hell, I better get in there and stop this." I went in, and the score was already 18-4. Raymond was killing Ernie. I stopped the game because I was afraid Ernie was going to catch the next flight back to New York.

That summer was the first year that Los Angeles State, which was a school in East Los Angeles, not far from downtown, implemented the quarter system. Instead of having its academic calendar broken into fall and spring semesters like Long Beach State and everyone else, L.A. State decided to go to four quarters. The coach at L.A. State was Bob Miller, and he was a real good friend of mine. L.A. State didn't have any money; they were even poorer than we were. They had just this little campus, not much of a program, and they didn't draw anyone. They were never a factor in the big recruiting battles of the day.

But one night that summer, Lois and I were driving to a CIF All-Star game to recruit some younger kids, and we heard a news report on the radio saying Raymond had enrolled at L.A. State.

"No, no, that's not true, that's not true," I told Lois. "He wouldn't do that."

But at the all-star game, word was buzzing around that Raymond was going to L.A. State and not us. I couldn't believe it.

"Bullshit, he's not going to L.A. State," I told them. "I saw him today. He's living in our dorm."

But when I got home, it was all over TV, "Raymond Lewis has gone and enrolled at L.A. State."

I scrambled to find Raymond, but I couldn't. I called Ella Mae. I called everyone. I went over to Watts. I tried everything. The story was Raymond got a new Corvette. That's it. L.A. State gave Raymond a new Corvette and was taking all of his high school buddies. They signed the whole team except for Randy Eckles. I thought I could go and find Raymond and get him back to Long Beach, but that's where L.A. State's quarter system came into play. Once Raymond enrolled that summer, he was officially on the team. The summer quarter at L.A. State counted as the fall semester at Long Beach State would have. It was over. Raymond was gone to L.A. State, and there was nothing I could do about it.

I was just devastated to lose that kid. The players on my team were kind of glad, because they knew that without Raymond, they would get to take more shots. But I was crushed. I thought we could have won a national championship with him. I thought we could have been better than UCLA.

The first thing I did was call Bob Miller at L.A. State.

"Bob, what did you do?"

"Tark, we had to have the kid. Our program needs Raymond."

"But you don't have any money. Where did you get the Corvette?"

And this is a true story: He told me he cashed in his teacher's retirement to get Raymond the Corvette. He spent his own money on Raymond because his program didn't have any boosters.

About a week after the deal went down, Randy Eckles came to my office and said, "Coach, you can't believe it. Raymond has that new Corvette. If I had a new Corvette, I'd drive it down to San Diego or up to Oakland or something. Show it off a little. Raymond hasn't left Watts yet. He is just circling Watts all day in his Corvette." That's the kind of kid Raymond was.

I honestly believe what Raymond thought was he could take the Corvette and then still come with us. I don't think he understood the quarter system and how he was stuck with L.A. State. I talked to him after, but he felt funny talking to me.

Freshmen weren't eligible then. So Raymond was stuck on the freshman team. L.A. State was in our league, so every time I went to scout them, I went early to see the freshman game, because I loved that kid. He averaged 38.7 points a game as a freshman.

That year, UCLA had the best freshman team in the country with Pete Trgovich, Dave Meyers, and Andre McCarter. That group would win a couple NCAA titles and each get drafted by the NBA. They had won 26 consecutive games when they came to play L.A. State freshmen. Raymond single-handedly destroyed the whole UCLA team. He dropped 40 on those guys, and L.A. State won by like 15. UCLA put a press on L.A. State at the end of the game, but it did nothing. You could have put the whole student body on the floor, and they wouldn't have been able to steal the ball from Raymond.

Well, every time I watched how good Raymond was, I kept getting upset. So at the games I sat next to my good friend—his mother, Ella Mae, and kidded her.

"Ella Mae, what kind of car are you driving?"

"I don't have a car, Coach."

"Geez, they should have bought you a car. You are the mother, after all. That's not fair. You ought to go ask Bob Miller for a car. It is only proper."

"You're right, Mr. Tarkanian. You're right."

Every Monday of that year, they had a sportswriters luncheon in Los Angeles and all of the coaches in the area—the Lakers coaches, the USC coaches, the UCLA coaches, the state coaches—would go. At those events, Bob Miller was so nervous that year that he couldn't even get coffee to his mouth. He just shook and spilled it all over the place. Ella Mae was driving him nuts. But I kept applying the pressure, and next thing you knew, Ella Mae got a Buick.

I don't know where they got money to buy the Buick, but they did.

At the end of the season, I called Bob Miller and said, "Hey Bob, are you going to the coaches convention at the Final Four?"

"Tark, we can't leave the city limits. Ella Mae has all our money."

I laughed. I just broke them financially. I wiped L.A. State out. And they haven't been heard from since.

The next year, Raymond played varsity ball. We had to play them twice. The first time was at our place, and we beat the hell out of them and won by 20-something. Raymond went eight-for-29 from the field. The key was we had Glenn McDonald, who was my great defensive player and would play a little bit for the Celtics. Glenn was quoted in the paper saying, "We wanted to win that game so bad because Coach Tark loved Raymond, and we wanted to prove to Coach Tark that we are a better team without Raymond." I guess my obsession with the kid was obvious. All of my guys were making comments in the paper about Raymond, saying he was overrated and saying he wasn't that good.

We played them again at L.A. State when we were ranked No. 3 in the country and our fans were so confident that they had signs that said, "Shoot Raymond Shoot." They thought what they saw in the first game was the real Raymond.

Well, it wasn't. The son of a bitch got 54 points on us. He beat us in overtime single-handedly. I went to a box-and-one and put Glenn, a NBA-caliber defender, on him, and it did nothing. In overtime, he made a move on Glenn that was so smooth Glenn wound up with a stress fracture in his ankle. Raymond literally broke Glenn's ankle. After the game, everyone was going nuts. Sonny Vaccaro, who signed Michael

Jordan to Nike and Kobe Bryant to adidas and has seen every great player for four decades, said it was the greatest one-game performance he had ever seen. Sonny still talks about Raymond that night.

Unfortunately for Bob Miller, Raymond didn't deliver in terms of wins and losses. L.A. State would win three and then lose two. The team never came together. It was completely disorganized. I was scouting over there once, and some guys showed up five minutes before the game. It was crazy. But Raymond led the nation in scoring; he averaged 32.9 points a game.

Then he declared hardship and went pro. He signed with about five agents and took money from all of them. Then all of these agents wound up suing each other. It was a disaster. Philadelphia drafted him in the second round. The 76ers' first-round pick was Doug Collins, who was our Olympic hero and a big-name player. Raymond was this guy from L.A. State. No one knew much about him.

They went to training camp, and Raymond naturally just destroyed Collins. It wasn't close. But he had a bad agent, and after he played so well, the agent convinced Raymond it would be a good idea to walk out of camp. They wanted a better contract than Collins had gotten. That wasn't going to happen, but Raymond held out for the entire season.

A year later, the 76ers invited him back and gave him a spot on their summer team. As the story goes, Raymond was playing well when the team came down the floor on a fast break. Raymond was open, but they didn't pass it to him, so he got frustrated and kept running, right out the door of the gym and never returned. That was it. He had had enough. The Philly papers started calling him "Phantom."

He drifted after that. No one knows exactly what he did, but he never played a minute in the NBA. He wound up on the streets. In 2001, he died after complications from leg amputation surgery. I guess he hadn't taken care of himself. It was a real sad story.

In the *Slam Magazine* piece, Raymond said, "I should have gone to Long Beach State and played for Coach Tarkanian." Then Raymond's father said he should have gone with me because "Coach Tark was the only one that actually cared about him. Instead Raymond took the money."

I agree. Boy, do I agree.

7

Wisin' Up

" Coach, they set me up with an apartment overlooking Waikiki Beach. Long Beach is nice, but it isn't Waikiki. **"**

—TOMMY HENDERSON

As good as we were during my five seasons at Long Beach State—it was incredible how close we were to being even better. We had some great players, mostly the junior college kids, but we almost had even more great players. If a couple of things had fallen right, we might have been the best team in the country.

Case in point: George "The Ice Man" Gervin was at Long Beach for 19 days. George, of course, would go on to be one of the 50 greatest players in NBA history, a slashing guard who perfected the finger roll with the San Antonio Spurs. He wasn't that good when I recruited out of Detroit in 1971, but he was on his way. Detroit was just a gold mine back then. In 1968, they had had huge riots in the city; they had burned a lot of the buildings down. It was very dangerous there. I think a lot of coaches around the country were scared to recruit there. Things got so bad that it was decided in an effort to get all of the kids home before dark, the Detroit public schools played their games in the afternoon. They tipped off at 3 p.m. and had everyone out of the building by 5:30 p.m. They actually still do that in Detroit. The result in 1968 was the players didn't get a lot of publicity. As good as George Gervin was, not many people had ever heard of him; he just wasn't on their radar.

But I had coached John and George Trapp, who were originally from Detroit. And their father, George Sr., just loved me. George Sr. called me one day to tell me about this kid named George Gervin, whom almost no one was recruiting. They had a city all-star game, so I went up to watch him play, and Gervin was just sensational. I thought he would be perfect in our system—I just knew he would be a star. With so few schools after him, it was easy to get him. He even enrolled in our school, moved into the dorm, and took classes. To help ease the transition, we even got Gervin's brother, who was third-team all-city in high school, enrolled at Compton Community College.

At the time, George didn't have much of a personality. He was real skinny, and his complexion wasn't real good. He didn't like to talk to many people. He was nothing like the guy he would become, a real showman. All he did back then was basketball. But he loved my assistant, Ivan Duncan. I don't know what it was, but he just loved being around Ivan, talking with him, listening to him, whatever. He'd sit in Ivan's office all day. And then if Ivan was making recruiting phone calls or was busy, George would sit in the hallway and wait for Ivan to finish.

We sensed he was getting homesick, though. Other than Ivan, George didn't like talking to many people. And this is where I made a major mistake and learned a very valuable lesson. Two of them, actually.

I had this kid named Eric McWilliams who was a juco transfer and played the same position as George Gervin. Eric was very outgoing. He had a really good personality, so I set it up that the two roomed together in the dorm. I thought that they had a lot in common and Eric would show George around campus, you know, make it fun for him.

I was living in Huntington Beach, which is about 15 minutes from the Long Beach campus. It was a Friday afternoon, and I was nervous because George was homesick, so I called Eric in just before the weekend and said, "Now Eric, if George gets homesick, or depressed, or anything happens, you call me immediately. I don't care if it is 3 a.m., just call me. I'll come over." I was scared George might bail out back to Detroit, but I figured that since the Los Angeles airport was about a 40-minute drive from our campus and George didn't have a car, he was stuck.

Well, all weekend, I heard nothing, not a word from Eric. I figured everything was fine. But when I got to campus Monday, Gervin was gone. He had packed up and gone back to Detroit. I went to Eric and said, "What happened?" Eric just shrugged, but then I found out that it was Eric who had driven George to the airport. I never even realized how stupid I had been putting those two together. Gervin played the same position as Eric. And Gervin was better. Everyone knew that, including Eric. There was no question that Gervin was going to beat Eric out for playing time, so Eric eliminated that problem by driving George to the airport.

After that I never allowed two players who played the same position to room together again. That was a young coach's mistake.

Of course, by the time Gervin landed in Detroit, it was too late to get him back. He was promptly enrolled at Eastern Michigan, not far from the city. It was the Eastern Michigan coaches who had sent George the plane ticket. He played two years there, was a first-team All-American in 1972, went hardship, and signed with the ABA. The rest is history. When he turned pro, they had his signing party at the Disneyland Hotel in Anaheim, and he invited me. I went, and he pulled me aside and said the biggest mistake he ever made was leaving Long Beach.

"George, why did you leave then?"

He said it was because his girlfriend was calling him all the time, and he really missed her.

The thing was he said that after he got home, he broke up with her about a month later. I lost George Gervin for a girlfriend who didn't even last.

And that was the second lesson I learned. From that point on, I found out whether a player had a girlfriend. If he was really close to his girlfriend, I brought her along, too. I got the girlfriends into school. I thought I had it covered by getting George's brother out to Compton, but there is the thing you forget. When you're an adult, you look back and say, "Hey, a high school girlfriend is nothing, it isn't supposed to last. We have all these girls in L.A.; he'll find another one." But the girlfriend can mean everything to an 18-year-old, more than even a brother. So why not bring her along? If I had gotten that girl from Detroit into Long Beach

State, I would have had George Gervin. He could have broken up with her in Los Angeles, and I wouldn't have cared. Hell, with him we probably would have won the national championship.

That's the thing with recruiting that a lot of fans don't understand. It isn't always about whether you like the player and the player likes you. In fact, it rarely is just about that. To this day, there are always the peripheral people, someone who has some juice with the kid. It could be a girlfriend, could be a teammate, could be a parent, could be a high school counselor, or could be a coach. But there's always someone. These are 18-year-olds. They don't make decisions by themselves—even if they think they do.

The key to winning in recruiting is getting the most important peripheral person on your side. The first person you have got to know is his coach. If it's an AAU coach, the street people—you've got to know them. And after losing "The Ice Man," I always got to know the girlfriend.

This stuff was especially important at Long Beach State, where we didn't have a big name or a fancy campus to fall back on. Kids had to come there because they liked us or the people around them liked us. There was no other reason to go there.

As tough as losing George Gervin was, my biggest recruiting loss at Long Beach was Tommy Henderson. Tommy was a great player who wound up a starter on our 1972 Olympic team. I didn't know anything about Tommy until I was back East recruiting another player. I went to watch that kid's all-star team and discovered Tommy, who was from DeWitt Clinton High School in the Bronx, New York. DeWitt Clinton is a legendary powerhouse, and because there were so many great players there, Tommy wasn't getting much attention. He was hardly being recruited at all. But Tommy was a six-foot-three guard, real strong, and I just fell in love with him. I wanted him so bad.

Tommy didn't have very good grades, so he wound up going to San Jacinto Junior College in Texas and had a great career. He was so good he made the U.S. Olympic team straight out of San Jac. That meant he was already one of the 12 best college players in the country. Well, by now, Marquette coach Al McGuire was recruiting him. If there was one thing I learned through the years, it was to not recruit against Al, especially for a kid from New York. Al always won. Always. And this was just another example. Tommy wanted to play with Al. It was done. I gave up.

But then one day Al called me and said, "Tark, get after Henderson, I am going to help you with Henderson. I can't take him."

I said, "Al, why? He's the best juco guard in the country."

"Because he's better than Allie."

Allie McGuire was Al's son. They played the same position, both point guards, and he didn't want to bring anyone in better than his son. So Al was backing off Tommy.

So we jumped back in when no one else knew that Marquette was about to jump out. That gave us a real advantage, and we got the guy. He was coming with us. I mean, it was over, we worked all of the angles thanks to Al. I was so excited because I thought Tommy could give us the star power to win a national title. But then word leaked out that Marquette wasn't taking Tommy, and half the country tried to jump in at the last moment. Tommy was hanging with us until a week before signing day. Then Tommy called.

"Coach, as a favor to Louis Shaffel [who was a pro sports agent from New York], I am going to take a visit to the University of Hawaii. But I want you to know I'll never go to school there."

I couldn't believe it. Man, I got nervous. But Tommy said not to worry; in fact, he said his flight back from Hawaii was landing at LAX on Sunday night. With signing day the following Wednesday, he said he didn't want to go back to Texas.

"When I land in L.A., I'd like to stay in L.A. I don't want to go back to San Jac because with the Letter of Intent, it's going to be crazy. Everyone is going to be down there trying to sign me, pressuring me."

"Well, Tommy, that's great," I said.

I started feeling better. Ivan and I immediately hatched a plan where we would meet him at LAX, but instead of taking Tommy down to Long Beach, we were going to hide him out at a cabin Ivan's dad owned on Lake Arrowhead, which is a real remote spot up in the mountains of Southern California. It was a couple-hour drive from Long Beach. We figured that once Tommy didn't show up in Texas, other recruiters would figure we had grabbed him and were keeping him in Long Beach. And they might come to Long Beach to find him and get him to switch or claim we were housing him illegally. So we were going to stash him up in the mountains, and no one would find him. And we wouldn't bring him back until after he signed with us. It was perfect. Ivan was going to stay up there with Tommy, and I was going to stay on campus. Then if anyone came around Long Beach looking for Tommy, I'd just shrug and say, "Well, he isn't in Long Beach." I thought we had a good defense mapped out.

Ivan and I went to the airport Sunday night to wait for Tommy. The plane landed, and we stood there at the gate. No Tommy. We looked everywhere for him and asked the stewardesses and everything, but he wasn't on the plane. He never left Hawaii. He wound up staying in Honolulu. The Hawaii coaches stashed him before we could stash him. They beat us to the punch.

Later, I talked to Tommy and said, "What happened? You were supposed to come to Long Beach."

"Coach, they set me up with an apartment overlooking Waikiki Beach. And I just couldn't leave. Long Beach is nice, but it isn't Waikiki."

Tommy went on to play nine seasons in the NBA. He was a starter on the Washington Bullets in 1978 when they won the NBA championship. I just always loved Tommy. He was the kind of big, strong guard I always favored. He was one of my favorite players who we didn't get. But as with George Gervin, I learned a valuable lesson in the recruiting game from him.

8

Sweet Redemption

"We still had Ivan's dad's credit card, and we didn't need to buy expensive plane tickets to Columbus, so we went back into the bar and bought everybody drinks all night long."

—JERRY TARKANIAN

As I mentioned in the first chapter, I was depressed in the spring of 1969 when I lost Bruce Clark. It really rocked me because I realized that no matter how hard we worked at Long Beach, no matter how much we did, the bigger schools were able to get the deal done better than we could. A place like USC had too many resources, UCLA even more. I mean, John Wayne? The kicker to the Bruce Clark story is that John Wayne was a USC alum, so for all I know, he actually did get the dad the job. But that was the problem. For alumni, USC had John Wayne; I had a bunch of young teachers. We were winning with smoke and mirrors at Long Beach State. We could get really good, but how could we ever beat UCLA?

I was so down in the dumps that I drove over to Pasadena City College to visit with my younger brother, Myron, who was the football coach there. I was sitting in his office complaining about the Bruce Clark deal when this kid named Vance Carr walked in. I had met Vance my last year at Pasadena City. He was a pretty good basketball player, and he had wanted to go to school there, but he hadn't registered in time and they had been giving him a hard time about it. I was leaving for Long Beach, so it wasn't a big thing to me, but I liked this kid.

The president of Pasadena City College, Dr. Sarafian, was like my father, so I had called and told him about Vance Carr. I even had taken Vance to the president's office and we had gotten him into school, even though it was past the registration date. I had just been helping the kid out, plus I liked the basketball coach at Pasadena, and I had figured Vance might be good for him.

Vance came into Myron's office and heard me talking about how I lost Bruce Clark.

"Coach, forget about Bruce Clark, I know an even better player. Why don't you recruit Ed Ratleff?"

Well, Eddie Ratleff was from Columbus, Ohio, and was one of the best players in the country. It turned out Vance had attended Columbus East High School, the same school as Eddie, so he knew all about him. But so did just about every college coach in the country. Eddie was a six-foot-six swingman and an incredible scorer, and everyone wanted him.

I said to Vance, "Hell, I'd love to recruit Ed Ratleff, but Ed won't even return my phone call. Every time I call, I can't even get through. I've been trying for a year. He won't come out here."

"Coach, Ed is a friend of mine," Vance said. "I could get him to talk to you."

"That's great, let's do it right now."

I pointed at the phone on my brother's desk, and Vance called Eddie. Vance got Eddie on the phone and talked to him for about 30 minutes, and then I got on the phone with Eddie. It was incredible. I would never have even gotten to talk to Eddie any other way. After we talked, Eddie agreed to come out for a visit. It was probably just to hang out with Vance or to see California, but I didn't care. I knew if we got him on campus, we had a chance.

Eddie had signed a Letter of Intent with Florida State. The Letter of Intent was a new thing in 1970, designed to lock a kid into a school. If you signed, it meant you were supposed to go there. It was a good idea, because there was too much poaching of players going on. You had to babysit kids until the first day of school. And even then, guys like George Gervin would leave. It was better for the schools, the coaches, and the players. So I liked the idea of the Letter of Intent, but at that time, we didn't have them in California. It was only in certain areas of the country. So we didn't honor them. It didn't matter to us if he signed somewhere— as far as Long Beach State was concerned, he was open.

For some reason, Eddie wasn't totally sold on Florida State, so he came and visited our place. He loved baseball. He loved baseball more than basketball, and he was a great baseball player. He wanted to play both sports in college. Well, the city of Long Beach had built a baseball stadium, Blair Field, that next to Dodger Stadium was the best baseball stadium in Southern California. The Los Angeles Rams had their headquarters there. It was a great field. Long Beach State only played about four or five games there—most of its games were on a campus field that wasn't so great. But I told Eddie we always played at Blair Field.

At that time, freshmen were not eligible for varsity basketball, they just played on the freshman team. If Eddie went to Florida State, the freshman basketball season overlapped with the start of baseball season, which meant he would miss some baseball. So I told Eddie that I would allow him to quit the freshman basketball team the moment baseball season started.

"I bet no other coach in America would agree to that," I said.

Eddie said I was right: No other coach had ever promised that. The thing was we didn't even have a freshman basketball team at Long Beach State, because we couldn't afford one. We only had eight scholarships anyway. So what did I care if the freshman season was shortened? We weren't planning on having a team.

We had a player named Sleepy Montgomery who was from Los Angeles and knew everybody in the area. He was a real character. I had Sleepy and Vance host Eddie on his recruiting visit. Vance was a host even though he didn't attend our school. All that mattered was that Eddie enjoyed himself. They showed him all over town, and at the end of the visit, Eddie told us he was coming to Long Beach State.

Then he flew back to Columbus, Ohio. Eddie's principal at East High School was Jack Gibbs, who had played football at Ohio State. On Monday, Eddie told everyone he was going to attend Long Beach State.

Gibbs called me up and said, "I don't know you, I don't know anything about Long Beach State. I do know Eddie fell in love with the place, and he wants to go to school there. But I'll tell you right now, he is not going anywhere I don't approve, his mother and father don't approve, and a high school counselor doesn't approve. Eddie is going to listen to us. If you want him, you need to send me some literature on the school, and you have to come out and meet these people."

"Fine, I'd be happy to do all of that," I said.

So I got George Trapp Sr. to write a letter about me, telling how I had handled his sons. I had the president of Pasadena City College send a letter. I got all of our catalogues and our schedules and sent them. I sent everything I could think of sending. Then I flew to Ohio and spent about five days hanging around Gibbs. He was a black guy, and he just loved all of the guys on the East High School basketball team. He just wanted all of the players to have a good future, so he was determined to get them all college scholarships—even the guys who weren't very good players, he wanted to package them with his good players. Columbus East was maybe the top high school team in the country that year. They had Eddie; Nicky Conner, who went to play at Illinois; and another good player named Bo Lamar.

Those days you didn't scout players. We didn't have the budget to fly to Ohio to watch a high school game, so we barely knew any of the kids. I just used to get these recruiting newsletters. It was very primitive. I had been reading up on Columbus East, and I knew all about Eddie Ratleff and Nicky Conner, but I didn't know anything about Bo Lamar. Ohio had a rule then that only two guys from one high school could play in the Ohio all-star game. So Bo Lamar didn't play and as a result didn't get much publicity.

While I was there, everything went well. The principal liked me, and we sat down one day, and he told me he wanted me to take the two other guys on the team. They were two small guys who weren't good enough for Long Beach State. I couldn't give them scholarships, but I told them him I would get them into a junior college in California. I knew some coaches who would take them. The principal was satisfied with that.

Then I decided to up my side of the ante.

"I would like to get Nicky Conner. Why doesn't Nicky come with me, too?"

"No," Gibbs said. "Nicky is going to Illinois. That is all set. Leave him alone."

So then the principal tried to get me to take Bo Lamar.

I didn't know Bo, so I said, "I can't take him. I'll put him in junior college, though."

"No, he's a four-year player, a good player, Coach. I think you're making a mistake."

Well, it turned out I was, because Bo Lamar was a terrific guard. In one year in college at Southwest Louisiana State, he averaged 28.9 points a game. He went on to play four seasons in the NBA and ABA. He would have been great for us, a total recruiting steal. I didn't realize it then, which was a mistake. But I didn't care, because Gibbs and I agreed on everything. I was getting Eddie in exchange for finding a place in junior college for the two other players. I flew back to Long Beach thinking everything had been finalized. Just to be sure, every night I called Eddie, I called his girlfriend, I called his mother and father, and I called the principal. Every single day. And then Ivan called Eddie every day. And then Vance Carr called Eddie. I didn't think I was going to lose him, but until he enrolled and was locked in, I was always nervous about these things. Fortunately the dad was really in my corner. He wanted Eddie to come to Long Beach.

About a week before Eddie was to arrive, I was in Pasadena with a bunch of guys I grew up with. Every year we get together for a big reunion, and that night I was in a bar and we were having a great time. Everyone was partying, drinking beer. But Eddie's dad called my home, got Lois on the phone, and told her that I needed to call him immediately. It was urgent. Lois tracked me down at the bar. I got all nervous and called the dad.

"Coach, you better get out here, we're losing the kid. Eddie is going to go to Southwest Louisiana. Jack Gibbs has swung his allegiance to Southwest Louisiana."

"Jack can't do that," I said. "Why would he do that?"

"Because Southwest Louisiana is taking those two other guys and Bo Lamar. So they get Eddie in a package deal."

Southwest Louisiana State had gotten into the picture at the last minute. Beryl Shipley was the coach at the time, and he said he would take the entire Columbus East team—well, everyone but Nicky Conner, because the principal wouldn't let Nicky go anywhere but Illinois. I don't know what deal Gibbs had going with Illinois, but it must have been impressive, because there was no wrestling Nicky away.

The next day, I was a wreck. Ivan and I tried to figure out a way to get back to Columbus as soon as we could. The problem was we didn't have any money. Our recruiting budget was tapped out, and a last-minute ticket was expensive. We just couldn't afford it. And it wasn't like we got paid much and could use our own money. I had four kids and a wife; I was broke. Ivan was no better.

Finally Ivan got in touch with his dad, who had some money, and explained the situation. His dad gave us his credit card to buy the plane tickets. There was a midnight flight to Columbus. Finally we had a way. So I called Eddie on the phone.

"Eddie, please, don't do anything until we get there. We're on a midnight flight. We get to Columbus around 7:40 a.m. Give us your word that you won't do anything until we get there."

"OK, Coach, I promise."

So Ivan picked me up around 9:30 p.m. I was so nervous that we decided to go to this great little bar in Long Beach where all of the coaches used to hang out to have a couple drinks. We were there about an hour when Eddie's dad called the bar.

"There's no need for you guys to come out."

My heart sank.

"Oh no, we lost him. We lost the kid."

"No, Coach, nothing like that. I just chased Beryl Shipley out of town. I told Beryl Shipley to get the hell out of here. Eddie's not coming along to Southwest Louisiana."

Man, was I relieved. We got Eddie. The dad came through for us, so we were ecstatic. It was over. We had him.

And to make matters even better, we still had Ivan's dad's credit card, and we didn't need to buy expensive plane tickets to Columbus, so we went back into the bar and bought everybody drinks all night long.

And I stopped feeling so bad about Bruce Clark.

9

Moneyball at UCLA

" They had a booster named Sam Gilbert who had them so far over the salary cap it was ridiculous. "

—*JERRY TARKANIAN*

I want to make it clear how much I liked John Wooden and how much I respected him. I still do. But I want to make it very clear that during the time when I was at Long Beach State and UCLA was winning all of those national championships, they had a booster named Sam Gilbert who had them so far over the salary cap it was ridiculous. He was the biggest cheater out there. It was the worst program in college sports.

But don't take my word for it.

"UCLA players were so well taken care of—far beyond the ground rules of the NCAA—that even players from poor backgrounds never left UCLA prematurely [for pro basketball] during John Wooden's championship years. If the UCLA teams of the late 1960s and early 1970s were subjected to the kind of scrutiny Jerry Tarkanian and his players have been, UCLA would probably have to forfeit about eight national championships and be on probation for the next 100 years.

"I hate to say anything that may hurt UCLA, but I can't be quiet when I see what the NCAA is doing to Jerry Tarkanian only because he has a reputation for giving a second chance to many black athletes other coaches have branded as troublemakers. The NCAA is working night and day trying to get Jerry, but no one from the NCAA ever questioned me during my four years at UCLA."

—Bill Walton, in *On the Road with the Portland Trailblazers*
(1978) by Jack Scott

No one has ever made my point on this better, or with more credibility, than Bill Walton, possibly the greatest UCLA Bruin of all time. And you know what happened when Walton wrote that? The NCAA probably sent another investigator after me.

I don't hate Wooden for that. I don't hate Sam for that. I actually got to know Sam and really liked him. He was a good guy. I didn't hate those guys at the time, either. I just hated that the NCAA just let it all go down, that they didn't care that the boosters behind their national champion were cheating. UCLA won 10 NCAA titles because John Wooden was a great coach and did a great job. You can't minimize that. The job he did was incredible. He had all of those great players, but he was always in charge. They always played hard for him and played together. Those teams had so much pressure. It wasn't just winning the NCAA title. It was going undefeated. Those teams couldn't make one mistake. And they didn't.

And Wooden is a great man. He was great to me when I was just a young nobody coach, and there was no reason for him to be so gracious to me. When Long Beach State hired me, I hardly knew him, but he told the Los Angeles media what a great thing it was and how I would do a great job for Long Beach.

In 1964 my Riverside team went undefeated and won the California state title. I was at the Final Four in Kansas City a couple weeks later, in a coffee shop with a couple of other coaches. UCLA was unbeaten and playing for the title. Wooden and his wife, Nell, came in. He barely knew me, but he came over to me and congratulated me on a great undefeated season. It was so nice.

"Thanks Coach, I sure hope it happens for you, too," I replied.

"Jerry, if we win the next two games and win the national championship I won't be any more proud of my players than I am right now. I am just so proud of what they have accomplished."

The way he said it was incredible. He's just one of the classiest and greatest men to ever coach basketball. I can't say enough good things about John Wooden.

But that doesn't change the way the NCAA allowed UCLA to operate.

Sam Gilbert was a contractor in Los Angeles who had made a ton of money and loved UCLA basketball. Talk about the perfect combination for a booster. Sam loved kids. He got them summer jobs in Hollywood that paid ridiculous amounts of money, he gave them gifts, and he got involved in recruiting. There was a longstanding joke among college coaches that when Sam got involved, you might as well back off. My players all hung out with the UCLA players, and they came back and told all of these incredible stories of how much money the Bruins were flashing.

Wooden knew this; it was no secret. He always said he wished Sam would stay away from his players. I had heard he even went to J.D. Morgan, the UCLA athletic director, and told him what Sam was doing, and J.D. told Wooden that he would handle Sam. But nothing changed. I talked to Sam many times, and he bragged about all of the things he did. He laughed about it. He wasn't hiding it. Even that didn't bother me. Hey, a school does what it does. I never turned in a school for cheating. Never. I came from an ethnic neighborhood in Euclid, Ohio, mostly Italian, and they would protect you for anything you did, except if you ratted. So I wasn't raised to do that. One time, late in my career when I was at Fresno State, a young coach cheated so badly on a player who had committed to us it wasn't funny. It was ridiculous, and he knew I had him. But I didn't turn him in, and the next spring I was at the Final Four having dinner with a bunch of people when the waiter came by and said the bill was taken care of. The coach came over, hugged me, and said, "I owe you. You saved me."

Throughout the years I said things about UCLA cheating in the media, but I didn't consider that ratting because I knew the NCAA would never do anything about it. The NCAA just never cared. The *Los Angeles*

Times once did a big investigation of Sam Gilbert and printed all of these facts in the newspaper, and no one cared. The NCAA didn't do anything.

What bothered me was that the NCAA decided to come after us at Long Beach State. We didn't have any money. We didn't have any boosters like Sam. We didn't even have the full allotment of scholarships. We couldn't even afford a pep band. Ivan Duncan said when the NCAA got here and saw our budget, they'd throw us a fundraiser. We couldn't have cheated like UCLA even if we had wanted to. But they came in, started an investigation of our program, started harassing us, and didn't stop until I beat them in federal court 26 years later for $2.5 million.

In the early 1970s, I wrote two guest columns complaining about the NCAA in the Long Beach newspapers, and that's what really set them off. That's what got them on my case. One time they had come down hard on Centenary, which is this little school in Louisiana that you probably never heard of. I defended Centenary, saying that there was no way they were cheating like the big SEC schools that bought everyone. Then the NCAA went after Western Kentucky, and I defended Western Kentucky, saying that Kentucky did more cheating in one day than Western Kentucky did in a year. I just thought the NCAA went after the little guy.

I was right. Because next thing you know, they were coming after us. But that's how they did things. One quote I gave about the NCAA gets repeated a lot, and that's that in the late 1980s the NCAA was so mad at Kentucky they gave Cleveland State two more years of probation. And it's true. The NCAA doesn't want its marquee schools in trouble. It sifted through everything we ever did because we were getting good, but it wouldn't ever dare take a look at UCLA, a team that won seven NCAA titles in a row. Seven! A team wins seven consecutive NCAA titles, puts together undefeated season after undefeated season, and recruits high school All-Americans from all over the country to sit on the bench—they never transfer, they never declare hardship—and it doesn't dawn on anyone at the NCAA that, gee, maybe they are cheating? But a team of investigators needed to get down to Western Kentucky on the double?

It was mind-boggling. Our problem was obvious. We got too good. I had all of these recruits now, I had Eddie Ratleff, George Trapp, and Chuck Terry, a great six-foot-six forward from Long Beach Lakewood High, and we won a lot of games. In 1970, my second year at Long Beach, we reached the NCAA Tournament for the first time in school history. Back then, the NCAA Tournament had only 32 teams, and the schools were divided up by region. The West Regional was the true West Regional, all of the teams in it were from the West. That meant for Long Beach State to reach the Final Four, we had to beat UCLA.

UCLA was not just a big game for a school such as Long Beach State, it was the only truly big game. UCLA was everything. In 1970, we were 24-4 and met UCLA in the second round of the NCAA playoffs. The Bruins had won the past three NCAA championships and were loaded with Henry Bibby, Sidney Wicks, and Curtis Rowe. To make matters worse, the game was at Pauley Pavilion, their home court. We weren't ready for that, and they crushed us 88-65. They were much better than we were.

We went back to the NCAAs the next year, though, and we were better and more experienced. We had Eddie, who no one could stop, and George Trapp, who was as good as anyone in the country. We were 22-3 when we reached the Elite Eight and faced UCLA in Salt Lake City. The Bruins were still the Bruins, but I thought we had a chance, because we weren't intimidated by them this time. After getting pounded the year before, I was determined to slow the game down and stay in it. And it worked. We played our 1-2-2 zone to near perfection. UCLA managed just six field goals in the first half. With 14 minutes left in the game, we were up by 11, and no one could stop Eddie.

Well, until Eddie fouled out for the only time in his career. UCLA stormed back behind Bibby and Wicks, but we still had a chance.

The score was 55-55 with four minutes left, and I went into a delay game, because I figured it was our only chance. I thought UCLA would come out and trap us, but they let us stall. I couldn't believe it. We ran the clock down to 2:30 when Bernard Williams, my point guard from Detroit, went in for a layup, but Wicks blocked it out of bounds. We got the ball and delayed again for another minute when Williams went in for another layup, but Larry Farmer blocked it out of bounds. We had the ball again, and the clock ran under a minute. I thought to myself, "We are going to run this clock down and get the ball to George Trapp, one-on-one for the final shot, and pull off the upset." I just knew George would hit the game-winner, because UCLA didn't mean anything to him. He wasn't nervous at all.

But with 45 seconds left, the ball went to Dwight Taylor, who was a great defensive player but had a terrible shot. I used to make a deal with him that he could only play if he never shot. But Dwight had the ball in the corner, and Bibby didn't even guard him. So Dwight went up for the shot. If I had known he was going to shoot it, I would have gotten a gun and shot him first. Dwight missed, UCLA got the rebound and went down to the other end, and Wicks got fouled and hit both free throws. UCLA won 57-55. We were so close. That was probably the greatest game in the history of Long Beach State basketball, because UCLA was historic. For our little program to play them that close in the Elite Eight was just incredible. UCLA, of course, went on to win the NCAA title. Again.

The next season, we might have been an even better team. I still had Eddie and George, and we had brought in Ernie Douse from New York City. We were good. We were deep. And that was the year we should have had George Gervin and Raymond Lewis. But I had added a seven-footer named Nate Stephens, who was like a modern player. Back then, most seven-footers were back-to-the-basket players, but Nate could run like a deer. He had a lot of potential, but he didn't always deliver.

Nate was really a strange recruit I had gotten from Eddie Sutton, who was coaching then at Creighton in Omaha, Nebraska. (Eddie later coached at Arkansas and Kentucky and is now the head coach at Oklahoma State.) Eddie used to be a junior college coach, so we had been friends for years.

"Tark," he called me up one day, "I got this seven-foot center. He wants to go back out West. He didn't like it out here because it's too cold. He might be interested in playing for you, and he asked me to call."

"A seven-foot center? Eddie, is he a legit?"

"Yeah, he's a legit seven-footer."

"Well that sounds good."

But I told Eddie I had to check with school officials before I took a transfer.

"I'm sure they'll be interested," I said. "Let me work on some of the details, and I'll get back to you."

The next morning I get another phone call from Eddie.

"Tark, Nate is on this plane. He lands at LAX in two hours."

It was that quick, and Eddie had him on a plane. I should have known right then and there that the guy had to be a little goofy or something.

Eddie hadn't even given me time to think about it or call around and find out about this guy. He just put him on the first flight to LAX. He just wanted him out of town. Who does that with a seven-footer?

Nate came out, and he wasn't a bad guy at all. He actually really tried to become a player. But he was a bit unusual. The other players called him "Nate the Skate," and he was just a silly guy. One time he stopped at a gas station right around the corner from Long Beach State, filled his tank up with gas, and then drove off without paying for it. The gas station owner was a fan of the basketball team, so instead of calling the cops, he called me and told me the story. He said Nate was even wearing a Long Beach State letterman jacket at the time.

I hauled Nate into my office.

"Why did you drive off without paying for the gas? If that gas station owner didn't know me, he would have called the cops on you."

"Coach, that wasn't me. How does he know it was me?"

"Nate, how many seven-foot guys in Long Beach State letterman jackets do you think we have running around here?"

You didn't have to be Kojak to figure that one out.

But that was Nate. Eddie had had enough of him, but Nate wasn't a bad guy at all. He wasn't a great player, though. He was a good player who always thought he could be a great player. That was a problem. But mainly, he just kept doing dumb stuff.

Nate became eligible for the 1971-1972 season, and he was part of a great team. We also added Leonard Gray, a transfer from Kansas. We started 16-1, and we were beating everybody by 10 or 12 points. But UCLA was beating everybody by 30 to 40 points. It was Bill Walton's sophomore year, and they were just annihilating even good teams. They scored more than 100 points in their first seven games of the season. Walton was named National Player of the Year despite being only a sophomore, and they entered the NCAA Tournament 26-0.

We got into the NCAA Tournament and won our first two games. We were 22-3 and were set to face UCLA in the Elite Eight in Provo, Utah. This was a big game for us—not only did the winner advance to the Final Four, but I really wanted to beat UCLA, especially after coming so close the year before. They were the kings of college basketball and obviously the Goliath to our David. It was even bigger than that in Southern California. UCLA was the school with all of the money, the powerful alumni, and the reputation. We were a small school and a small program. We had begun to get some media attention that wasn't very favorable, taking shots at our junior college players and transfers. There was an implication that we weren't on the up and up, all the while Sam Gilbert was hovering around the Bruins.

But we were very good, and I thought we could beat them. That isn't to say I was underestimating them. They were unbeaten and had Bibby, Keith Wilkes, and Bill Walton, who was the best college player I ever saw. I knew we needed something special to happen for us to beat them. I thought we needed to sneak up on them, and to do that, we needed them to be overconfident.

A couple days before the game, I told our guys, "Now we've got UCLA next. In the press, I want you guys to all be real nice to UCLA. I'm not going to say anything but nice things about them. I am going to say they are much better than us. I am going to say we aren't that good. Don't believe what I say to the press; just believe what I tell you. We've got a shot. But we need to sneak up on them, and then we're going get them this year. But if we run our mouths and get them riled up, we'll get beat. So when the press comes to talk to you, only praise UCLA. Say you feel lucky just to be on the court with the Bruins. OK?" Everybody seemed to agree. They knew I was serious.

So the press came by, and they interviewed me. All I did was talk about what an honor it was to coach against Wooden and UCLA and all of that stuff. And I overheard some of our other players talking about how great UCLA was and how they just wanted to give it a good try. So I was all excited. The players were following the plan. I figured the plan was going to work.

We flew into Salt Lake City, and someone handed me a copy of that morning's *Los Angeles Times*, which had a big headline: "The Redhead Is Overrated." I almost fainted on the spot. Here was this article with none other than "Nate the Skate" saying all of these negative things about Walton. Nate said he had been watching UCLA on television, "and they're all pumping up this Walton guy." He called him "this Walton guy" like Walton was just any old player. Then he called him "the redhead." Nate said when he was at Creighton, he had played against some kid who had been leading the NCAA in rebounding at the time, and he just annihilated him. But that player was some big white kid, nowhere near Walton's caliber. Which Nate didn't understand, so he said, "I've been watching the redhead play, and he's way overrated."

I almost died right there. I just couldn't believe it. I gave Nate so much hell for that, I can't even describe it. Here was my big plan—to lay in the weeds, sneak up on UCLA, and score one of the greatest upsets in the history of college basketball and the greatest win in the history of Long Beach State, and advance to the Final Four, where we would win the national championship in just our fourth year as a Division I school. The greatest Cinderella story ever. And here was Nate saying this Walton guy was overrated.

The game started, and Walton just annihilated Nate. He killed us. Nate had about three traveling calls in the first minute. Then Walton blocked about three of his shots. UCLA beat us, and Nate finished with like two or three points. Walton had about 19 points and 20 rebounds. After the game, the press came running in to Nate, and they asked him what he thought of Walton now.

Nate said, "That redhead's got some soul in him."

Some soul in him? I about died again.

The 1972-1973 season was my last at Long Beach State, but I thought I might have my best team. We rolled through the regular season with a 22-1 record and another top-10 ranking. UCLA was again looming in the Elite Eight, but we got upset by San Francisco before we got another crack at Walton and the Bruins.

It was about this time that the NCAA got on us. I later found out in court proceedings that UCLA athletic director J.D. Morgan had turned us in to the NCAA. He wanted to hurt our program because we were getting close to knocking UCLA off. To my face, J.D. had always been nice to me. He used to come up to me and say in this slow voice, "Jerry, what a marvelous job you do," and all of this bullshit.

J.D. was a powerful guy, though, and if he wanted the NCAA investigating us, then the NCAA was going to investigate us. They got us on some ridiculous things, nothing like what was happening up in Westwood, and I let the NCAA know about it. And then they let me know about it, which started our longtime feud. But I don't regret it. They can say what they want, but the NCAA will not investigate or punish the big schools like they investigate the small schools. They won't. They never have, and they never will. And I have been right about that from day one.

10

Al McGuire

❝It was like 2:30 p.m., but if Al wanted to have a drink, I was going to have a drink, too.❞

—*JERRY TARKANIAN*

During my time as head coach at Long Beach, I was lucky enough to become real good friends with Marquette coach Al McGuire. Al was one of the greatest coaches I ever met. He was also one of the smartest people I ever met. He went on to win the 1977 NCAA title at Marquette and then quit to become a famous television analyst. He did a number of our games at UNLV, but our friendship went back before then.

Even though Al always, always beat me for recruits, I liked the guy. When it came to recruiting, he had a way of getting things done that no one else could. It wasn't even fair. This was especially true for a player from New York, where Al had grown up. If we would come across a New York kid who we liked and then found out Al was recruiting him, too, we'd just drop out. It wasn't worth the effort, because Al was going to win. Even if we had been involved with the kid a year ahead of Al and had some good contacts, Al could come in at the last minute and beat you. That's how strong Al McGuire was in New York.

But he was good in other towns, too. In 1971, I got involved with two players from Pittsburgh—Ricky Coleman and Maurice Lucas. Maurice was a great, great player; a six-foot-nine forward who could just rack up double-doubles for you and just dominate in the paint. He went on to a 13-year career in the ABA and NBA. Ricky was a six-foot-two point guard whom I really liked. They were teammates at Pittsburgh's Schenley High School. Their senior year at the Dapper Dan Roundball Classic, the Pennsylvania All-Stars just destroyed the U.S. All-Stars, which was rare. But it was all because Pittsburgh had Ricky Coleman and Maurice Lucas. I thought if we could get them both to come to Long Beach, we would be in great shape.

When they came to visit Long Beach, I quickly gave up on the idea of signing a daily double. Ricky Coleman was great; I thought we were going to get him. But Maurice was a real jerk. He was real aloof, he didn't seem to be enjoying himself, and he didn't seem very impressed with Long Beach. That's OK; it happens sometimes in recruiting. The last thing you want is a kid at your school who doesn't want to be there.

During campus visits, I always made a point to sit down with a player one on one, talk, get to know him, and answer any questions he might have about me, the school, or the town. When I sat down with Maurice, he immediately pulled out a piece of paper with a list of things that he wanted in exchange for coming to Long Beach. He had all of these demands—money, cars, insurance policies, and all sorts of stuff like that.

"Maurice, you're going to college, this isn't pro ball. You don't get paid or get to make a list of demands to play college ball."

I had never had a kid be so up front about what he wanted so I wasn't getting involved in that. I had had a bad feeling about this kid, and the demands just confirmed it. So I told Maurice no way. Maurice was surprised by my answer, and then he told me he had a guidance counselor at Schenley who had said this was how the recruiting game worked. Maurice said the counselor made up the list of demands.

"Well, Maurice, you tell that counselor that he's got it all wrong. That's not how it's done."

After that, I wrote Maurice off. I figured he was going somewhere else, and even though I loved him as a player, I wasn't going to waste any more time on him. So I didn't pay any attention to him the rest of the trip. I just ignored him. I put all my focus on Ricky Coleman, because I thought we still had a chance to sign him. I was just all over Ricky. And Ricky was having a good time. He was an 180-degree turnaround from Maurice. He seemed to really like the school, the area, and the other players. At the end of the visit when I drove them to LAX, I didn't say a single word to Maurice, and I just spent all my time trying to close the deal with Ricky. The visit went so well, Ricky thanked me for having him out to California.

The two of them headed back to Pittsburgh, and I thought we were going to get Ricky. But sure as hell, about three days after he was home, Ricky committed to Jacksonville. I couldn't believe it. I thought Ricky was a lock. But Jacksonville got in there on me and pulled Ricky at the last minute, and there was nothing I could do to change his mind. It was done.

Then about three days later, Maurice called me up out of the blue and committed to us. I couldn't believe that, either. I said to myself, "God, this is strange, why would Maurice commit to us when he looked so miserable on the visit and I didn't even pay attention to him?" But he was a real good player, so I just said, "Maurice, that's great." On the phone he was very positive about coming to Long Beach.

There was no binding National Letter of Intent then, so a verbal commitment only meant so much. What I wanted to do was get some publicity out of it and get the story of Maurice committing to Long Beach in the newspaper, which would help keep other coaches away. The problem was there was a newspaper strike in Pittsburgh. Maurice committed to me on a Friday, and there was no paper in Pittsburgh to announce it to. Maurice's people wanted it to be big news, so they asked me to wait until at least Monday before we announced it, that way maybe the newspaper strike would be over. I agreed.

I shouldn't have, because Al flew in on Saturday and got Maurice in one day. In just a couple of hours, Maurice broke it off with us and committed to Marquette, where he would go on to be an All-American. Al was good with people, and he just got it done like that. He hadn't even been recruiting Maurice. But Al had that way about him. People just flocked to him. I called Al up.

"Al, what did you do? Did you meet those guidance counselor demands?"

"No, I just took him to a place to eat that didn't even have plates. You had to eat on paper."

That's all Al would say. That's how he explained it. And I guess the kid loved it. He just loved Al, always did. So that was it. It only took one meal for Al to beat me, and Al gave me hell about that one for years.

You could never figure out what Al was doing. The first time I met him was during the 1970-1971 season. We were in Milwaukee to play UW-Milwaukee on a Thursday and then Marquette on Saturday. When we got into town, the phone rang in my hotel room, and it was some booster from Marquette. He said they were having a luncheon that day and Al McGuire would like me to come. At this point, I had never met Al, and I said, "God, that'd be great. I'd love to just meet Al, get to know him."

So I went to the luncheon and met Al. I thought it was a nice thing for him to do. At the time I was just this young coach, a nobody, and Al was a big-time guy.

As we were walking out, Al said, "Hey, my assistant scouted you guys. He likes your club. Have you seen us play?"

I said, "No."

At that time there was no way a program our size had money to scout teams in person. And because there were so few games on television, you couldn't even get tape. We used to go into games blind; we barely knew the other roster. It was a big advantage for Marquette to have seen us play when we hadn't seen them play.

But Al said, "You want to go to practice?"

"What?"

"Come to practice and see our guys."

I couldn't believe it. Why would a coach invite me to practice a couple days before we played, giving me a chance to scout his team?

"Yeah, Al, I'd love to go. Are you sure you don't mind?"

"Hey, we saw you play. You should have a chance to see us play, so come to practice. It will help even things out."

I said to myself, "God, this is strange." So, I got in his car, and we drove to the arena in downtown Milwaukee where practice was going to be held. We parked the car, got out, and started walking toward the arena. Al pointed at this place.

"See that bar there. That's my bar." Al owned the bar. "Let's go have a drink."

"Ah ... OK."

It was like 2:30 p.m., but if Al wanted to have a drink, I was going to have a drink, too. We went in there, and we had a drink.

"What time's practice, Al?"

"Three o'clock."

I looked at my watch, and it was like about seven or eight minutes to 3 p.m.

"Al, it's about seven minutes to 3 p.m., don't you want to get over to practice?" I just wanted to alert him.

"Yeah, OK, one more drink and then we'll go."

So we had another one, and then it was about three or four minutes after 3 p.m. I figured, "Hey, if Al doesn't care if we are late to practice, I don't care. That's not how I do things, but whatever."

Finally we got up to leave when a buddy of Al's came into the bar and said, "I want to have drink with your friend here. Let me buy you two a drink."

Al agreed, so we sat down and had another drink. By the time we left the bar it was 3:15 p.m.

When we walked into the gym, they were going through layups. Jim Chones, their great center, was blocking shots, throwing them in the bleachers and stuff like that. In the layup line, guys would double-pump and everyone was just screwing around. There was no intensity at all.

Al had a kid from Evanston, Illinois, named Bob Lackey who was six foot six and really tough. He had attended junior college in Wyoming, where I had tried to recruit him. He visited Long Beach State before signing with Marquette. I asked Al how he beat me on Lackey, and he just said he recruited him "out of a barbershop in Evanston, Illinois." I never even knew what he was talking about. But that was Al.

When I walked into practice, Lackey saw me, immediately came over, gave me a hug, and started talking with me. I pushed him back because I was afraid Al was going to see this and get mad at me for pulling Lackey out of practice.

"Bob, you have to go back to practice. I'll talk to you after."

Lackey just laughed and said, "Al won't mind. Don't worry, Coach. Al won't mind." The kid called me "Coach" and his actual coach "Al."

Lackey went back to practice, and a little while later, Al blew the whistle. He took off his tie, but he still had street shoes on.

"All right, you guys, we're gonna be working against the press here. Start practicing."

They started practicing, but the whole time the players were bitching at each other, the coaches were bitching at each other, everybody was bitching at everybody. At one point, Al was bitching at Dean Meminger because Dean was not running hard.

Meminger grabbed the ball, slammed it down, and said, "Aw shit, Al, when you recruited me, you told me we were going to run. We haven't run since I got here."

Everybody started laughing.

I had never seen a practice like that. The coach had a couple drinks in him, the kids called him by his first name, and no one was afraid to bitch at each other. I just couldn't believe it. I went back to the hotel and told my assistants that it was the worst practice I had ever seen. I told them I thought we had a real chance to spring the upset, because Marquette was feuding, undisciplined, and ripe to get beat.

Then they came out on Saturday and played a flawless game. They played an absolutely flawless game. They beat us in every facet of the game, just ran us out of the gym. We had no business even being on the same court with those guys. It was incredible. We were getting pounded, and my assistants were looking at me like I was nuts.

But that is the way Al did it.

After that, Al and I became really good friends. One year it was October 12, three days before practice started and Al called me.

"Hey, Tark, I am going to New Zealand tomorrow for two weeks and I stop through LAX. Why don't you jump on the plane and come with me to New Zealand?"

"Al, practice starts on October 15, I can't go to New Zealand. Don't you have practice?"

"I don't go to practice until November 1. I let my assistant, Hank Raymonds, handle it until then."

I was speechless.

In the fall of 1972, I asked Al if I could come to Milwaukee to hang out with him and talk hoops. He was such a smart coach I thought I might be able to learn something. One afternoon, we were sitting in Al's office talking when his secretary buzzed in and said Maurice Lucas was waiting outside and wanted to see Al.

Al told the secretary, "Tell him I'm not here. Tell him I'm not here." Al hung up and said, "Let's go out the back door."

We sneaked out the back door.

"Al, why won't you talk to Maurice Lucas?"

I couldn't understand it, Maurice was a star. My door was always open to all of my players, even the benchwarmers.

"What do I want to talk to him for? He's either got a problem, or he wants to get in my pocket. One of the two. And I don't need either one of those."

I laughed at that as we walked across campus only to be spotted by Maurice. He had apparently left the office and stumbled upon us.

He yelled from across the quad, "Al! Al!"

He came running over, and before he could say a word, Al started in, "Maurice, where you been? I've been looking all over for you. I got Coach Tark here, and I want to take him out to lunch. But Maurice, I left my wallet at home. Can you loan me $20?"

Maurice was stunned. He stopped right in his tracks, and he didn't know what to say.

"Gosh, Al, I would give you the money, but I don't have it with me. I was going to ask you for some."

"That's all right. We'll get it somewhere else."

Then he slapped Maurice on the back, and we immediately took off. Maurice was standing there like he didn't know what had hit him.

Once we got out of earshot, Al said to me, "That's what you've got to do. You ask them before they ask you." He was so sharp, so street smart. Al was something else.

A couple years later, some of the boosters at Long Beach State had a dinner for me on the *Queen Mary*, which is docked in the Long Beach port. The chicken pie guy in town was our big booster, actually about the only booster we had. He owned all of the old chicken pie shops in Orange County, and there were a lot of them. He had a ton of money. Well, he loved Al McGuire, so to make him happy, I got Al to come out and speak at the banquet.

We put Al up at the Golden Sails Hotel in Long Beach. Sometimes Al liked to be by himself. As colorful and personable as he could be, there were times he didn't like entertaining people; he was kind of a loner that way. He liked to go off by himself or just stay in his room.

That night the chicken pie guy and I went to pick Al up for dinner, but as we were leaving the hotel, Al said, "Let's go get a drink in the lobby bar."

So we stopped in the bar, and they had a little music playing. We sat down and ordered a round of drinks when Al immediately got up and asked this girl to dance. The chicken pie guy and I sat there having glasses of wine, and we watched Al and the girl dance. At one point, Al pointed the two of us out to the girl, and we gave a little wave back. Then, the next thing I knew, Al left with the girl. Before one song was even over, they went right out the door. I never saw him the rest of the night.

I had to go have dinner with the chicken pie guy all by myself.

So the next day, I saw Al.

"Al, how in the hell did you pull that off? You didn't even finish one single dance with her."

He said he told the gal that the chicken pie guy and I were gay and we'd been harassing him all night. He asked if she'd help bail him out of a jam and leave with him.

Then, once he was outside, he left her, snuck back in the hotel through a back door, and went to his room to hang out by himself. He didn't pick up the girl; he just didn't want to have dinner with my booster and me. He figured that would be boring. He knew if he left with a girl, we wouldn't follow; we'd just let him go off thinking he was picking up a girl. I laughed, and then I started thinking, "You know, we were sitting there with a glass of wine, smiling and looking at Al, giving him a little wave. We probably looked like we were gay."

That's how sharp Al McGuire was.

11

Seduced by The Strip

" Every time I thought of something new to ask for, [they] said, ' No problem.' "

—*JERRY TARKANIAN*

I never lost a home game at Long Beach State. I never lost one as a junior college coach, either, but it was the run at Long Beach that I was most proud of. Five seasons, and any time we played on campus, we won. That was one of the reasons I knew I had to leave Long Beach. My final season there, we were ranked No. 3 in the nation, had brought in All-America-caliber players, and won every single home game—and we still struggled for fans.

I had thought I could turn Long Beach into a Long Beach State town. I thought the city would embrace us, rally around us, and make us its team. Although we made some progress, the reality was Long Beach remained a UCLA town or a USC town. Or a Lakers and Dodgers town. We didn't draw well. We didn't have wealthy boosters. We didn't have the connections to get our guys good summer jobs. We didn't dominate the media coverage.

I thought that if I could get to a place like that, a college town desperate for a winner, then I could lead the school to a national championship. But I couldn't do it at Long Beach State. I loved that school, loved my players, loved the boosters we had, and loved living in Southern California. But as long as I was there, I knew we had to work magic. I knew when it came to recruiting, there was always a bigger school capable of getting things done like USC did with Bruce Clark.

I may have been the only person who thought Las Vegas, Nevada, was a college town. When I said it, people laughed at me. But I saw a community outside of The Strip, neighborhoods and churches and Little League fields. And the local college, the University of Nevada–Las Vegas, was a focal point for those people. I had taken my Long Beach teams up there a few times, and UNLV had good crowds even though the team wasn't all that good. The fans were there. The city was desperate for a winner, and because there were no local professional franchises, I thought UNLV basketball could be the pro team of Las Vegas.

And I knew UNLV had good boosters. It was those boosters who hired me. That was the way UNLV worked back then. It wasn't the president or the athletic director who hired me; it was the boosters. Those were the guys who wanted UNLV to be a basketball powerhouse, and they were determined to get me. I had been offered the job twice before—once when I was at Riverside City College and once after my second year at Long Beach. Both times I turned it down because I didn't think the timing was right. I felt a real loyalty to my players.

This time, the boosters were determined to get me. They sent a couple guys from Las Vegas to Long Beach. Davey Pearl and Sig Rogich were very influential Las Vegas residents, and they came and offered me the job. Then they called me every day. It wasn't an easy decision, because I really did love Long Beach. But every time I thought of something new to ask for, Davey or Sig said, "No problem."

At Long Beach, we didn't have a secretary. UNLV said it would get me one. At Long Beach, I didn't have my own office. UNLV said it would build me one. At Long Beach, my assistants had to teach class. UNLV said they could just be coaches. On and on it went. A courtesy car, better pay, more support. It was tempting.

In all probability, I would have never left, but after the 1972-1973 season, it broke in the papers that I was going to UNLV or Arizona State, which was interested in hiring me if its coach retired. The Long Beach president was trying to get me to stay, but he told me he could handle it if I left for Arizona State because he perceived that to be a step up. But UNLV he considered a lateral move at best. He said leaving for Vegas was a slap in his face. I kept prolonging the decision because I kept thinking about how much potential UNLV had. Finally, the Long Beach president said I had until Friday to decide.

I woke up Friday morning and the birds were chirping, it was a beautiful day in Southern California and I said, "You know, maybe we ought to just stay." I was all set to stay, but then I read an article in the *Long Beach Press-Telegram* that quoted the president saying that if I were going to stay at Long Beach, they would have a press conference on campus. But if I were leaving, I would have to hold it somewhere else. I was pissed off at the president for that. That was the thing that did it. I thought I had done enough for Long Beach State that I had earned the right to have a farewell press conference on campus.

So I took the job. I was 43 years old. UNLV announced the hiring, scheduled a press conference, and brought me up to Vegas. At that point, I realized I hadn't even met the university president yet. The boosters had done the whole thing.

Just before the press conference, I said, "Hey, I want to meet the president."

"Oh, you'll meet him, you'll meet him tonight," they said.

"No way, I'm not going to have any press conference until after I meet the president."

I didn't want to disrespect the guy. I had no idea how he would take it. So I made a big deal about it, and they made arrangements for me to meet the president. He was leaving anyway. We were going get a new interim guy, so it didn't really matter. But I went up and met the president. If it wasn't for me, that wouldn't have even happened. That's how strong the boosters were at UNLV. It was amazing. They ran the athletic department.

UNLV was just a small school then. Las Vegas was just a small city, just getting going. UNLV was a good school academically, we had some great professors, but it didn't have the most stringent entrance requirements. One thing I had going for me was the state of Nevada had passed a law that said anyone who had six college credits with a C (2.0) average had to be admitted to UNLV. And junior college credits counted. They wouldn't be eligible to play right away, but they would be admitted as full-time students, and then you'd go from there. That was a big advantage, because we could get in on some recruits who were poor high school students, get them into a juco in California for six credits, and then bring them to UNLV. We could recruit kids other schools couldn't.

My first year at UNLV was the hardest I ever had in coaching. First of all, my wife was pissed off at me for going. She kept saying all along it was "your decision, your decision." But then after I made it, she locked herself in the closet, cried, and gave me shit about it. My daughter Pamela was a junior in high school, and she didn't want to leave school and her friends. So to make her like me again, I went out and bought her a new car, a Ford Maverick, and she still didn't want to go, she was still pissed at me. Then every weekend that first year we were in Vegas, she drove back to Huntington Beach to be with her friends. So I was just miserable.

Then the NCAA came in and put Long Beach on probation. If I had known that was coming, I would never have left Long Beach, I would have stayed and fought the NCAA. But I didn't know. I still fought them, even if I shouldn't have. Two of my coaching friends Lou Henson and Hugh Durham both told me if I would have just let them hit me over the head with a hammer and thanked them for it, then everything would have been fine. But I fought them. I went and had a press conference in Long Beach, and we went through each allegation, one by one, proving how bogus they were, calling the NCAA names. It just made the war bigger. So that was just a miserable time in my life. The most miserable year I ever had.

The team I got had all these leftover guys who weren't that good. I brought in some good recruits right away, some guys I had stashed away at jucos and some others I found at the very end. But the old guys and the new guys didn't even speak. There was no harmony at all. Our guys didn't even play hard. I just didn't like the team. There was no warmth. We lost our home opener, my first home loss in 11 seasons, and in Vegas, one thing you don't want to do is bomb out on opening night. I think that set the tone for the season.

I never had a radio show in Long Beach and that was one of the things they promised me at UNLV. But after we lost that first game the guy who ran the radio show told someone, "Tell Tark to shove that radio show up his ass." The show was cancelled after one loss. After we won the next couple of games, I got the radio show back, but that is how tough a town Vegas can be.

Nowadays, when a coach leaves one school, he takes half his old team with him to the new one. I see it all the time, and it blows my mind. When I left Long Beach State in 1973, I probably could have taken three-quarters of that team with me. They all wanted to go to UNLV with me.

If there was one whom I would have considered taking, it was Roscoe Pondexter. His younger brother, Clifton, was the No. 1 high school player in the country, and wherever Roscoe went, Clifton was going. Everybody, including me, wanted Clifton. Plus, I was so close with Roscoe that he drove Lois and me to LAX when we flew up for our UNLV press conference. He begged us to let him go to UNLV. He said he wanted to transfer and bring Clifton.

I said that wouldn't be right. I talked him into staying. I told him that he was already settled at Long Beach and it was a great school. I loved Long Beach, and I didn't want any hard feelings, so I personally talked him out of leaving. I wanted to leave on good terms. I thought taking the players would be the wrong thing to do, but I see it all of the time now. About halfway through that first year, I think I cursed myself for that policy.

One day we went into Reno to play the University of Nevada. We had a pregame meal at this big restaurant, the Primavera, and there was hardly anybody in there. My two assistants so hated that team that they ate across the street; they wouldn't even eat with the players. My players wouldn't even speak to each other; they split up into these little groups. We had three guys sitting here, three here, three here, three here; they were all spread out in this empty restaurant. The waiter came up to me and asked if I could get these guys to sit closer.

"Coach," he said, "is there any way you can get your team together?"

"Shit, I have been trying to do that since October."

We went 20-6, which isn't bad, but we should have been better. I remember at the end of the year, they said if we won our last two games, we got an NIT bid, which was a big deal because UNLV was so down that it had never even been to the NIT. The fans were all excited, and this was going to be a good momentum builder in recruiting.

So we won our last two games. The last one was at home, and as we came off the court at the Las Vegas Convention Center, all of our fans were chanting, "NIT! NIT!"

But then one of my assistants grabbed me and said, "Coach, do you realize if we get an NIT bid, we're going to have to spend two more weeks with these assholes?"

"Yeah, you're right."

I was all depressed just thinking about it, so I went into the locker room, and I told the players, "We're not going to the NIT. Instead we're going have a meeting. A lot of you guys aren't coming back next year, we're getting rid of you."

I went right through the whole thing. I just laid down the law. They all knew I was serious about it, because who turns down the first NIT bid in school history?

But I hadn't come to Vegas to be in the NIT.

12

The Power of the Pen

(Hell, I coached there 19 years, and I bet in all that time, I didn' t pay for 19 meals.)

—*JERRY TARKANIAN*

Las Vegas in 1973 was an entirely different place than it is now. Now it's the fastest-growing city in the country; thousands of people move there each month. The city can't keep up with the housing demand, and traffic is incredible. Back when we went there, it was kind of small, lots of open space. And because of its reputation, people didn't want to move to Vegas. It wasn't the attractive place to live that it is today.

In the 1970s and 1980s we had to convince people there was more to Las Vegas than just the casinos. And it wasn't easy. Back then, the mob had a lot of influence in Vegas; they had a big say in the casinos. As a tourist destination, Vegas was so much better then, because the mob's major concern was getting the first count in the casino cage. Once they got their money, they were as happy as hell. They didn't care what it cost to get the gamblers in, because that wasn't their business. So food was free; rooms were real cheap. You could get a room at a real nice hotel for

$19. You could get a steak-and-egg breakfast for 99 cents. Casinos would do anything to get you in the door so that first cage count was strong.

And it wasn't like you saw the mob guys. They had people rent a casino and other guys run it. They were just getting their share, taking some out of town. So you wouldn't see them. They were usually back East somewhere.

But casino gambling got so lucrative that in the late 1980s, corporations came in and bought up the casinos and the hotels. Corporations have accountants, stockholders, and things like that. They want a profit in every department. Food and beverage has to have a profit. Rooms have to have a profit. When the mob controlled it, their only concern was the cage. It used to be they catered to all of the big gamblers. They'd bring in the big hitters and wine and dine them and treat them great. Now they bring a few in but keep a close watch on them. It isn't the same.

The concern of some parents was that Las Vegas was a bad place for their kids to live. But it wasn't like that. My players usually stayed near campus and hung out with other college kids. They weren't going to casinos; they were going to get pizza with the other kids. They might get a meal at a casino restaurant, but that was it. It really wasn't what everyone thought it would be for the players. In all my time at UNLV, there was only one player who had a gambling problem. But we had the casinos so wired that the moment he entered one, we would get a call.

Still, we had to deal with that all of the time. A recruit would come visit the campus, and then go home and tell people how much he loved Vegas and wanted to come there. Then the assistant coaches at the other schools recruiting him would tell the kid's mother that if he came to UNLV, the mob or the hookers were going to get her son. And the mother would be all shook up, and I would have to fly back out and meet with her again to smooth it all out. The University of Arizona assistant coaches used to always do that to us.

I got to know a lot of people in the casino business when I got to Las Vegas. One of the first was Ash Resnick, who was a big-time casino guy in the 1970s. Ash was a great basketball player originally from New York, a Jewish guy, who was one of the original Boston Celtics. UNLV could only pay me so much money, so in an effort to supplement my income, the boosters set it up for me to work as a public relations guy at Caesar's

Palace. I'd greet people and things like that. I worked with Ash. That's how linked the city and the school were then.

Eventually the *Las Vegas Sun* newspaper wrote an article saying I shouldn't work in a casino because it was a bad image for the school. So the university pulled that deal from me. But to tell you how Vegas worked, the school made it up to me by arranging for me to receive the same amount of money to write a column for the *Las Vegas Sun*. That was even better because it was easier to do.

But while I worked for Ash, we became great friends. Ash's problem was he could never get a casino license. He had been moved out of Caesar's and was running the Aladdin and wanted to take an ownership stake in it. But he had some ties back in New York that made it tough for him to get a license. So he applied for one and had to go to Reno for the hearing in front of the Nevada State Gaming Control Board, which determines who gets a casino license. Ash asked me and some other guys to go up and testify on his behalf because he knew the background check would be trouble.

It was me, Sugar Ray Robinson, Joe DiMaggio, Wayne Newton, and a Catholic priest. We went up to Reno and spoke at the hearing, but we got beat 3-0. You could appeal the decision to another hearing in Vegas, but they said if you got beat in Reno, it was almost impossible to win in Vegas.

But Ash wanted to try. So we all got ready to speak again on behalf of Ash. There was an article in the paper about my going up to testify on his behalf, and one of our college vice presidents called me.

"You have to pull back and not testify. Ash can't get a license, and this is hurting your reputation."

"Hey, Ash has been my friend ever since I came to town."

One thing about me is loyalty is the most important thing. I wasn't going to turn my back on him.

So this time he had just Wayne Newton, the Catholic priest, and me testify. It was such a big deal, part of it was televised. And this time we won it. It was the first time the board in Reno said no and the board in Vegas said yes. So Ash got his license, and for several months there, I had the *power of the pen* at the Aladdin hotel. It was the first time I had ever experienced anything like that. The power of the pen meant you could get anyone you wanted room, food, and beverage at the casino. And when the bill came, you just signed it. You never had to pay. You could get anything you wanted on the bill, anything at all. You want a piece of filet mignon, you just sign for it. Bottle of champagne? Just sign for it. Anything. In Vegas. Just ask. The power of the pen is a big thing in Las Vegas.

So for several months, I could bring in any coach I wanted; get him room, food, and beverage; and just sign for everything. It was the most incredible time. Finally they cracked down. But until then, it was incredible. I had no idea things worked that way.

That's how Las Vegas was, though; people would do anything to help you out, to get you to come to their place. Once we got it going and started winning a lot of games, getting a lot of attention for UNLV, and entertaining the fans, it was the best. I never got the power of the pen again, but it was close. I couldn't get anyone I wanted a room, but I could sign for almost everything else.

Everybody treated me like I was the king of Las Vegas, but the thing that made it big for me was I never really felt like I was a celebrity. Then people said I was the only guy in town who didn't know I was a celebrity. I'd go everywhere, but I'd always mix with everybody because I enjoy mixing with people. I didn't need a high-rollers area or a VIP section. I like regular people, working people.

I used to eat all the time at Piero's, an Italian place run by my friend Freddie Glusman, a tough Jewish guy. He's hard on his workers, but he pays them well, and they all like him, but they all fear him. I would eat in there almost every day. Not six times a week, all seven. And I always took guys into Piero's. I took the coaches and media out to eat in there the night before games. I took Jimmy Valvano, Gene Keady, all of the coaches. I took Bobby Knight there once, and Freddie loved it; he got an autographed basketball. I would take Dick Vitale, Digger Phelps, Billy Packer, all of the broadcasters, and then they'd mention Piero's the next day on television. I got them national publicity.

One day I was in Piero's, and the guy who owned the Palace Station came up to me and introduced himself.

"I want you to know, you have done more for Vegas than anybody in the history of the state."

"Oh, that's so nice of you to say."

"You've made people realize that we have other things out here, and it isn't just gambling. We have a community. We have fans who support the university."

The people in Las Vegas just loved UNLV basketball. Hell, I coached there 19 years, and I bet in all that time, I didn't pay for 19 meals. I probably paid for one meal a year, and I ate out every night. And I was eating gourmet meals.

People couldn't do enough for you. The guy who ran the Dunes would call me because I wasn't coming down enough. He'd say, "Tark, are you mad at us. Is something wrong?" So we'd go down there, Lois and the kids and everything, eat a fancy, expensive meal, just so the guy would know I wasn't mad at him. It was unbelievable. I had to eat a prime rib dinner for free just to show I wasn't mad at a guy.

The offseason was great. I'd go have lunch with the football coach and some of our staff and eat out by the pool of some casino.

High school coaches used to love to come to Vegas, which was a big help in recruiting. Mothers may have been worried about Las Vegas, but high school coaches weren't. They loved Las Vegas. The NCAA said I couldn't get them comped rooms, but rooms were so cheap it hardly mattered. We had a great friend who owned a motel in Vegas called the Klondike Inn. We would refer everyone to the Klondike Inn, where the rooms were real cheap. Opposing teams would even stay there sometimes because it was off The Strip.

We used to have high school or juco coaches in all of the time to watch practice. Everyone wanted to come for a weekend, so on every game weekend we would have 15 coaches in from Southern California or around the country in to watch practice. Then at night I did what they wanted to do. I went to a bar with them, had some chicken wings, and drank all night. I just hung around. Or my assistants took them out on the town. By the time we got it going really good in the 1980s, I was older and I went to Piero's and all of these fancy places every night. But my assistants went to the chicken wing places and kept them out at the bars all night. I was getting too old for that. Las Vegas can wear you out.

They don't do comps like that anymore in Vegas, but it was fun then. When I first came to town, it was just so easy.

In 1990, we won the national championship on a Monday. That Saturday, my daughter Jodie was getting married. All of the groundwork had already been laid, all of the arrangements had been made, but after we won the national championship, we got treated like royalty. It was incredible. Southern Nevada Wine picked up all of the booze. It was just great. The wedding wasn't completely free, but a lot of things were free. I was expecting to pay a ton, but then I found out somebody else paid for it because they were so happy we had won the national championship.

We met all sorts of celebrities through the years. I remember one time around New Year's we played Maryland, which was coached by Lefty Driesell. Lefty is a great friend of mine, so on New Year's Eve, I took Lefty to a party at the Riviera, and we sat at the same table as Elizabeth Taylor. Lefty couldn't believe it. Frank Sinatra used to have parties that started at 2 a.m., right after his last set at Caesar's. You wouldn't even go to the party until 2 a.m., which will tell you what kind of party that was.

We had a lot of big entertainers at our games. Bill Cosby used to come often and sit right behind our bench. We had Don Rickles, Mike Tyson, George Foreman, Lola Falana, Diana Ross, Sammy Davis, and Wayne Newton. We had all of those people at our banquets at one time or another. When entertainers were in town, they wanted to come over to the games. We were like a big show. George Foreman came to my retirement dinner and presented me with his championship belt.

I got to know Mike Tyson pretty well. You couldn't believe it, but he didn't seem like the same guy in the ring. Here was a guy who bit Evander Holyfield's ear off but then could be such a nice guy. He was very intelligent and was always great to Lois and me. My son Danny saw him one time, and Tyson asked all about me, how I was doing. He told Danny, "Be sure to say hello to your dad." He could act like a real nice, normal guy, and then next thing you know, you would read something crazy about him. One of my real good friends in town owns a sports car dealership, and he said Tyson would come in and buy three or four $100,000 cars at one time. Then he'd just give them to people.

One time Tyson had a Rolls Royce, and he hit a tree. The car wasn't totaled or anything, just damaged. It was still a Rolls Royce. The police showed up and were going to write up a report, and Tyson said he didn't want to get it repaired or deal with the crash, so he gave the cop the keys.

"Oh, you take it. You keep the car."

"No, I can't do that," the cop replied.

I'm not surprised Tyson went broke.

Occasionally we used celebrities to recruit, but not often. When kids would come for a visit, the people at the hotel arranged for them to go see Bill Cosby backstage or Diana Ross, something like that. We figured that might help. Or if their parents came along on the visit, we'd set it up so they would run into a big star who would say something good about UNLV basketball. But then the NCAA came out with a deal that we couldn't have them meet those people, so we had to stop.

Another time, the NCAA came out with a rule that we couldn't put them in nice casinos because it wasn't the typical place where college students would stay. We couldn't put the players in the big fancy spots on The Strip. I thought that was unfair, so I got a list of where UCLA and Cal–Berkeley were putting their guys, and they were putting them in the best places in town. So I sent that to the NCAA.

"Hell, look where they're putting their guys, the best hotels in Los Angeles and San Francisco. Incredibly expensive places. Do you think that's the typical place college students would stay?"

But the NCAA didn't care.

Our school decided to put recruits up at Circus Circus because it was kind of a family place. That was the best we could do. Some new incredible casino would open, and we'd have to drive right by it and stop at Circus Circus. But what could we do? The NCAA was just always screwing with us.

13

Frank Sinatra

" Mr. Sinatra wants you to know that he has all the confidence in the world in you. And Mr. Sinatra knows that you can get this straightened out, and Mr. Sinatra just wants to thank you beforehand for straightening it all out. "

—FRANK SINATRA'S SECRETARY

When I first came to Las Vegas, Frank Sinatra did a fundraiser for the university every year. Sinatra could raise $100,000 in one night, which was an incredible amount of money in the early 1970s. But that was how big Sinatra was. That's how strong he was. Through those fundraisers, I got to know Frank well, and anytime he was in town to perform at Caesar's, he'd take Lois and me to dinner at the Palace Court, his favorite place.

Sinatra loved our program, but we could never get him to come to an actual game. He was just so busy, so in demand. We left tickets, and then he never showed. But he called us after big victories, things like that. He watched on TV. The night we won the national title, when Lois got back to our hotel room, the phone was ringing, and it was Sinatra, calling to congratulate us and to tell us he was proud of us.

That was the kind of guy he was. He was just a great guy. Obviously, he was an incredible entertainer, but he was really just a great guy to be around, a real friend. When you think about how many people he knew and how busy his schedule was, for him to take the time to call us or have dinner with us in Vegas was just incredible. I really valued that.

Sinatra was a very, very powerful guy. And he had very, very powerful friends. So whatever Frank wanted, Frank got. I found that out the hard way. My second year in Vegas, I got an invitation from Sinatra's secretary that he was going to have a fundraiser for his mother. His mother's dream had always been to build a retirement home for Italian entertainers. So they decided to have a big fundraiser at the Stardust Hotel to raise money for it. I got invited, and it was $2,500 a person, and I was expected to bring Lois. This was 1974, and that was a pretty damn good amount of money. I mean, I was only making $48,000 at that time with four kids, and they expected me to spend $5,000 on a fundraiser for Frank Sinatra's mother to open a retirement home for Italian entertainers? So I got the invitation, and I just didn't even respond to it. I hoped they wouldn't notice.

Then about 10 days before the event, Sinatra's secretary called.

"Mr. Sinatra is really hurt that you haven't responded to his invitation. Mr. Sinatra wants you to know that from the university, he has only invited you and the college president. The fact that Mr. Sinatra hasn't heard from you has made him really, really disappointed."

I was reeling then. I had only been in Vegas for two years, but I knew that one thing I didn't want was a man like Frank Sinatra disappointed in me, because I just had no idea what that might entail.

So I threw it all on Lois.

"God, I thought Lois sent it in. We were planning on going, of course."

I didn't know what the hell to say. So I went home and told Lois about it.

"We've got to go, $5,000 or not."

So we wrote the check and went to this function at the Stardust. I figured I was going to run into a lot of the boosters whom I knew, good friends, people from Vegas. The room was packed, but I looked around and I didn't see anybody in there I knew except the university president and the local district attorney and his assistant, who were good friends of mine. There were only about 10 guys from Vegas in the entire room. Lois and I sat at our table. The guy to the right of me was from Phoenix. He was with his wife, and he was in the computer business. We started talking.

"Are you friends with Frank?" I asked.

"No, we've never met him."

"Why are you here?"

"We were told to be here for business reasons."

The guy to the left of us was from Chicago, and he said the same thing. He didn't know Frank and had no idea why he was invited, but he was told in no uncertain terms that for "business reasons" he and his wife needed to come to the banquet. I couldn't believe it. All of these guys flying in from all over the country to pay $5,000 to have dinner, and they didn't even know Frank Sinatra. That shows you how strong the guy was—Sinatra could get guys there, because they were told to be there.

The district attorney was a good friend of mine. He came over.

"Jerry, let's go over and say hello to Frank."

Sinatra was sitting at a head table, with about 15 people up there. Well, I didn't want to bother him, but they said, "No, no, Frank would like to see you." So we went over, and they tapped Sinatra on the shoulder, but I stayed to the background. I didn't want to impose. Well, Jilly Rizzo, who was Sinatra's bodyguard, saw me.

"Frank, Frank the Coach is here."

So Frank got up and gave me a big hug. Then this guy jumped up— and I didn't even know the guy—and started saying, "Jerry, Jerry Tarkanian!"

He came over, shook my hand, and it was Tommy Lasorda, the manager of the Los Angeles Dodgers. Tommy was at the head table, sitting right with Sinatra. We became pretty good friends from then on.

I can't even imagine how much money they raised for that Italian entertainers retirement home.

Jilly was not just Sinatra's bodyguard; he was legendary in his own right. Jilly was a very powerful guy because he was so close to Sinatra. When I first met Jilly, they said, "Jilly is so loyal to Frank that when Frank dies, Jilly wants to get buried instead." So whatever Jilly wanted, he got, because no one—and I mean no one—dared cross Sinatra. Everyone understood that.

Jilly had a son who lived in Vegas and worked in one of the casinos. In the late 1970s we played our games at the Las Vegas Convention Center, which only seated 6,700 people. We got so good that our games became the hardest ticket to get in town. Articles were written in the papers that it was a lot easier to get tickets to the Frank Sinatra show than it was a Rebels basketball game.

But I had a pass list at the back door of the convention center where I could get guys through without a ticket. I would put my friends and my family on there, so they could all get in for free. I had Jilly's son on that pass list, because that made Jilly happy and in turn that made Sinatra happy. Then one year, we got a new athletic director, Al Negratti. He came in and eliminated the pass list. He said we had to get the athletic budget up and declared, "Everybody's paying, and there's no pass list." He was a real hard ass. I was nervous because that meant Jilly's son was out, and that meant—well, I didn't even want to think about what that meant. I went to Al and told him about Sinatra.

"You know, Sinatra raises $100,000 a year for the school, and you're going to take away his pass list?"

"Yep, he's got to pay."

The guy wasn't budging.

So I called Jilly and I told him, "We got a new AD and he's just a hard ass. He's eliminated the pass list, and there's nothing I can do about it. I can't get your kid in. I'm sorry."

About two days later I get a call from Mr. Sinatra's secretary.

"Mr. Sinatra understands that you are having a real problem with this new athletic director, but Mr. Sinatra wants you to know that he has all the confidence in the world in you. And Mr. Sinatra knows that you can get this straightened out, and Mr. Sinatra just wants to thank you beforehand for straightening it all out."

And that was the conversation, the *entire* conversation. She hung up after that. "Mr. Sinatra has all the confidence in the world in me? He knows you can get this straightened out?" That's the way Sinatra was. He didn't want any excuses, just get it done, get Jilly's kid into the damn game. I was so nervous I couldn't stand it. I did not know what to do, so I went to the university president and described the situation. I told him about Sinatra's confidence in me and everything. The college president has the real power on a campus, and he understood. So he overruled the athletic director, we got the pass list back, and I finally felt at ease.

One night in 1976, I was having dinner with Frank at the Palace Court at Caesar's. He asked me about the team and mentioned that he was really excited about the future. Then he said, "Jerry, if there is anything I can ever do to help out, let me know."

Well, I thought there was something he could do. I had gotten to thinking that Sinatra could be real helpful in recruiting, especially if we hooked him up with some Italian-American kids back East. I thought that if we could ever send Sinatra into a recruit's home, have him meet the Italian mother, well, it would be over. They'd do whatever Sinatra told them to do. I figured it would be a lock. How could they turn down Frank Sinatra? So I told Sinatra my plan, and he loved the idea. He said to set it up.

Well, it turned out that year there were only two kids like that who we wanted. One was a big Italian kid from Long Island, a six-foot-10 center. Sinatra was supposed to meet with the family, but there was a scheduling problem. He was only able to call them on the phone and talk up UNLV. The kid wound up signing with South Carolina, where Frank McGuire, who was from New York, coached. Sinatra knew Frank McGuire from New York, and he liked him. So when Sinatra called me up to ask how we did, I told him the news.

"Well," he said, "we didn't get him, but at least he went down there with my friend, Frank."

I wasn't as excited about that.

The best player was Mike O'Koren, who everybody in the country wanted. Mike was a six-foot-seven forward, a slasher who could really play. He was from Jersey City, New Jersey. Sinatra was from Hoboken, New Jersey, which is right next to Jersey City. We learned that Mike's mother loved Frank Sinatra. I figured if we got Frank into that living room in Jersey City, there was no way we wouldn't get Mike O'Koren. This time the schedule worked out, and Frank Sinatra went and talked to his family, met the mom, signed autographs, and everything. He may have even sung them a couple songs. He sat right in that living room and told them to send their boy Mike out to Las Vegas. They were all excited.

And then we didn't get him. After all that, he signed with Dean Smith and North Carolina, where he was a three-time first-team All-American before playing eight seasons in the NBA. I just couldn't believe my plan had backfired. We went 0-for-2 on Sinatra's recruits. Dean Smith might be the greatest recruiter in the history of college basketball. Forget about signing Michael Jordan, James Worthy, and the rest. Dean Smith beat Frank Sinatra on a kid from Jersey City. Impossible.

The worst part came in 1977, when my UNLV team played North Carolina in the Final Four. O'Koren was just a freshman, but he killed us. He had 31 points on 14-of-19 shooting. We couldn't stop Mike O'Koren and wound up losing to Carolina 84-83. Every time he scored, I was ready to curse Sinatra for not closing out that recruiting deal. If we had gotten O'Koren instead of Carolina, we would have won the national title.

That Frank Sinatra, he could really sing, but he sure couldn't recruit.

14

Runnin' Rebels

"Here I am trying to sell Las Vegas to her while Oral Roberts is selling God."

—*Jerry Tarkanian*

W hen I got to UNLV, the team was just called the Rebels. The UNLV Rebels. No one called them the "Runnin' Rebels" then, because they never ran. Neither did I, though. When I was at Long Beach, we didn't have the talent to win by running the ball. My teams used to slow it down, play a ball-possession game, and win with defense. That's the only way to beat more talented teams. I liked to use a 1-2-2 zone on defense, a far cry from the pressure man-to-man most people associate with me.

But I had to adapt. My second year at UNLV, I thought we were going to be pretty good because we had David Vaughn, a seven-foot center. A big guy is a key to the 1-2-2 zone. But that summer, Louis Shaffel stole him from us. Shaffel was a sports agent from New York who had been involved in the recruitment of Tommy Henderson when I was at Long Beach and had helped me get Ricky Sobers, a real talented guard, to come to UNLV. Ricky was also from New York and had a summer job in Shaffel's office. I liked Louis, and he would hang around our place. But one day I was in Montana speaking at a coaching clinic, and I got a call from my assistant.

"You won't believe it," he said. "Louis Shaffel came in and took David Vaughn. He signed with the Virginia Squires of the ABA."

"Oh, no," I thought. "Now I don't have a big man at all."

I had one big guy, Louis Brown, but he was unpredictable. He was a hell of a player, but I knew that if he knew he was our only big guy, he was going to give us all kinds of hell. He needed some competition to keep him focused.

No one thought we were going to be any good. All we had was Ricky Sobers, and he was a pain in the ass as a junior. I didn't even want Ricky on the team anymore. In fact, when Ricky's old coach got the job at Oral Roberts, I tried to get Ricky to transfer there. I called Ricky in, and I told him he should be loyal to his old coach, really laying it on thick. But he didn't fall for it. He wouldn't go. But that talk changed his whole attitude. He eventually became a great, great guy and a great player for me. Ricky Sobers is the best guard I ever coached.

What I had was a bunch of six-foot-five freshmen and sophomores who were good athletes. But no big man at all. I met with my assistants and said, "We've got to get out of the zone. We can't play the zone. We have good athletes. We've got to play pressure man defense." I figured that we could use our small size to our advantage by making bigger teams run the floor. I knew we had to try something. My staff and I went down to the University of New Mexico and met with the Lobos head coach, Bob King, who was a great man-to-man coach. Then I flew down to Lexington and spent time with Kentucky coach Joe B. Hall, and we discussed pressure defense. That's where I got most of my theories.

After that, we hardly ever played a zone. Once I went to man, I loved it, and our fans loved it. Of course, as long as you win, fans are happy. It hardly matters how you play. But I do think the pressure man-to-man defense was a better fit for Las Vegas. When you think Vegas, walk-it-up ball doesn't really fit. They want a show, they want flash, and they want excitement. And that's what we gave them.

It is rare for a coach to completely change his offensive and defensive philosophies in the middle of his career. At my retirement dinner, John Wooden said I was one of the few coaches ever who changed his game 180 degrees. Pete Newell has said over and over again: I'm the only coach he's ever seen who went from a zone to a man and pressure defense and ran at the same time. Pete used to think you couldn't run and play pressure defense, because it took too much out of you.

We had a great run after switching to man-to-man. My second year, we were picked third or fourth in the league, and we wound up winning the thing. We went from averaging 78 points a game my first year to 91 my second. And the fans loved it. In 1975-1976, my third year, we averaged 110.5 points a game. That's a lot of points in a 40-minute college game, and back then there was no shot clock. We played a game against Hawaii–Hilo where we had 85 at halftime and won 164-111. It was incredible. We started the season with 23 consecutive victories and finished 29-2, and with our style, we became a big hit across the country.

We were a lot better by then, though. We had brought in Reggie Theus out of Inglewood, California, one of the most important recruits of my career. Reggie was a six-foot-seven guard who UCLA got in on a bit at the end, but he stayed loyal to us. Reggie went on to play 13 years in the NBA and become a Hollywood actor, and now he's the head coach at New Mexico State. Reggie was just such a positive person; he helped us prove good kids could come to The Strip. We got Tony Smith, a great guard out of Saginaw, Michigan, when he decided to transfer from the University of Houston. We got tipped off on that one by Michigan coach Bill Frieder, who couldn't take Tony in Ann Arbor but was so scared Tony would transfer to Michigan State that he helped us out. We got Glen "Gondo" Gondrezick out of Boulder, Colorado, because I loved his energy and thought he was a great kid.

Then there was Eddie Owens, who was a smooth, six-foot-seven swingman out of Houston. I used to never recruit players from there because if the University of Houston wanted them, you had no chance of getting them. It was locked up down there. But Eddie's high school coach didn't want him to go to UH, so we jumped in. The problem was to get him we had to beat Oral Roberts. Not just Oral Roberts University, the Christian school in Tulsa, but the actual Oral Roberts. Eddie's mom was very religious, and Oral had gotten involved in the recruiting process for the school he founded. Here I am trying to sell Las Vegas to her while Oral Roberts is selling God.

I flew down with a National Letter of Intent and sat in the Owens's living room, pleading my case. Eddie wanted his mother to sign the papers; he wanted to come with us. But the mother was against it and said she had promised Oral Roberts a visit the next day. I knew that if that happened, I wouldn't get the kid. You just can't beat a preacher like that. So I decided I just would not leave the house until Eddie and his mother signed. I figured I would just wait them out. Finally, at 1 a.m., the mother gave up and signed, probably just to get me out of the house so she could go to bed. I had the worst headache that night, but on the way out of there, I looked at the signed letter, and it made me feel a little better. No player in UNLV history ever scored more points than Eddie Owens.

This was the core of the Runnin' Rebels, the team that would take us to the 1977 NCAA Final Four and truly put UNLV basketball on the map nationally. What was amazing was we could have been even better.

I had Michael Cooper, who would go on to an incredible career with the Los Angeles Lakers, wrapped up when my friend, Norm Ellenberger, who had just succeeded Bob King as the head coach at New Mexico, stole him from me. Cooper was at Pasadena City College. I had Pasadena wired. That was my hometown, and I used to coach there. My brother was the football coach. The school president, Dr. Sarafian, was like a father to me. The athletic director, Skippy Robinson, played football there, and I had known him for 30 years, so he was in our corner. Everybody was in our corner. They wanted me to take Michael Cooper in 1977.

But in 1976, I had Gondrezick, Eddie Owens, and three wing players, and all of them were coming back. I didn't have the spot for Cooper so even though I knew he was good, I couldn't recruit him. But in Pasadena, they had it so locked up for me to take Cooper that no other school could even get in there. Then one day Skippy Robinson called.

"Tark, this kid's not going to be eligible anyway next year. He's only going to have 36 units; you need 48 to transfer."

"God, that's great."

That meant we could take him and redshirt him. He would sit out one year, take 12 credits, and then get eligible. Then when Gondrezick and Owens graduated, he could move right in. It was perfect.

At the end of August, I was expecting Cooper to show up at UNLV when I found out he was at the University of New Mexico. Not only that, New Mexico claimed he was going to be eligible for the upcoming season. I couldn't believe it. I called down to Albuquerque.

"Norm, how the hell did you get him eligible? He only passed 36 credits, he needed 12 more to get eligible, that is another semester at least. . . . There was no way you got him eligible."

"Tark, the kid had a hell of a summer. He had a hell of an August in the classroom."

I just laughed. Norm laughed. It was funny.

I don't know if they stashed him somewhere and got him 12 credits in like two weeks, or they just manufactured a transcript. I have no idea, and I didn't care. They got it done, and we didn't; that was the bottom line. Norm was my great friend, anyway. Every summer, he and his staff would come and spend a few days in Las Vegas, and we would take them out on the town. Then a couple of my guys and I went to Albuquerque, and he'd take us out. Every summer. We talked basketball and hung out. We were really close.

Probably a little too close, actually.

One year, Norm had an assistant coach from Compton, California, who was a real good dresser and a well-spoken guy. But he was backstabbing Norm. One season they had a revolt among the black players, and they wanted to get Norm. The team was divided, and Norm almost got fired over it.

We were set to play New Mexico in Vegas on national television. We had a 78-home-game winning streak going. I sent my assistant down to scout New Mexico, and he came back and said the players had quit on Norm. UNM was like 4-4. We were 8-0 and just rolling. The night before the game, I took Norm and one of his assistants out to dinner in one of these gourmet rooms at a casino, and we had a good time. We went out on the town after that, and all night Norm and his assistant just badmouthed their team and how much they hated it.

I was actually feeling for Norm. He was my friend, and he was in a tough spot. Then the next afternoon UNM played incredible, and my 78-home-game win streak went up in smoke. To make matters even worse, the star of the game for the Lobos was Michael Cooper.

"I will never feel sorry for an opponent during the season," I told Lois. "I don't care if it is my best friend."

It might have affected us, because I might have been a little too loose, too confident. A team reflects the personality of the coach. Before the game, I felt sorry for Norm, but when they beat us, I wasn't feeling bad for Norm anymore. I was feeling sorry for me.

The 1976-1977 team was one of the greatest in school history, Michael Cooper or no Michael Cooper. I had Eddie Owens, Gondo, Reggie Theus, and the "Smith Brothers"—Sam, Robert, and Tony Smith. They weren't related, but it was a good nickname. We still weren't big; we had a six-foot-eight center, Larry Moffett. But he was a heck of a rebounder, and he started our break. And what a break we had, what a bunch of athletes.

We averaged 107 points a game. Our pressure defense caused an average of 28 turnovers. We just swallowed teams up. The city of Las Vegas was completely behind us, tickets were tough to get, and we had this big light show to introduce our team. It was great. We entered the NCAA Tournament with a 25-2 record.

The NCAA gave us the most ridiculous draw, though. We were in the top five of the polls, and they paired us in the opening round with second-ranked San Francisco, who had Bill Cartwright and had been undefeated until the last week of the season. I always thought the NCAA tried to stack the brackets against us, and this was one case where it was obvious. How could two top-five teams meet in the first round? It didn't matter in the end. We just ran them out of the gym. In one 90-second stretch, we scored 12 points, and we wound up winning 121-95.

In the second round, we beat Utah 88-83, and I thought we would get a regional final matchup with UCLA, with the winner going to the Final Four. That was the game I wanted, because of all of the losses we had had at Long Beach State. But Idaho State upset UCLA, and the game never happened. In fact, I never played UCLA again, although I tried for years to schedule them. We avoided a letdown against Idaho State to win 107-90 and sent UNLV to the Final Four for the first time in school history.

The Final Four is a dream goal for every college coach, and it was no different for me. All of the focus is on you, and it really makes your career. The only downside to the weekend was when we arrived in Atlanta, there were constant rumors that the NCAA was about to put us on probation. That is the way the NCAA used to work; you didn't even know what was going on. Now they have to be more up front about it, but back then, you weren't sure.

When we got to Atlanta, the talk was nonstop. The NCAA was not happy that I had not only survived the Long Beach investigation, but was now at the Final Four. Almost every coach they go after gets fired or winds up at a much smaller school where they're out of the spotlight. LSU coach Dale Brown and I were about the only ones they could never take down. That was because UNLV stuck by me, and I appreciated that. Most schools would have fired their coach after an investigation, but UNLV hired the state attorney general to conduct an investigation, and when he turned up no major violations, they decided to stick with me.

When I got to Atlanta that weekend, a coach told me there was no way the NCAA would let UNLV win. He promised me the referees would ensure that we lost, because there was no way the NCAA would allow me to win a national championship. I thought about that, but I didn't want to believe it.

We played North Carolina in the Final Four, and that was the Mike O'Koren game I described. We were the highest-scoring team in the country, and Dean Smith at UNC liked to employ the Four-Corner offense, where his team stood in the corners and just held the ball until something broke open. If they got the lead, they would hold the ball for minutes and minutes. O'Koren got inside our defense and killed us. As for the referees, well, UNC shot 28 free throws. We shot five. That's all I can say.

We lost 84-83. And then I really got worried about probation. In August, the NCAA hit us with two years for a bunch of garbage. We were banned from the NCAA Tournament for two years, which really took the wind out of our program and hurt our recruiting. But it didn't kill us. The NCAA tried to get UNLV to suspend me, but I sued them because they violated my rights. And I was right. So I kept my job. The NCAA didn't get me that time, which is why they just kept trying harder.

15

Taking on the Big Boys

" If he is driving a Cadillac, he' s going to Kentucky. "

—JERRY TARKANIAN

During the summer of 1978, a friend of mine, Irwin Molasky, asked me to help him film a movie, *The Fish That Saved Pittsburgh.* Irwin was in the film business with Lorimar Productions and was a big-time UNLV booster. The movie starred Julius Erving and featured a lot of big-time players. Irwin made me the technical adviser. I spent about three weeks in Pittsburgh while they filmed the movie, and it was a lot of fun. They put me up in a real nice hotel, and I always liked Pittsburgh, anyway. It's a great town.

I got to be real good friends with the guy who owned the oyster houses in Pittsburgh, Louis Grippo. He had some connections with people in Vegas, and he was great to me. Louis's son played high school football at Catholic Central High School, and he would pick me up in his limo, and we'd go watch football practice. The quarterback on that team was Dan Marino, and even then you could tell he was great.

One Sunday morning while I was in Pittsburgh, I read the newspaper, and there was a big article about this great player from Lebanon, a small city in central Pennsylvania. His name was Sam Bowie, he was seven foot one, and he was considered the No. 1 recruit in America. If Sam were a high school senior today, no one would recruit him, because he would be the No. 1 pick in the NBA draft. He was that good. Back then, though, every school in the country coveted him.

I didn't really know much about Sam, because a guy like that wasn't even on my radar. We never had a chance with a top recruit like that. Las Vegas is a long way from Pennsylvania, and we never were able to beat the big schools such as North Carolina, Kentucky, or Indiana for recruits. So I didn't know anything about Sam. I was just reading the article for the fun of it when I came to the part where they listed the schools he was considering, and we were one of the schools. It said "UNLV" right there in the Pittsburgh paper.

I couldn't believe it. We had never even contacted him. I didn't even know about him. I thought it might be a misprint, but I had to find out, because according to this article, Sam Bowie, this seven-foot-one kid from the middle of Pennsylvania, was considering playing for me.

On Monday, I called his coach at Lebanon High School and introduced myself.

"It said in the Pittsburgh paper that Sam was considering us, but we haven't even recruited him. Is it true?"

"Yes, it's true."

What happened was the kid was trying to figure out where he wanted to go to school, and he sat down with a guidance counselor and filled out a survey with some things he was looking for in a college. He wanted a place where he could start as a freshman, and our starting center was a senior. He wanted good weather, and Vegas has great weather. And he wanted to major in hotel management, and we had the best hotel management school in the country. It wasn't in the survey, but he also said he wanted a school with pretty girls, and UNLV had pretty girls. With those four things, Vegas came out strong. We were in there.

So I got all excited. The next day I drove about five hours to Lebanon to visit with him. Sam and his family were interested, so we stayed in touch. We thought we had a great shot. Sam came out to visit and really liked our school, our players, and the city.

My assistant George McQuarn was on Sam. He really worked hard recruiting him, but this was when I was reminded why I didn't like to bother with top-five or top-10 recruits. No matter how hard we recruited Sam, we couldn't recruit him as hard as the University of Kentucky. UNLV was a better situation than Long Beach State, but it was a long way from the level of a Kentucky.

One day as we were getting ready to go to practice, McQuarn came running into the gym.

"I just called Sam Bowie; his dad is in the hospital."

"George, just forget practice. Just get on a plane."

Back then, we needed to get advance money from the school to pay for a trip, but obviously we didn't have time. But I wanted McQuarn on the next flight. So I gave him some money right out of my own pocket.

"Just get on a plane," I said. "Get back there. Be with his dad in the hospital. This will really help us with his recruitment."

I figured no other school would be there that quick, and Sam and his father would really appreciate how much we cared and be impressed that I sent an assistant coach all the way across the country to be by his side.

So George hopped on a plane, flew all night, and got in there. He called me from the hospital.

"Coach, you won't believe it. I'm here at the hospital, and the whole Kentucky staff is here, Joe B. Hall and everyone. They came in on a private jet."

I was like, "Oh, man, Kentucky is incredible."

One thing I almost never did was miss practice to recruit. As much as I enjoyed recruiting, nothing excited me like practice. I just lived for practice, putting the team together and teaching the game. Plus I thought it was unfair to the current players to miss practice to recruit future players. Even though I had a great staff of assistants, I wanted to be there. So I almost never missed practice. I'd go seasons without missing one.

Except for the four times that year when I caught a midnight flight back East. We played a game, and then I caught a redeye flight, into Harrisburg, Pennsylvania, the closest city to Lebanon, and landed about 7 a.m. I remember the lady at the airport rental car office.

"Where you going?"

"I'm going to Lebanon."

"Oh, are you going to see that Sam Bowie kid?"

"Yeah."

"Thank God for that kid. He sure increased our business."

That was how heavily recruited Sam Bowie was; coaches were all flying in and renting cars.

I got in the car, drove to Lebanon, and checked into the only hotel they had in town, the Rodeway Inn, about 9 a.m. I slept until about noon, and then I went over to school and saw Sam during his lunch hour. Then I hung out with his coach and then watched Sam practice. Then after practice, I went by his house and met with his mom and dad for a little while. Then I drove back to Harrisburg and caught the last flight back to Vegas. I was back at practice the next day.

Here was the thing with a school like Kentucky. That winter, every time I checked in the Rodeway Inn, I asked the person behind the desk who else—any other coaches—was staying there. I wanted to see who else was snooping around Sam Bowie. Every time I asked, they said Leonard Hamilton of Kentucky was registered. Leonard was a UK assistant; he's now the head coach at Florida State. I was pretty good friends with Leonard, so every time I checked in, I called his room. But he never answered the phone. When I went over to watch practice, he was never there. Later, when the recruitment was over, I asked Leonard about it.

"Leonard, every time I checked into the Rodeway Inn, you were registered, and yet you were never there."

"Oh, Coach, we kept that room all year just in case we wanted to fly in, we'd have a place to stay."

I was blown away. I thought, that's really nice that the University of Kentucky has that kind of budget. They rented a room for the entire year just to recruit one player. That was how naïve I was. What I later found out was the reason Kentucky rented the room for the entire year was they gave the key to Sam, and anytime he needed someplace to go hang out or do whatever he might need to do, he just went to the Rodeway Inn. Maybe they got it for him so he had a place to concentrate on his studies. I don't know. All I know is it wasn't Leonard Hamilton using that room, Sam Bowie was.

We wound up losing him to UK in January. His high school coach called me and said that Sam was driving a Cadillac. It was an older one, about four years old, and Sam wouldn't say where he got it.

"I think the kid's going to go to Kentucky," the coach said.

"Yeah, I know. If he's driving a Cadillac, he's going to Kentucky, and we're not going to get him."

I knew it was over. I vowed to never recruit against Kentucky ever again. Anytime I was after a player and Kentucky got in there, I would back off. It was futile.

Kentucky was just in a different league than everyone else. In 1978, I got a call from Eddie Einhorn, who scheduled games for the television networks asking if we would play UK on senior night. No one else would do it. My philosophy was to play anyone, anywhere, anytime. Eddie and the networks loved me for this. I'd play Kansas at Kansas. I'd play Princeton when no one would play Princeton. Anyone. I loved big games. I wasn't returning any good players, and Kentucky was loaded—they wound up winning the national championship that year—but I figured why not?

So we went back to Lexington, and boy was that a hell of an experience. Their pregame was so full of pageantry that they introduced everybody. It took 20 minutes. Rick Robey was one of their big superstars that year, a real beloved player, and for senior night, they not only introduced Rick and his parents, but introduced all of his relatives. They had half of the crowd out there. It was the damnedest thing, and the place was just nuts. It was absolutely bananas. Those Kentucky fans were crazy.

We actually led at the break, but then they blitzed us the second half. They just wore us down. I'll never forget that place, though. After the game, Happy Chandler came out and sang "My Old Kentucky Home." The entire arena stayed and sang along, even the players locked arms and rocked back and forth and sang every word. I mean, talk about impressive stuff. Even though we lost, I stayed out on the court just to see this scene. I was standing out there with a couple of my boosters, including Don Chandler, Happy's son who was a host for some casinos in Vegas, and I said, "This is the big time. We're finding out what the big time is like."

Tark the Shark

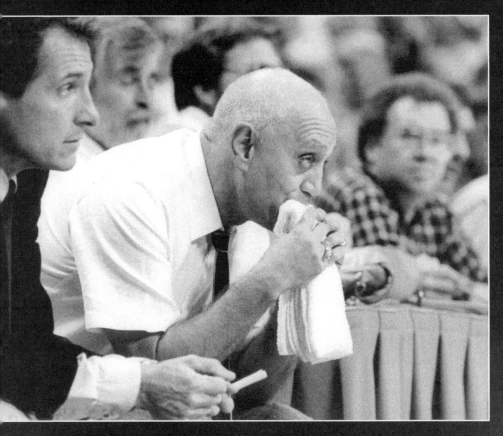

Courtesy of UNLV

Early Beginnings

I (top row, sixth from left) grew up in Euclid, Ohio, as the son of Armenian immigrants. My background made it easier for me to relate to future recruits. *Author's Collection*

The birth of my first child, Pamela, inspired me to move from my first head coaching job at San Joaquin Memorial High School to Antelope Valley High School. *Author's Collection*

As our family grew (me with my son Danny), I moved from coaching at the high school to coaching stints at Riverside City College and Pasadena City College. *Author's Collection*

Long Beach State

At Long Beach State we really had something going, but I (with my son Danny) realized we were never going to beat out the bigger schools. *Author's Collection*

Al McGuire (left) and I became friends while I was at Long Beach State. I always admired John Wooden (right), even though UCLA had an edge when our teams faced off. *Author's Collection*

I took right to Vegas and Vegas took to me. Jodie, Lois, Pamela, George, Danny, and I enjoyed many a dinner out on the town. *Author's Collection*

Wayne Newton and I testified twice on behalf of a friend, Ash Resnick, in front of the Nevada State Gaming Control Board to get Ash a casino license. *Author's Collection*

As the coach of UNLV I became a bit of a celebrity and even got a part in a movie, *Honeymoon in Vegas,* with Nicolas Cage. Here we are on the set with my granddaughter, Dannielle Lois. *Author's Collection*

The Rebels' Biggest Fans

When we opened the Thomas & Mack Center at UNLV in 1982, Diana Ross performed with the current UNLV players joining her onstage. *Author's Collection*

convinced Frank Sinatra to help me on the recruiting trail, but he went 0-for-2 against Frank McGuire and Dean Smith. *Author's Collection*

Bill Cosby loved UNLV. When he was in town doing his comedy shows, we would sometimes take potential recruits backstage to meet him. *Photo by Greg Cava*

Richie Adams was a guy I recruited out of one of the toughest neighborhoods in the Bronx. *Photo by Greg Cava*

Freed from NCAA sanctions and in need of talent, I went back to Brooklyn and signed Sidney Green (right) in a wild recruiting chase. *Courtesy of UNLV*

When I needed a point guard during the 1980-1981 season, all I had to do was look right down the hall for my son Danny. *Author's Collection*

A Hell of a Run

Larry Johnson (No. 4) and Stacey Augmon (No. 32), as well as Greg Anthony, Anderson Hunt, Moses Scurry, and David Butler, were the center of the UNLV championship team.
Author's Collection

Whoopi Goldberg (center) came by the locker room to celebrate with the team after we won the national championship.
Photo by Greg Cava

President George H.W. Bush got me an extra year out of Larry Johnson when Johnson promised the president he would return and get his degree.
Photo by Greg Cava

The End of an Era

After ending my career at Fresno State, I have closed the door on ever oaching again. *Photo by Greg Cava*

16

Hold That Phone

" He said, ' That' s like telling a girl you' re going to marry her; you don' t have to.' "

—*WINSTON KARIM*

T he perception is that when we were at UNLV, we got all of these great recruits, all of these All-America players. That wasn't true. In my 19 years at UNLV we only signed three McDonald's All-Americans directly from high school. Rarely did we get a recruit other people wanted. We were always getting guys who were great athletes, junior college guys, or transfers. The facts back that up.

It is not that I wouldn't occasionally try. After losing Sam Bowie, I knew I still needed someone good to jump-start our program back to the Final Four, so my attention shifted to talent-rich Brooklyn, New York. Two years before, I had gotten real close with Winston Karim, who was a guy who hung around the playgrounds in Brooklyn and coached guys. The kids loved Winston, and Winston loved the kids. He was very influential in recruiting at the time. Winston was close with Albert King, so if you wanted to recruit Albert, you had to get to know Winston. I did. I went to Brooklyn and hung around with him all day. We didn't get

Albert King—he went to play for Lefty Driesell at Maryland—but I
developed a good friendship with Winston. Two years later, that was a big
help.

We got sidetracked at UNLV in 1977 when the NCAA came in and
put us on probation. It was the most ridiculous investigation ever, and we
eventually fought it all of the way to the Supreme Court. But at the time,
it crushed us. They hit us with a two-year ban on NCAA Tournament
play and a two-year ban on national television, which really hurt
recruiting. I thought we had Albert King wrapped up, but once probation
came down, we lost Albert. Then, to make matters worse, Reggie Theus
declared hardship after his junior year because we couldn't go to the
Tournament anyway. We went on to have two of my toughest seasons,
going 20-8 in 1977-1978 and 21-8 in 1978-1979. Just keeping the guys
motivated was difficult, but I had some real quality people.

By 1979, I needed some players, and freed from the sanctions, I
thought I could get one. So I went back to Winston and got involved in
one of the craziest recruiting battles of my career, for the signature of
Sidney Green.

Sidney was a six-foot-nine, 210-pound forward who was just
dominating everyone at Thomas Jefferson High School in Brooklyn. His
senior year, Sid averaged 35 points and 25 rebounds. And that was against
some serious competition in Brooklyn, not at some nowhere high school.
I didn't initially get involved with Sidney because he was supposed to be
a lock to attend South Carolina, where Frank McGuire, who hailed from
New York and had lots of contacts, was coaching. But South Carolina
played Syracuse at Madison Square Garden during Sidney's senior season,
and naturally, Sidney went and watched. The Gamecocks lost 71-64, and
Sidney was so surprised at how slowly they played that he backed off
them. He wanted an up-tempo team. The only reason Sid had been
interested in going to South Carolina in the first place was because all of
the people he knew in New York had been pushing McGuire.

In the middle of the 1978-1979 season, I was reading an article in
Basketball Times that said McGuire had lost Sidney because of his team's
style of play. About a week earlier, I had discovered Sam Bowie was
driving that old Cadillac. So I decided why not get involved with Sid? I
called up Winston and told him I was coming in. Winston was very, very

close with Sidney, so I thought we had a great chance, even though Louisville, UCLA, and half of the rest of the country were after him.

I flew to Brooklyn and met with Sid and Winston. Then, after the season, I went back to New York for weeks and just hung around trying to get Sidney to commit to us. I went by Sid's high school, and it was like a coaching reunion. Sid got out of school at 1 p.m., and we'd all be in, Oregon, St. John's, Louisville, and me. There were about five coaches every day waiting for Sid to get out of high school to say hello to him. It was the damnedest thing you've ever seen.

After school, Winston and I went to the park to watch Sidney play. When I got to the park, all of the guys around the court—street guys—said, "Hey, Coach Tark! Tark the Shark!" They broke up their dice games, came over, shook my hand, and said hello. These were like drug dealers and gang leaders and real tough-looking guys. I didn't think they knew much about college basketball, but I was wrong. It was like I was welcome there. It was really strange, but they had all heard about my reputation with black kids. They knew I gave kids a fair shake, and they appreciated it, I guess. I had all sorts of credibility with the Brooklyn street guys.

Every day I stayed in Brooklyn, Sid went to the parks, and we sat and watched the playground games. Usually after a few games, Sidney came over and asked to go for a drive. So he, Winston, and I got in the car, and Sidney had us drive him over to an apartment building.

"Coach, you guys mind if I stop here? I got to stop here."

Of course I didn't mind. I was willing to do whatever Sidney wanted. We stopped, and Sid went inside for a little while and then came down. We began to realize Sidney was having us drive him over so he could visit his girlfriend. He ran up while we sat in the car waiting. Then after a little while, he came down, we took him back to the park, and he played more ball. People think recruiting is glamorous, but this is what it is.

I liked our chances with Sidney, but Louisville was in there pretty good, too. Denny Crum, the coach, sent in Otis Wilson, a star linebacker who had played at Sid's high school and then at Louisville. Otis went on to play for the Chicago Bears. He was supposed to close the deal. Well, I was hanging out at the high school, and I started hanging out with Otis. And he and I hit it off really well.

"I'm here to get Sid for Denny Crum," Otis told me, "but if I can't get him, I'm going to push him toward you guys."

And that's what he did. So I got Louisville's guy, Otis Wilson, to help me, and Denny didn't even know it.

After a week of this, Sidney finally said he was going to sign with UNLV. I was excited. I had the National Letter of Intent with me, and I was all ready to make it official, but he said he wouldn't sign until May 1. That was the date his brother got shot, and for sentimental reasons, a tribute I guess, he wanted to sign on the anniversary. It was late April, and I wanted to just stay in Brooklyn until May 1, because I didn't want to leave Sidney's side for even one day. But I had to get back to Las Vegas because my son Danny was receiving the Nevada High School Athlete of the Year award. I just couldn't miss that.

"Sid, I've got to go home Saturday because my son Danny is getting this award. I've got to be there. I can't hang out in Brooklyn forever. You've got to sign before I go."

"Coach, I can't sign until May 1. But I'll write you a note."

"OK, you write me a note."

I thought he was going write me a note saying he was going to sign on May 1 and all of this. Something that at least looked official. But he took this little scrap of paper, scribbled on it, and handed it to me.

It read: "I'm coming, Sid."

That was it.

Well, after weeks in Brooklyn, that was all I was getting. So I flew home on a Friday for Danny's ceremony. Right when I landed in Vegas, I called Sid to see how he was doing.

"Coach, I'm going visit UCLA this weekend because I always wanted to visit UCLA. But I won't go to school there, Coach. I promise."

I was about ready to faint. UCLA? I was gone five hours, and UCLA was in there? UCLA had already scheduled a recruiting visit?

"I'll call you during the visit just to make you feel safe," he promised.

Well, I was worried. Larry Brown was the coach at UCLA then, and he knew how to get things done. So I didn't want him going to UCLA for even one minute. I figured when Sid saw that big, beautiful campus, saw all those NCAA banners hanging in Pauley Pavilion, and met those rich boosters, my little note wouldn't be worth a thing. But what could I do? He got on a plane and visited, and we never heard from him all weekend. He didn't call.

Now I panicked. I knew I had to get to New York to salvage this deal. Sidney's flight from Los Angeles was supposed to get back to New York at about 9 p.m. I booked a flight and got in around 10:15 p.m. I called Winston.

"How'd it go with Sid?" I asked.

"He loved it. It's a tossup between you and UCLA."

"That son of a bitch, how could he do that? He gave me his word."

I pulled out the note and said, "He gave me this note saying: 'I'm coming, Sid.'"

"Coach, I mentioned that to Sid, and he said, 'That's like telling a girl you're going to marry her; you don't have to.'"

Well, I was nervous now. Winston and Sid came and picked me up at LaGuardia. We drove around Brooklyn all night.

"Sid, how in the hell can you talk about UCLA?" I asked. "You committed to us."

"Coach, they had the prettiest girls I've ever seen."

"What do you mean? You can't meet girls any prettier than we have in Vegas."

"Yeah, Coach, they were prettier than in Vegas."

He went on to tell us he went to a party at the home of Jim Brown, the great football player. He just went on and on about how many beautiful girls there were at this party.

"Look, Sid, I am sure there are lots of pretty girls in Los Angeles and at the party and all, but all you can handle is three or four girls. A man can't handle more than that, and I'm positive you can find three or four girls in Vegas who are just as good looking as the girls in Los Angeles. What more could you need?"

Sidney seemed to like that argument. After a couple hours of driving around, I thought we pretty much got UCLA out of the picture. I was still nervous as hell, though. Then UCLA assistant Larry Farmer called and told Sidney not to sign with anyone on May 1 until he and Larry Brown came by his apartment. Farmer said they were flying back East and would stop by Sidney's place right after they signed Rod Foster, who lived in New Britain, Connecticut. I jumped on that.

"Sidney, you aren't even their No. 1 guy."

But Sidney was still interested.

The Greens scheduled a party at a local restaurant to celebrate the signing. It was supposed to start at 6 p.m. Winston and I went to Sidney's apartment about 4 p.m. to sign him. There were no guarantees, though. We all just sat in the living room, I had the National Letter of Intent out on the coffee table, but Sid wouldn't sign. But he wouldn't say he wouldn't sign. I was so nervous, Sidney's mother said I got up and went to the bathroom like 12 times in one hour. She was in my corner.

She kept saying, "Sid, you owe it to Coach Tark."

"Yeah, I'm going to sign with you, Coach."

But then he wouldn't sign. It was clear he was waiting for Larry Brown to call.

The apartment had one phone, and it was in the kitchen. We were all in the living room, but Winston was standing in the door to the kitchen. And he would slide into the kitchen and, without anyone realizing it, take the phone off the hook. That way when Larry Brown called, he would get a busy signal and not get through. Later I found out Larry Brown had tried to call the apartment about 50 times but just kept getting a busy signal.

The problem was you could only leave a phone off the hook for so long before it made that loud busy signal. So Winston put it back on the hook for a couple of seconds and then took it off again. But during one of the times the phone was on the hook, it rang. Sid jumped up. I about passed out. But Winston grabbed it.

"Hello?"

It was Larry Brown, but Winston just nodded his head and then covered up the receiver.

"Hey Sid, it's Oregon coach Jim Haney."

Well, Sid didn't want to go to Oregon.

"Tell him I'm not here."

So Winston went back to the phone and said, "Sorry Coach, he's not here right now."

And that was that. Larry Brown never did get through to Sidney Green. Finally Sid figured Larry wasn't calling, so he signed with UNLV.

And we all went and had a party. I don't know what Larry Brown did that night.

17

The Lakers

" His body was found in the trunk of his Rolls Royce. "

—*JERRY TARKANIAN*

I n 1977, the Los Angeles Lakers offered me their head coaching job. For a basketball guy from Southern California, this was the ultimate. The Lakers are the Lakers. It was almost unbelievable that someone like me—just a kid from Pasadena who wasn't a great player and didn't play at a famous college or for a famous coach, let alone in the NBA—could get offered the Lakers job. After all, just nine years before, I was the coach of Pasadena City College.

So obviously, I was interested. Jack Kent Cooke was the owner, and he was very interested in me. Despite all of that, I didn't really want the job. We had just reached the Final Four at UNLV. I thought we were building something memorable, and as much as I was in awe of the Lakers, being a pro coach concerned me. I loved practice. I loved teaching basketball. I didn't like games. In the NBA, it's all games and almost no practice.

But Lois wanted me to take it. A guy I grew up with, Vic Weiss, was acting as my agent. He was a real close friend. We grew up together in Pasadena, and he played football at the University of Pacific. He was a tough little guy. He got in the car business and made a lot of money. Every time we'd have one of our reunions, he'd buy for everybody. I never had a clue about contracts and things, but he had a good business sense, so he was my agent. He wanted me to take the job, too. He and Lois were double-teaming me. But I didn't really want it, and Cooke wasn't offering that good of a salary. It was $70,000 a year with a $2,500 raise each year. That was just about what I was making at UNLV.

I had a special deal at UNLV, too. I was a full-tenured professor, which meant I could never be fired.

What happened was when I was at Long Beach State, being the basketball coach wasn't a very big deal. To be the coach, you also had to teach class, and to do that, you had to have a rank. So I was the men's basketball coach and an assistant professor. I only taught one class—basketball theory—but it was as an assistant professor. And that was my pay scale. My chance of a raise was based on my rank as a teacher, not on how well we did on the court. That was the system for all coaches at Long Beach. The year that we had almost beat UCLA, my athletic director, Fred Miller, had been named athletic director at Arizona State. He had wanted me to go there with him as basketball coach. I was close to taking it; I always thought Arizona State had a lot of potential. Even Lois thought I was going to go to Arizona State.

At the time, I was in New Jersey recruiting a player from East Rutherford High School, whose coach then was none other than Dick Vitale. I had been hanging around Jersey recruiting this player when we were all getting ready to fly to Pittsburgh for the Dapper Dan Roundball Classic that Sonny Vaccaro put on each spring.

Dick then was like Dick is now. He was promoting the hell out of his player, Les Cason, telling everyone how good he was and drumming up interest. Howie Garfinkel, who runs the Five-Star Basketball Camps in Pennsylvania each summer, had Cason as the best forward since Bob Pettit. So all of this attention got me to go back East and try to get Les Cason.

I was at Vitale's house, and we were preparing to go to the Newark airport. The phone rang, and it was Sam Cameron, who was the editor of the local paper, the *Long Beach Press-Telegram*. He tracked me down at Vitale's. The editor of a newspaper is a very strong position, but I didn't realize how strong it was at the time. Sam always liked me; I had a good relationship with him.

"Jerry, you can't go to Arizona State. We don't want to lose you. What's it going take to keep you there?"

He thought I was going to ask for some more money.

"Sam, I want to be a full professor with tenure."

I figured that would move me up on the pay scale, plus it provided job security. You can't fire a tenured professor. Once you get that, it's like having a job for life. I had a young family, four kids by then, so that was important.

"Jerry, you got it. You're a full professor with tenure."

"Sam, you can't make me a full professor with tenure. You are the editor of the newspaper; you aren't the president of Long Beach State. You don't even work for Long Beach State."

"Jerry, just sit by that phone. Within 30 minutes, you'll be getting a phone call from the president. You're going to be full professor with tenure."

I couldn't believe it. I hung up and told Dick, and he couldn't believe it either. We had to get to the airport to fly to Pittsburgh, but we decided to wait for a couple minutes for the call.

It didn't come, so we left for the airport. I figured there was no way the editor of the local newspaper could get me a full professorship, and Sam was just talking a big game. But when I checked into my hotel in Pittsburgh, the lady behind the counter said I had a message from Steve Horn, the president of Long Beach State, asking me to call him. I called.

"Jerry, I met with the faculty today, and you've done so much for this university that we think it's only right that we make you full professor with tenure."

I acted like I didn't know what was going on, like this was the first I had heard of it and I hadn't already talked to Sam Cameron. So I accepted, turned down Arizona State, and stayed at Long Beach.

That shows you just how strong a newspaper editor can be. And it shows what newspapers sometimes do behind the scenes in communities. They like to pretend they are objective, but the editors and publishers do all sorts of stuff. I didn't care, all I knew was I was full professor with tenure. I don't know if any coach in the country has ever had that.

When UNLV recruited me to take their job, I insisted that they do the same thing. And they did. It was great because it gave me the security that if I ever got fired from coaching, I always had my teaching job at a full professor's salary. When I first went to UNLV, I had no idea it would turn out like it did; for all I knew, we would lose and I'd be fired. So that security was great. The only downside was I never got to negotiate a contract, because every year, I just got the regular raise they gave all professors. So I didn't get quite as much money as I would have had otherwise. That was the tradeoff. But UNLV paid me well, so even if I didn't make what some of the top coaches did, I did fine.

People in basketball were amazed I had that deal. One time I was offered the Phoenix Suns head coaching job. I was thinking about it, and I talked to Cotton Fitzsimmons. He was involved with the Suns.

"Cotton, my only problem was that I'm full professor with tenure at UNLV, and I don't want to give that up."

Cotton couldn't believe it, and he said, "Tark, if you've got that, if you've got tenure, don't take this job."

So leaving that lifetime security for the NBA, where they fire coaches all of the time, was risky. Still, it was the Lakers, so I went in for the interview. Pete Newell, who had been my all-time idol when he coached at Cal, was the general manager. He, a few other front-office people, including broadcaster Chick Hearn, and I were at Jack Kent Cooke's home in Beverly Hills. We talked about the team, and Cooke said they needed a rebounder. Newell agreed. So Cooke started to talk about Sidney Wicks.

"Maybe we can get him in a trade?" Cooke suggested, waiting for Newell to reply.

Silence.

"Well Peter, can we win if we get that?"

"Well, I don't know if we can get a rebounder."

"Peter, I just said Sidney Wicks. Weren't you listening?"

And then he just jumped all over Pete Newell. He yelled at him in front of everyone. I said to myself, "God, I can't do this. I'm not going to work for a guy who's jumping all over Pete Newell. This is Pete Newell after all. What will he do to me?" That scared the heck out of me.

Cooke was one interesting guy. He insisted I tell no one but my agent and wife that I was considering coming to the Lakers. His favorite saying was "Less is More," so that became Lois's and my code name for him. He used to say the less someone said to the media, the better. Less is More. He always told me that if anybody, and he meant anybody, asked me about the Lakers job, I was supposed to say nothing. Less is More. He called me up on the phone and disguised his voice.

"Jerry this is the *L.A. Times.* I understand that you're going to be the new Lakers coach," he said.

"I have no comment."

Then Cooke would go, "Atta boy, Jerry."

He was goofier than hell.

But in the end, I accepted the job. I don't even know why, but I did. I guess it was the Lakers mystique. But it got leaked out to the newspapers, and once the news broke, the people in Vegas got a hold of me. They all made me feel like I was betraying them if I left because they all stood by me during the NCAA problem in the late 1970s. And now, if I up and left just as they were hit with the probation, I was being disloyal. They made me feel bad.

I was supposed to fly to Los Angeles for the press conference at 10 a.m. They had a private plane ready to come and get me. At 7 a.m. I woke up.

"I'm not taking the job," I thought.

I called Cooke, and I turned it down. He called Lois.

"I don't know how this guy could be a coach; he can't even make a damn decision," he said.

That was his comment. But I just couldn't get that vision of him jumping all over Pete Newell out of my mind. I couldn't work that way.

Well, two years later, he sold the team to Jerry Buss, and Buss offered me the job. I told Vic Weiss to ask for an outrageous salary.

"Hell, I got to have at least $200,000 per year for five years, or I am not even talking to them."

Vic called me back and said, "The new owner said, 'No problem, you got it.'"

Now that was a lot of money then, and this new guy was saying, "No problem." God, I was stunned. And, as it turns out, soon after the Lakers drafted Magic Johnson, and the rest is history. So Buss, Magic, and I could have been rookies the same year.

I was ready to take the job, the five-year contract was all set, and the only thing we were hassling on was season tickets. I had a car for me and a car for Lois. Then I wanted some tickets for my brother's family. So I wanted like 10 tickets, and I think they were offering like four. It was nothing. It was going to get done. I actually went looking for high schools. I drove up to Palos Verdes and met with the coach there because I wanted Danny to go that high school. Danny could have played high school ball with Bill Laimbeer.

While all of this was going on, we kept the secret here in Las Vegas. No one knew about it. Or at least not many people. The Lakers wanted it to be a secret, and I didn't want anyone in Las Vegas to know I was leaving.

Vic called on Friday night and said Lois and I should drive to the Balboa Bay Club, a real fancy resort in Newport Beach, down in Orange County. He said he was about to go to Jerry Buss's office to get everything worked out, and then on Saturday morning, Buss wanted to meet with us and sign the deal.

Friday, Lois and I drove down to Newport Beach. I stopped at a pay phone in Barstow, California, out in the desert and called Vic to see how everything went with the tickets. Vic's wife said he wasn't home yet and she hadn't heard from him. We checked into the Balboa Bay Club and still hadn't heard from him. At 8 a.m. the next day, his wife called and asked if we had seen Vic. We hadn't. She said he never came home Friday night and she thought he was with us.

No one knew what happened. Then we got the word: He was murdered. His body was found in the trunk of his Rolls Royce in a hotel parking garage in North Hollywood. His hands had been bound behind his neck and he had been shot twice in the head. It was obviously an execution. It wasn't some random murder. We were all stunned. No one knew what the hell happened. It was just unbelievable.

The Long Beach newspaper ran an article that said the Vegas mob got him because he was trying to get me to leave UNLV. It said the mob didn't want to lose me as coach of the Rebels. But that was crazy, you know. I never believed that story. Another story was that Vic had gotten into the fight game, which he had, and it had something to do with that. I have no idea, though. The murder was never solved.

They even featured it on the television show *Unsolved Mysteries*. Lois and I were home in Las Vegas one night watching the show, and on came the story of Vic Weiss. They made some claims, everything from his ties to organized crime, to the idea he was running drugs for Carroll Rosenbloom, who owned the L.A. Rams. But they didn't know what it was, either.

Anyway, Jerry Buss was wonderful. He called and said, "Just take your time." If nothing had happened, I would have taken the Lakers job that Saturday morning. No question. But because there was the murder, everything got put on hold. About two weeks later, Buss flew up to Las Vegas, and we met at the Desert Inn. I turned it down. I was crushed because of Vic at the time, so I was no longer positive about moving.

Plus, by that point I had so many people, so many influential people, talking to me about staying at UNLV. Word had gotten out. People said, "Jerry, this whole town has stood by you, supported you, and if you leave right now, it would be a slap in their face." They said UNLV had stuck by me through probation, when a lot of schools wouldn't have. The one thing that's always been one of my problems, I guess, is I've always been very, very loyal to people. That stuff gets to me. So I turned the job down and decided to stay at UNLV. I've always wondered to this day what it would have been like if I could have gone to the Lakers.

Consider that with Magic Johnson, they went on to win five NBA titles. But after Vic was killed, I never thought of leaving Vegas again. I never even interviewed for another job.

18

Family Ties

"Lois was furious with me. She kept asking me how I could choose Dixie Junior College over the University of Southern California. I didn't have much of an answer."

—*JERRY TARKANIAN*

I loved Reggie Theus. I loved Larry Johnson. I loved Greg Anthony. I loved all of my players, really. But when it comes to the player I loved the most, it's no contest. It's my son Danny.

In coaching, you often talk about having a father-son relationship with your players because when they arrive on campus, they're usually still teenagers. You even tell their parents in the recruiting process that you'll look after their child as if he were your own son. So the best coach-player relationships become almost that close. But when it's actually your own son that you're coaching, it's like nothing else.

I actually never wanted Danny to play for me because I used to talk to Al McGuire about it. When Al was at Marquette, his son, Allie, played for him. Al used to tell me that he would never do it again. It had worked out well, but Al said it was tough. He didn't like the pressure on his son, and he thought it was tougher on Allie than on him.

The other reason I didn't want Danny to play for me at UNLV was because I knew how much pressure comes with playing Division I athletics, especially at a high level like UNLV. Big-time college sports look like a lot of fun, but only when you win. You miss a couple of free throws at the end of a game, and you get crushed. The fans and the media have no patience with players, even if they are just college students. In a town like UNLV, where there is no professional franchise, we were the pro team. So at times we were treated like that. It can be really tough. And I wanted to shield my son from that.

I wanted him to go to University of Redlands in Southern California, which has a smaller athletic department. I thought Danny could go there and play all he wanted and not worry about the pressures of big-time sports. I thought that would have been perfect for him.

When Danny was a senior at Bishop Gorman High School in Las Vegas, a lot of people thought he was a better football quarterback than basketball point guard. That might be true, but he definitely liked basketball better. He only played football because all of his friends played. But there was a high school coach in Vegas who went on to coach pro football in Canada, and to this day he swears Danny would have been in the NFL if he would have played football.

Bishop Gorman is a private Catholic school. When I came to Las Vegas, it was the only private high school in town, and everybody wanted their kids to go there, so it was incredibly competitive. Before I accepted a job, I checked into it, and there was a waiting list to get in. I had an understanding that as long as I was UNLV coach, all four of my kids had a guaranteed slot at Bishop Gorman.

Bishop Gorman was a heck of a place. It was where the best of Las Vegas sent their children. All of Danny's high school friends were sons of doctors, casino owners, and things like that. It is a very powerful school. Those are the kind of people who help you for the rest of your life in Las Vegas. That's why so many people wanted their kids to go there.

Sports at Bishop Gorman were a huge deal. They used to have tailgate parties before football games, and because of the casino connections, they would fly in this gourmet food. Like someone would decide they should grill shrimp before the game, so they'd get the catch of the day flown in from Louisiana. Stuff like that. It was crazy, all for a high school. Danny's senior year, Bishop Gorman went undefeated and won the state football title.

Danny visited a few different schools for both football and basketball, but he kept getting pressured by football coaches to play that sport only. Most of them said football came before basketball. Danny just couldn't decide between the two sports. He wanted to play both, so finally he told all of the football coaches that he was just going to play basketball.

Eventually he was going to attend the University of Nevada in Reno. I was in favor of that, because I always thought Reno was a great school and a great town. One of my daughters went there. The basketball coach was Sonny Allen, whom I really liked. Sonny played the game with the point guard handling the ball all of the time, so I thought it was a perfect fit for Danny.

The thing with Danny is he had great grades. He went on to graduate third in his class from the University of San Diego Law School. Danny was Nevada's nominee for Rhodes Scholar. He didn't make it, but he was the state's nominee. Harvard and Princeton were both recruiting him for football, but he never followed up on either one because they were too far from home. I regret that now. It would have been great for him to go to an Ivy League school.

Danny was all set to go Reno. His car was packed and everything. I was in Hawaii on a Nike trip when a newspaper reporter called me and said Sonny Allen's kid, Billy Allen, who was a very good point guard, had backed out of a commitment to Missouri. He had changed his mind and decided to go to Reno to play for his dad. Well, I knew that if Billy Allen was on the team, Danny wasn't going to be playing much at point guard. Reno was no longer a good place for him.

Then Sonny Allen started telling me, "You know Tark, they could play together at the same time."

I said, "Sonny, you're full of shit. You know, you're talking to another a coach here."

So I called Danny and told him to wait until I got home. It was a hectic time. As soon as Danny backed out of Reno, Stan Morrison, the basketball coach at USC, tried to get involved. Stan was a great talker, and he sounded good on the phone, but I knew his starting point guard had two years of eligibility remaining, so playing time would be limited. So I was against USC.

Lois wanted Danny to go to USC because of the school's great academics. She saw the opportunity for Danny to get a top-flight education at a school with strong alumni ties. It made sense. And Danny wanted to go to USC, too. So it was a hell of a battle to keep him from going there.

I understood why she wanted Danny to go to USC, because it's a great school. And the thing is, my whole life I wanted to be a Trojan. I grew up in Pasadena, which was a Trojan town, and I coached in Long Beach State, and all of the people who ran the town were Trojans. A lot of them had businesses in Long Beach, so they were Long Beach State boosters, but their loyalties were to USC. They were Trojans.

Up until after I had a lot of success at UNLV, my dream job would have been USC. That was what I always wanted. But once I got it rolling at UNLV, things were too good to leave. Every time something happened at USC, the boosters would push for me; all of my old friends called and tried to get me to come back. But there was no way that I could go. UNLV was 10 times better than USC could ever be.

But their alums were great. When I was coaching at UNLV, during the summer I spent about a month at the Balboa Bay Club in Newport Beach. The guys who ran it were Trojans.

One time, this rich USC alum told me, "Tark, I know you got some guys with money out at UNLV, but you bring them down here and match them up with the USC alums. If we take $100 bills and start throwing them into Balboa Bay, they'd run out a week before us."

I loved those USC guys. One year they had a chili cookout in Newport Beach, and I became a judge and I had a lot of fun with that. Wilt Chamberlain was a judge with me. I got to know Wilt real well.

I once asked Wilt, "Is it true what they said about you having sex like 20,000 times?"

And Wilt smiled at me and said, "Coach, they shortchanged me. It was a hell of a lot more than that."

Anyway, we didn't know what to do with Danny. It was August, school was about to start, and Danny needed to go somewhere, so I sent him to Dixie Junior College in St. George, Utah. It was a last-minute deal. I used to have a basketball camp at Dixie, and I liked the town of

St. George. It was real clean. The coach was a good one, and I knew him real well. And it was only about a two-hour drive to Las Vegas. I thought it would be a good fit.

But that was a battle. Danny wanted to go to USC, and Lois wanted him to go to USC, and going to USC made a lot of sense. And I went and talked him out of it and sent him to a small junior college in St. George, Utah, which didn't make much sense to anyone but me.

Lois was furious with me. She kept asking me how I could choose Dixie Junior College over the University of Southern California. I didn't have much of an answer. She finally stopped asking me, though, when she threw me out of the house. That's how mad she was—she told me to get out. I couldn't even bargain my way onto a spare couch, I was out of the house. I had nowhere to go, so I called my friend Mike Toney, who was a greeter down at the Desert Inn. He got me a room, food, and beverage at the Desert Inn. I was there for three or four days. It was perfect. It was like a little vacation.

It turned out Dixie was a great fit. Danny went there and loved it. He had a great year. He made All-Conference as a freshman, and at the end of the year, he was one of three nominees for their outstanding student award. Not outstanding athlete, outstanding student. Lois, who had started talking to me again, and I drove up for the award, and one of the other finalists was the college president's son. We figured there was no way Danny would win, but he did. It was the first time in the history of Dixie College that a non-Mormon got the award. They said that one reason he got the award was that he never missed Catholic Mass. He'd always go to Mass, and the Mass was in an old barn building. It wasn't a real nice place. So they respected that.

Being a junior college, Dixie was a temporary stop for Danny. He still needed to go to a four-year school. Because he had been academically qualified out of high school, he could transfer to a four-year school after just one season of juco ball. Even though Danny was really progressing as a point guard, we never talked about him going to UNLV. I still didn't want to put that pressure on him. And he never mentioned it, either, so it was just not brought up. I figured he'd go to Utah and play for Jerry Pimm, who was a great coach. Besides, I had enough problems already.

That year, 1980-1981, we were really struggling. After the two-year NCAA ban, we had gone 23-9 and reached the NIT Final Four, which is not bad but was not at all satisfying to me. The NCAA probation had hurt our recruiting, and it showed. Then that year, we had my worst season as a college coach, 16-12. I thought I had good players, such as Sidney Green, but it wasn't working out. Our problem was at point guard; we didn't have a good one. We needed a leader. We needed to get back to dominating.

Dixie was in a tournament that year, but I couldn't go to the game because we were playing at Air Force. Lois drove up without me. Danny made the All-Tournament team, and he was out on the floor to accept his trophy when someone told him that Air Force beat UNLV in a big upset. Danny was devastated. He turned to Lois.

"Mom, can you believe they lost? I've got to go to UNLV."

That's when it started; maybe Danny should come to UNLV. I kept thinking about what Al McGuire told me, but then I kept thinking about having my son around me all of the time and coaching my son. I just thought it would be really special. So I decided I would take Danny, but only if he was good enough. It wouldn't be fair to him or the other players or UNLV to take him if he wasn't good enough. And as a father, it's difficult to judge your son.

We were recruiting two other junior college point guards, too. So I called my assistants, Tim Grgurich and Mark Warkentein, into the office.

"Now, you guys decide who's going to take our final scholarship. You look at the choices and decide."

I figured I was biased. They said they thought Danny was the best of the three guards we were recruiting, and so I said, "OK."

They played a junior college all-star game in St. George, and we went as a staff and decided after the game we were going to make the decision.

"I want to make it very clear to you guys that if we say Danny is the guy we're taking, then Danny is coming in and starting. I'm not bringing him in and sitting him on the bench."

We all went up, and Danny got MVP.

At UNLV, Danny was a three-year starter. In 1983-1984, his senior year, he set the school single-season assist record with 289. Our three-year record under Danny was 77-19, a period that jump-started our program to new heights that we would eventually ride to a national championship. So it turned out the point guard I needed all along was living right down the hall from me.

19

Rollin' Again

❝ I figured they must have thought we were narcotics officers, you know, what other dressed-up white guys would go to that building? So as we ran up the stairs, I yelled out, ' I am Richie Adams' s coach. I am Richie Adams' s coach.' ❞

—*Jerry Tarkanian*

From 1977 to 1982, our average record was 20-9. For a lot of coaches and schools, that's very good. For UNLV and me, it wasn't. I had a hard time dealing with losing. All I could think about was how to get my team better and how to make things better. My focus was all basketball all of the time. I couldn't think of anything else. Even worse than losing were the times my team didn't play harder than the other team, when my players didn't give 100 percent. For me, that was completely unacceptable.

The disappointment weighed so heavily on me that I couldn't shake it even when we did turn it around. In the 1982-1983 season, we won our

ROLLIN' AGAIN 133

first 23 games and climbed all the way to No. 1 in the national polls. Then we lost to Cal State–Fullerton in a huge upset. In the locker room after I screamed at my team, "You guys, I'm getting tired of losing!" Everyone made a big joke of that, the coach of a 23-1 team sick of losing, but I was.

That was a breakthrough season for us at UNLV, the year the Rebels came back. The core of the team was Sidney Green, Spoon James, Danny Tarkanian, Larry Anderson, and Anthony Jones. We were back to our old selves. That was the year we opened the Thomas & Mack Center on our campus, an 19,000-seat state-of-the-art arena. So it was a good year to be good.

The week we opened the Thomas & Mack was the first time we were ever ranked No. 1 nationally in any sport at UNLV. It was a great accomplishment. Everybody said there was no way we'd ever sell 19,000 seats for basketball. But the second game we played there sold out. The Thomas & Mack was huge for us; it was a great recruiting tool because it was as good of an arena as anyone in the country had. Plus it was right on our campus, just a couple blocks from The Strip.

When it got going, it was so loud you could sit next to someone and not hear a word they said. Then there were the high-roller seats on the floor, which became the place to see and be seen in Vegas. It got nicknamed Gucci Row because of all the big-timers and celebrities who would sit there. We were on television all of the time, and those seats were shown on TV all game long. So it was like a fashion show over there. All of the women tried out their best dresses and outfits and made their husbands get seats on Gucci Row. It was all about status. There were only 72 seats, but when we opened the building, season tickets went for $1,800 a year. That eventually got up to about $2,400. It was unbelievable. UNLV was making more money on those 72 seats than Long Beach State made in its entire building when I coached there. The Thomas & Mack was just an incredible environment, like nowhere else in college basketball.

We had a good team that year, but it wasn't full of a lot of highly recruited players. What we realized was we weren't going to get the player who was great at everything. Those guys would go to North Carolina or Kentucky. So we started recruiting specialists. Danny Tarkanian was our point guard, and he could handle and pass the ball as well as anyone. But he wasn't a great shooter, so he rarely shot. Jeff Collins was our off guard, who transferred in from Arizona. He was six foot three and a great athlete; he could defend and get to the rim, but he couldn't shoot.

Larry Anderson was our small forward, who we beat Pitt and West Virginia on. He couldn't create his own shot, but he was a great pull-up jump shooter. So we had him just do that. Paul Brozovich, a six-foot-10 white guy, was our power forward. Tim Grgurich had coached him at Pittsburgh but when Grg left there, the new coach didn't want Brozovich, so we took him out of loyalty to Grg. He couldn't jump. He couldn't shoot. But he played hard, and he could pass the ball, and he was a tough guy.

Eldridge Hudson was our sixth man, a real good forward. Eldridge was from Carson, California, but he was such a tough, tough guy that none of the Los Angeles schools had recruited him. UCLA had no interest. I went to Los Angeles for a game once, and Joey Meyer of DePaul was there, too; it was DePaul and us for the kid. We both sat right behind the Carson bench when Eldridge's coach called a timeout, and the whole team huddled. The coach was drawing up a play when Eldridge said, "This shit isn't going to work. This shit isn't going to work!" He turned to the coach.

"Sit down, Coach, you're just screwing things up."

Joey Meyer heard that, got scared, and left. On the way out, he said, "I can't coach this." So we were the last big school left, and we got Eldridge. I figured I could coach him. Eldridge hurt his knee as a freshman and was never the same player, but he played hard and was a joy to coach.

Then we had Sidney Green, who was a great one, but despite all of the effort we spent recruiting him, hadn't panned out. His first three years with us, he struggled. There were games he put up good numbers, but he wasn't a consistent player. During Sidney's freshman year, we played Wyoming, and they beat us. Sidney had no points and no rebounds. He went like 0-for-10 from the field and didn't get a rebound. He was terrible.

After the game, a reporter asked me, "Well, what did you think of Sidney Green?"

"Hell, I could get no rebounds and no points right now. In fact, I could get at least one rebound. I'd just run under the basket every time they shot, and one might fall on my head."

But by the time Sidney was a senior, he played great. He wound up the second all-time leading scorer in UNLV history, averaged 22.1 points a game that year, and was the fifth pick in the NBA draft.

That was our team, and we just had everyone do what they could do. All of them had some kind of weakness that had kept other schools from recruiting them, but together they were great. And that helped our recruiting philosophy the rest of my career. We wanted specialists. We weren't all over the country recruiting all-stars. We only recruited in cities where we had some contacts. Almost all of my players came from Pittsburgh, Detroit, Baltimore, New York, Southern California, or occasionally a local Vegas kid. That was it.

The guy who we actually lost that season was Richie Adams, who was six foot eight and as talented as anyone. Recruiting Richie was really incredible. He played on an unbelievable high school team in New York, but Richie didn't have any grades; he wasn't eligible to go to a four-year school. Tom Davis was up at Boston College then and got a hold of Richie and placed him at Massachusetts Bay Community College near Boston. But something happened so that Boston College could not get him in, so Tom's assistant called my assistant, Tim Grgurich, and we got involved at the end.

Richie was immediately excited about coming out to Vegas and committed almost right away. But we still had to have him sign a National Letter of Intent. So Tim and I flew to New York. Richie lived in Fort Apache the Bronx, the worst neighborhood in all of New York at that time, maybe the entire country. I had planned on going over to Richie's home in the evening, but at the hotel they told me no cab would go in there after dark, so we went in the afternoon.

Richie lived on the 22nd floor of a tenement building. The elevators didn't work, so we had to run up the stairs, 22 flights. We passed by all of these winos, bad guys. They were drinking beer, shooting up. I had a tie on, and Timmy was in a sport coat. Two dressed-up white guys. I figured they must have thought we were narcotics officers, you know, what other dressed-up white guys would go to that building? So as we ran up the stairs, I yelled out, "I am Richie Adams's coach. I am Richie Adams's coach." I was afraid someone might stab me. I ran up 22 flights of stairs faster than you can believe. We got to the top and signed him.

My son Danny used to call Richie "a follower," and it was true. We had trouble with Richie; he had a bad attitude his first season and then sat out 1982-1983. He even returned to New York for a while. It was too bad, because he was a great player. But when we went No. 1 without him, it really made an impact. Richie came back later for a while and was a good player. He was a great guy when he was in Vegas, but eventually he got back to his peer group in New York and fell into the street life. He is in prison in New York now, and he kicked away a good pro career. I could never truly reach him.

Without Richie, though, we were not some ultra-talented team. But everybody fit together perfectly. We played incredibly hard, especially on defense. We were just a great team. We entered the 1983 NCAA Tournament with a 28-2 record, and I thought we were good enough to get back to the Final Four.

But we ran into N.C. State, and that was the year they won it all. We led that game the whole way, but we missed five free throws the last minute and a half. We had a one-point lead in the final seconds when they got the ball to Dereck Whittenburg. We defended him beautifully. He was forced into a tough shot and missed. Eldridge Hudson went up for a rebound, but he had a bad leg and he timed it wrong. He came down when he should have been going up, and Thurl Bailey came out of nowhere and tipped it in with two seconds to go, and we got beat by one. But that was how it was for N.C. State that year. They kept winning NCAA games in crazy fashion at the buzzer, the most famous being the championship game victory over Houston, when Whittenburg threw up an air ball and Lorenzo Charles caught it and laid it in for the title. They were incredible that year.

The thing I was proud of that season was we got back to being a real blue-collar team, the way most of my best teams were. For all of the flash we had in Vegas, all the pregame light-and-smoke shows, we always were a blue-collar program.

I always considered myself a blue-collar guy. That was my background. I never was a fancy dresser or anything like that. Back then I drove an Oldsmobile that the school had provided for me. Our football coach drove a Cadillac. It didn't make any difference to me. I just didn't pay any attention. I just wanted a car that ran. But we had been No. 1 for a while, and the Cadillac dealer saw me in an Oldsmobile.

"Coach, why aren't you driving a Cadillac?"

"I don't know, this is what they gave me."

"Come on down tomorrow, I want you to drive a Cadillac."

"God, that's nice."

So I went down and got a Cadillac; it was a hell of a lot nicer than the Oldsmobile. I started driving the Cadillac when school started for the 1983-1984 season, and Eldridge Hudson saw me in it.

"Hey, Coach, see, we had a great year, and you got you a Cadillac."

"Yeah, you son-of-a-gun, if you'd got that rebound against N.C. State, I would have been driving a Mercedes!"

My assistant coaches were the best. I had Mark Warkentein, who was one of the best talent evaluators I have ever seen. He is currently with the Denver Nuggets.

No one in basketball was better at working guys out and getting them better than Tim Grgurich. He's still the best. He works now for the Portland Trailblazers. Back then, that was all he cared about. He just wanted to coach. He didn't necessarily like to work with the media very much. He didn't like to work with the boosters very much. He didn't really like to work with administrators. He just wanted to practice. Tim was a real blue-collar guy. His favorite shirt was a Barbary Coast golf shirt. He always wore that thing. And he was never into having his picture taken. He was an assistant coach, and he wouldn't show up for a team picture. He came to our postseason banquet once, but only because we had Reggie Williams in for a visit. Grgurich would always try to get the banquet scheduled during a recruiting period so he had an excuse to leave town and miss it. He didn't want to be part of it.

Grgurich used to drive this old car, and he wouldn't go down and get a new one. He could have had a new Cadillac or just about anything for free, but he didn't care. So we convinced him to get a new car.

"Grgurich, what kind of car do you want?" I asked him.

"A Toyota pickup truck. If you get me a car, I'll just park it in my front lawn and never drive it. I want a Toyota pickup truck."

A Toyota pickup truck? You can have any car you want, and you choose a Toyota pickup truck?

We always had a really good part-time coach. I would bring in someone like Tates Locke, some head coach who had just been fired. I felt bad for those guys who had given so much to the game. After what the

NCAA tried to do to me, I knew how they felt. So I gave them a job for a year, and it was great for them because it kept them in the business until they got back on their feet.

We had guys in the right slots, and then we had a lot of continuity. It wasn't as though we had to change every year. We just keep the same guys in the same slots. And it really set the tone for us heading into the future. Once we got things rolling with that 1983-1984 team, I knew we had a chance to be great every year.

20

Back to the Final Four

66 Wade, I can' t talk to you about transferring; we' re playing you tomorrow night. *99*

—*Jerry Tarkanian*

For all of the recruiting services and media attention on high school players, some of the best guys we ever had at UNLV we kind of discovered during the recruiting process.

The best example was Armon Gilliam, who attended Bethel Park High School in Pittsburgh but was known then as a wrestler and a football player. He played basketball, but as a junior he was the sixth man on the junior varsity team. He had a football scholarship offered to him by Clemson, but he fell in love with basketball. As a senior, he started and averaged 13 points and 10 rebounds, but by no means was he major college material. He decided to stick with basketball, though, and went to Independence Junior College out in Kansas.

We were recruiting Spoon James then out of San Jacinto Junior College in Texas. Spoon was a six-foot-six forward whom I had recruited myself because I thought he would really help us. Mark Warkentein went out to scout Spoon, and San Jacinto just happened to play Independence.

That's when Mark noticed Armon, who was six feet, nine inches and 240 pounds of muscle. Armon didn't start for Independence, but Mark loved his potential.

"I think we can get Spoon," Mark said when he got back to Vegas. "I think he likes us. But Coach, there's a guy on the other team who I love. He's got a big body, he looks like a warrior, and he's from Pittsburgh."

Once I heard he was from Pittsburgh, I knew we could get him. My other assistant, Tim Grgurich, was from Pittsburgh. I had spent three weeks in Pittsburgh during the filming of *The Fish That Saved Pittsburgh* and had become friends with Louis Grippo, the oyster house guy. We had connections. Mark said we should take Armon and redshirt him. He was just a freshman, but because he had good grades, he was eligible to transfer right away. So that's what he did. It turns out we didn't need all of those Pittsburgh connections, because no one else really recruited Armon. Right at the end, Lefty Driesell at Maryland tried to steal him. He came in hard. This was after the season, so there was no way Lefty had even seen Armon play. I called Lefty up.

"What in the hell are you doing trying to steal Armon away from us? He's committed to us. Besides, you've never even heard of this guy."

"Yes, but I figure if you were recruiting him, he had to be a good player."

But we held off Lefty and got Armon.

Armon, of course, wound up an All-American, a Wooden Award finalist, and the No. 2 pick in the 1987 NBA draft, right behind David Robinson. How's that for a find? But Warkentein and Tim Grgurich were the absolute best talent evaluators in college basketball anywhere. You can't minimize the value of that. A lot of head coaches hire these young guys who are smooth talkers but don't know basketball well enough to scout a player. They just recruit the obvious superstar or whatever the recruiting services say.

Mark and Tim knew basketball. They knew it as well as anyone in the world, and I think their post-UNLV careers prove that. Mark saw something in Armon Gilliam that no other assistant or head coach in the country saw. That's a valuable assistant. We landed an All-American who led us to the 1987 Final Four without having to really beat anyone for him.

Our starting lineup in 1987 was at forwards Armon and Jarvis Basnight, neither of whom was heavily recruited. We had Freddie Banks, a local kid, and Gerald Paddio, who was a six-foot-seven kid from Rayne, Louisiana, who attended Seminole Junior College in Oklahoma. He was a good recruit, but he wasn't one of the big, big recruits.

Then there was our starting point guard, Mark Wade. He had originally gone to Oklahoma. But as a freshman, not only did he barely play, he was behind Billy Tubbs's son as a backup. He was OU's third-string point guard.

We played at Oklahoma his freshman year, and we were sitting in our hotel in Norman when Wade showed up. I couldn't believe it.

"Coach, I want to transfer to UNLV."

"Mark, I can't talk to you about transferring; we're playing you tomorrow night."

He wanted to transfer, but I didn't know how good he was, so we stashed him at El Camino Junior College in Los Angeles the next year. Mark played well there, but I still wasn't sure. The El Camino coach was one of my best friends, and he kept telling me that Mark was really good and we ought to take him. This was where the recruitment became a juggling act.

We were trying to get Tommy Lewis out of Mater Dei High School in Santa Ana, California, with our last scholarship. Tommy was six foot eight and would go on to be named a McDonald's All-American his senior year. The only thing I didn't like about Tommy was the guy who ran him, Pat Barrett, was a real character. He's still down there; he's real big with Nike. He handled Tyson Chandler during his high school days.

Eventually it got to be such a disaster, but at the start we felt for sure the kid loved us. Tommy wanted to come with us. But he kept putting us on hold because of Barrett. Barrett would come to me and tell me, "Oh, Syracuse has offered him $100,000," and things like that. And I said, "You're full of shit." The other problem was if you took Tommy Lewis, you had to hire Barrett as a graduate assistant. Barrett needed to get his degree, so he would go for free in exchange for looking after Tommy. Well, I didn't think we needed someone to look after Tommy. But Barrett saw this as his chance. I didn't want to do it, but we liked Tommy so much that we said we'd take Barrett as a grad assistant.

That didn't end the recruitment, though. The whole thing was crazy. Tommy would never completely commit. Finally, I had a home visit set up in Santa Ana with Tommy Lewis. I went to the home, and I was really fed up that Tommy kept putting us on hold while all of these guys he knows were asking for things. Grgurich and I were in his home.

"Tommy," I said, "I'm tired of this. What's the deal?"

"It's between you and Syracuse."

"Tommy, what the hell? You are a Santa Ana kid, a Southern California kid, and it is between us and Syracuse? What? Do you like the weather better there? What do you like?" I started comparing the programs, I went right down the line and said, "Is there a program in the country any better than ours?" Finally, I had enough, I just said, "If you want to go to Syracuse, just go to Syracuse. Just quit bullshitting us."

I laid it right on the line to him, because I always figured he wanted to come.

"No, no, Coach, I want to go with you guys."

So he committed to us. He was a big commitment for us, a big-time player.

I would have stayed right in Santa Ana and guarded Tommy if I could have, but I had to fly up to Portland, Oregon, right after the home visit for a Nike speaking engagement. I didn't feel good about it. Even though Tommy was great, I didn't like this recruitment at all.

The whole time, we had Mark Wade on hold, even though he wanted to come with us. But right then Mark figured out what was going on with Tommy Lewis, got pissed off, and said he was going to go to BYU.

After the speech in Portland, I went out to eat with Rollie Massimino of Villanova, Jimmy Valvano of North Carolina State, and a whole bunch of coaches. I was all nervous. I wasn't myself.

"Tark, what's the matter?" Rollie asked.

"I don't feel good. We're getting that Tommy Lewis kid. He committed to us."

"Oh, you're getting Lewis. He's a hell of a player. How could you feel down when you're getting Tommy Lewis?"

"I don't like that I have to have Pat Barrett around."

The next morning, Warkentein called and woke me up.

"Coach, you're never going to believe it, Tommy Lewis committed to USC today."

"What?! They weren't even in the picture two days ago."

Stan Morrison was the coach at USC then, and he went out and got all of the USC alums down at the Balboa Bay Club—some of them were my friends—and he sold them on the fact that they had to have Tommy Lewis. He convinced them that for USC to ever be good at basketball, they had to get Tommy Lewis, because it would turn around recruiting in Los Angeles for USC. So these guys got on the bandwagon for him and pulled Tommy from us. And at the same time, they got the two kids from Philadelphia, Hank Gathers and Bo Kimble. They got all three of them to USC.

I always liked Stan, because I honestly think of all of the coaches, he wanted to do it the right way. He was an honest guy. Stan coached at Pacific when I coached at Long Beach. We went and played them when we were undefeated and ranked in the top five in the country. The place was going absolutely crazy, and the game was nip and tuck. Then right near the end, they missed a shot, but the refs blew the whistle and called a foul right as one of their guys tipped the missed shot in. And the ref also counted the basket. I went crazy.

"No, no, it didn't go in. It didn't go in on the original shot; it was the tip that put it in. The basket shouldn't count!"

I screamed at the ref, and the fans screamed at me to sit down, and the refs told me, "Sit down, Coach. It counts." Everyone was on my case.

Then Stan walked out on the court, tapped the ref on the shoulder, and said I was right.

"The ball didn't go in on the original shot so it shouldn't count."

The ref reversed the call. They took the points off of the board. I'll never forget that. I've never, ever heard of a coach doing that. We went on to win the game. If Stan had kept his mouth shut, Pacific might have won. But he did the right thing.

After the game, the press asked me if in the same situation, I would have done what Stan did, and I said I would hope I would, but I couldn't say I would because I wasn't put in that position. I don't know if I would. It is easy to say you would, but in reality you never know. But Stan did it. Stan was really trying to be a realistic, honest guy. He had real ethics. When he went to USC, he tried to do it right, but he got his ass kicked. He couldn't get any players. Everyone was coming into Los Angeles and cheating. So I think he figured he'd better get these guys or he was going to lose his job. So I didn't care that much that USC did that. I figured if someone was going to steal Tommy Lewis from me, it might as well be Stan. I owed him one.

Tommy would have been a disaster at UNLV. One day in the middle of the next season, we had a day off from practice. I flew to Los Angeles for a speaking engagement but had some free time in the afternoon. I called Stan to see if I could go to his practice.

"Yeah," he said, "come on over, Tark."

I went to USC's gym, and they had this balcony there where you could sit and watch practice. I sat up there, and this asshole, Pat Barrett, Tommy Lewis's grad assistant, was up there, too. The whole practice, Barrett knocked Stan.

Barrett kept asking me, "What do you think of that? Why would he do that? Isn't that stupid?"

Here is this "grad assistant" ripping Stan, who is a heck of a basketball coach. I just kept defending Stan all the way through.

"Yes, that's a great drill. I think I am going to steal that drill and use it at UNLV."

That recruiting class didn't help Stan much. Tommy wound up transferring to Pepperdine. Bo Kimble and Hank Gathers transferred to Loyola Marymount. Stan got fired; it all got ruined. Stan was really an honest guy. I think if you asked me who the most honest coach I ever dealt with was, Stan would be it. But at the end, he had to do some sketchy stuff. I was surprised, because Stan had been so honest, but that's the business. He was going to get fired either way.

Meanwhile, I ended up with Mark Wade. Once Tommy went to USC, we convinced Mark to back out on BYU and come to UNLV because Las Vegas would be a good place for him and he could feel real comfortable there. Mark forgave us for going after Tommy and signed. He became our starting point guard, and in 1986-1987, he broke Danny's school assist record by ringing up 406 in one season. I got lucky on that one. I got the better player for us even if he was my second choice. That's the thing in recruiting. Getting the big-name player isn't always worth it.

That 1987 team didn't win the national title, but I think it was every bit as good as the 1990-1991 team that did. In 1986-1987, we lost only one game before the NCAA Tournament. We just destroyed everyone. A month before the Tournament, we had a game at Auburn, who had a very good team that year, and we just stomped them. It wasn't even close. Right then I felt we could win it all. We reached the Final Four in New Orleans with a 37-1 record and ran into Bobby Knight's Indiana team. It was a hell of a game, one of the best ever in the Tournament, but they had a great team. We got 38 from Freddie Banks, who hit 10 three-pointers, and 32 from Gilliam. Wade had 19 assists. We played great and still lost 99-95. Indiana was a strong team, though. They went on to win the title two days later.

21

You Wouldn't Believe It ...

" Well, today's your lucky day. My son wants to go to UNLV, and for about $15,000 or $25,000, you got him. **"**

—*John Williams's mother*

The one NCAA investigator I really liked and had any respect for was Bob Minnix, who works now at Florida State. He always treated me well, and I always had a little rapport with him. Most of the other guys there were useless, but I liked Minnix. When you get investigated continually for a couple of decades, you tend to get to know everyone at the NCAA. Being under constant investigation really limited how we could do things. I knew if we stepped out of line, the NCAA would be right there. We were getting shadowed nonstop.

Year after year, we had great teams, but we never had the great player who could get us over the top. In the late 1970s, we had Reggie Theus, and that was what we needed. But then we couldn't get another great one. We always had good players, but we kept losing the great ones to Georgetown and UCLA. We were hamstrung.

Recruiting back then was unbelievable. There was so much cheating going on, it got comical. At one point during the early 1980s, Ned Wulk, who coached Arizona State, was president of the NABC, the coaches' association. There had been a bunch of recruiting scandals, and everyone thought the game was corrupt. So the NABC tried to improve the image of coaches. On TV that year, they ran this ad over and over again; I must have seen it 30 times. Ned Wulk came on and said, "I'm Ned Wulk, president of the National Association of Basketball Coaches. The NABC is very concerned about cheating in intercollegiate athletics. If you know of any cheating, please call this number." And they flashed the number on the screen.

That spring, we took a transfer from Arizona State. He was a great scorer, and we were excited to have him. Then he pulled up on our campus in a brand new sports car.

"Where in the hell did you get the car?" I asked him.

He said Arizona State bought him the car. I figured, "Hey, keep driving it. I didn't buy it, so I'm not going to take it away from the kid." In 1978 I had a transfer, Brett Vroman, from UCLA and he showed up with a car the Bruins bought him. That's why when I was asked by a reporter why I took so many transfers, I said, "I love transfers. They already have their cars paid for." I wasn't kidding.

It was around April when I found out about the sports car. June comes, and the player came to my office.

"Coach, I've got to get $1,300 for my car insurance, and I don't have it. What am I going to do about the car insurance?"

"Call Ned, he bought you the damn thing," I said.

"Oh, I can't call Ned."

"Fine, I'll call Ned."

I shooed the player out of the room and called Ned.

"Hey, Ned, your former player came by to see me today. He needs $1,300 for his car insurance."

"Well, Tark, we can't do that. That's illegal."

"Ned, you bought him the car. Pay for his damn car insurance."

"Tark, we wouldn't do anything like that. That kid's lying."

He went on and on. But Arizona State had bought him the car; it's a true story. Every time I saw that stupid NABC commercial, I wanted to dial up that number on TV and say, "Hey, Ned, I know a coach who's cheating." But I would never turn anybody in.

That's how recruiting was back then, though; especially in the SEC, which was just a joke when it came to cheating. In my career I never even bothered recruiting in the Deep South. I had a speaking engagement in the 1990s, and Darryl Dawkins was on a speaker deal with me. Darryl, of course, was a six-foot-11 center who was the first to ever rip down a backboard in a game. He used to call himself "Chocolate Thunder," and in 1975, when he was a senior at Maynard Evans High School in Florida, he became the first player to ever bypass college and go straight to the NBA. Darryl is a great guy with a lot of personality.

After I finished my speech, Darryl gave his and then took questions from the audience.

So somebody asked, "Darryl, you were the first one to go pro out of high school, but if you had attended college, where would you have gone?"

He said he was always going pro because of the money. His mother was completely against college because she figured why play for free? His mother didn't even want him to take a single recruiting visit, but one SEC school convinced him to take one.

"When I took my visit," Darryl said, "the head coach and the assistant took me out to eat. And the head coach said to me, 'Darryl, we want you in the worst way, and we're going to make you the best player you can be, and we're going to make you a good student, but we're not going to cheat. We're not going to violate any rules, and we are not going to cheat. If you want somebody to cheat, don't come here, because we're not going to do that.' And I thought, 'Shit, why the hell did I waste my time coming here?'" Darryl said that the head coach excused himself to the restroom, and the assistant handed him a big envelope. Darryl looked inside, and it had $15,000 in cash in it. The assistant said, "Now don't tell Coach that I did this, or I'll lose my job."

Darryl said he went home and gave the $15,000 to his mother. She couldn't believe it. Darryl was still going pro, but if this was what college recruiting entailed, maybe it wasn't such a bad thing. She said, "Darryl, I think you ought to take some more campus visits."

In 1984, we lost to Georgetown and Patrick Ewing in the NCAA Tournament at Pauley Pavilion in Los Angeles. At the game that day was

John Williams, who was a six-foot-eight power forward from Crenshaw High School, and he could do it all on the court. He was rated as one of the top five high school players in the country, just the kind of guy we could never quite get. We had been recruiting John all year, but he was still undecided.

John came into our locker room after the game. I was really down after the loss, because it was Danny's last game. John walked me out to the rental car I had in the parking lot. Usually I would be working hard to get in with a player like John Williams, but this loss hurt. I was just really frustrated, and John put his big arm around me.

"John, the problem is I've got a lot of good players. I don't have a great player. Everybody's got a great player, someone like Patrick Ewing. I've got to get a great player."

"Don't worry, Coach, I'm coming to UNLV. I'll be your great player. I'm coming with you guys. I give you my word."

So that cheered me up. It helped ease the pain of the loss. My entire staff felt great because we were going to get John Williams. This was the guy we felt could put us over the top. All we had to do was keep him with us until signing day, which was about a month away. A couple weeks after John said he was coming with us, my assistant Mark Warkentein got a call from John Williams's mother. She told Mark the ceiling in her kitchen had collapsed and some wiring was out of place.

"Boy, that's terrible," Mark said. He knew what was coming next.

She told Mark she wanted it repaired, and she wanted us to do it. Mark told her that we couldn't do something like that, but she had it all worked out, she said we could pay her sister, and the NCAA would never know.

Mark came to me.

"Well, what do I tell her?"

"Well just don't tell her anything. Let me talk to her when I go to Crenshaw for a home visit next week. I'm going to give her a speech about how they're jeopardizing John's future when they ask for things like that. And then I'll point out that if they play it straight, John is going to make all this money in the long run in the NBA and so forth."

A couple days later, I went to Los Angeles to speak at the CIF dinner, which was held at the offices of the *Los Angeles Times*. John Williams was there to get an award, so his mother was also there. The next day they were going to have the McDonald's All-America game. I went, and John Williams killed everybody. He put on one of the greatest shows ever in that all-star game. He was so much better than every other player in the country that it wasn't even funny; it was like men against boys. At halftime, Bob Minnix of the NCAA came up to me.

"Tark, I hear you're doing pretty good with John Williams."

"Yeah," I said, "we've got the right of first refusals. If we match the offer, we're going to get him."

And Bob just laughed like hell. That's what I liked about Bob. Anyone else at the NCAA would have cited me right there.

Just then I saw another big-time coach who had flown in to take a shot at John. He was there with his assistant, who had a briefcase with him. The only time anyone would bring a briefcase to an all-star game was if it was filled with cash. Why else would a coach have a briefcase?

I said to Bob Minnix, "I'll tell you what you ought to do, Bob. You ought to walk over and steal that briefcase full of cash and then go down to Florida and buy a condominium. Just pay cash. You're an NCAA investigator, what is the coach going to do? He can't ever turn you in. They can't even say a word to you. They won't even report it stolen. Just seize the money."

And he just laughed like hell again.

I told another coach at the McDonald's game, a national championship coach, about John Williams and how he had committed to us, but it was going to get crazy.

"You know," I said, "I can get the kid for $10,000."

"Tark, that's a bargain. You can't get anybody that good for $10,000. John Williams is worth five times that."

The next day Warkentein and I went to John's house, and there was a guy I didn't know sitting there. He turned out to be the father of Kenny Fields, who played at UCLA.

"Hell, who's this guy?" I asked.

And John's mother said, "My agent."

"Agent for what?"

"Well, today's your lucky day. My son wants to go to UNLV, and for about $15,000 or $25,000, you got him."

This woman was crazy. I was paranoid because of the NCAA. I was convinced they were out to get me. She was so bold, I figured it was all just a setup or something. I figured the NCAA had the house wired, and they were trying to trap me. So I jumped up and ran out of the house without saying a word. I was gone.

I was standing outside the door when Warkentein came out to get me and find out why I bolted out of there.

"Mark, you go in there and tell them we've got nothing to do with that stuff. You go in there and just tell them we can only give them room, food, and beverage, and we can only give them books and tuition, whatever the NCAA allows. Make sure you mention the NCAA. Whatever they allow, that's all we're giving them."

I told him to look around for wire taps and tapes and all of that. I was paranoid.

John's mother was crazy. It was funny. That spring I heard a story that when the organizers of the McDonald's All-America game called to invite John to play, she got on the phone and said, "My son will play on one condition, you give me a franchise." She thought she could get the McDonald's All-America people to get her an actual McDonald's.

That home visit ended our shot at John Williams. He made me too nervous to stay involved. When I left, I walked to my car, and there were Walt Hazzard of UCLA and Dale Brown of LSU, both waiting to get in. They were coming from all over for a shot at John Williams.

I really liked Dale Brown. He has been one of my best friends in coaching through the years. He's the only other guy besides me who fought the NCAA and survived. Everybody else got buried. A week later, John Williams was at the Dapper Dan Roundball Classic, the national all-star game Sonny Vaccaro ran out of Pittsburgh, and his recruitment was still open. We were out, so it was anyone's game. Everyone was trying to get in, making bids, who knew what? It was one of the wildest recruiting deals of all time.

One of my best friends, Mike Toney, was there helping Sonny out. He and Sonny were real close, so Mike's job was to drive college coaches to and from at the airport, stuff like that. After the Dapper Dan game, he gave Dale Brown a ride to the airport.

"Hey, Mike," Dale said, "you must be up on the gossip, where's John Williams going to go?"

"He's going to the highest bidder."

"Well, who's that?"

"You. You're the highest bidder."

Dale denied it, though; he said he didn't know. It was funny.

But John Williams did sign with Louisiana State. People started calling John Williams "the Louisiana Purchase." His mother didn't even know what LSU was. She was from Los Angeles. LSU was just some letters, but they signed. The story circulating was he got $100,000, but that was bullshit, and I'll explain why in a second. His mother just started all of those rumors. Dale was a great friend of mine, and he told me he heard the same thing and just laughed.

An amount like $100,000 for a player was ridiculous—although in the 1990s there was a federal case against Michigan and its booster Ed Martin where it came out that Chris Webber received $240,000 during his time at Michigan. Juwan Howard and Jalen Rose got paid a ton, too. That didn't surprise me, because I tried to recruit Jalen. And all of this was from the feds, not the NCAA. But a hundred grand for a player was unheard of money.

John Williams might have been worth it, though. John played only two seasons for Dale Brown, but he led LSU to the 1986 Final Four and was the 12th pick of the draft that year. His problem was his weight. In the NBA, they used to call him "Hot Plate" because he couldn't refuse one. He got up to about 300 pounds. But he really knew how to play the game. He was just a great player.

The reason I don't believe Dale Brown really paid John Williams $100,000 came two years later, when we were at the Final Four. I was hanging around the hospitality suite Nike had set up at a hotel when Mrs. Williams came in. I couldn't believe it. I hadn't seen her since I sprinted out of her living room. I didn't even want to talk to her.

But she talked with Mike Toney.

"I'll tell you something about them people at LSU," she said, "they're all liars. LSU promised me $150,000. Then they promised me a Cadillac. But they didn't deliver."

"What'd they give you?" Mike said.

"Nothing. They got me a job, but they wanted me to actually go to work."

It was funny. She was crazy.

"Coach Tark was the only coach that told me the truth," she told Mike. "The only one. After all the promises fell through, I kept saying,

'Coach Tark told us right off the top, he couldn't give us anything.' When we asked, he ran right out of the house."

I just wished the NCAA had wiretapped *that* conversation.

22

... If I Told You

" Then there was Lloyd Daniels . . . "

—JERRY TARKANIAN

One time I recruited a valedictorian.

The kid's name was Clifford Allen, he was six foot 11 and had been a star player at Carson High School in Southern California. He lived with his summer league coach, Issy Washington, until he got into some trouble with the law for stealing something and got sent to the El Paso de Robles Juvenile Detention Center, north of Santa Maria. We kept in touch with him even though he was in jail, and we weren't the only school. That's how good Clifford was. In the juvenile center Clifford earned his GED. He was released, and after paying his debt to society, he was fair game. He moved back in with Issy. UCLA coach Walt Hazzard was after him, too, but Clifford liked us and decided to sign with the Runnin' Rebels.

At the time, UNLV was a good school, but it didn't have much of a national profile. We had gotten a new president, and he wanted to make UNLV a national school, not just a regional one. So he came up with an idea that no matter what high school a student attended—in Las Vegas, in Maine, in Seattle, wherever—if he or she were named valedictorian of the graduating class, he or she automatically qualified for a full academic scholarship to UNLV. The president figured we would get some real good students in from all over the country and that would help our reputation. It was a good plan.

One of my assistants heard about the new program, and because we had Clifford signed, he joked, "Hell, Clifford was the valedictorian of the El Paso de Robles GED program. He should qualify for a full academic scholarship." We all laughed, but then I got to thinking, maybe that was a good idea. If Clifford were on an academic scholarship, that would help his image, particularly coming from jail, and it would free up another scholarship for us.

I sent one of my assistants to the juvenile center and got the prison worker who ran the GED program to sign a deal that said Clifford was, indeed, the valedictorian of the program. I even scheduled a meeting with a UNLV committee to see if we could get Clifford qualified.

But a week before the meeting, Clifford stole Issy's car. I guess it wasn't the first time, so Issy had warned him that if he did it again, he would turn him in to the cops. And that's what Issy did. Because Clifford was on probation, he had to go back to prison. And there went my valedictorian.

Eventually Clifford went to a junior college in Texas and was phenomenal, and a bunch of schools got back in and tried to recruit him. But he got in trouble down there, too, and went back to prison. He was considered the finest big man in the country his senior year of high school, but he never amounted to much. He was a real waste of talent because he could have made a lot of money in the NBA if he had just stayed out of prison.

We recruited Chris Mills, who was from Los Angeles and would wind up getting half the country in trouble. He was playing in Vegas during the summer of his junior year in high school. One day he came in to the office with his dad.

"I want to commit to you guys. I want to come here."

I was like, "God, that's great Chris. We're really happy."

But then one night after a game, we were having a party over at Piero's, my favorite restaurant. Chris Mills's father was going to be there, and he was with this guy, Al Ross, who claimed to know my friend Mike Toney and wanted to talk to Mike. Mike had coached football at Michigan State, where Al had gone to school. Now Al was an attorney.

At the party, he said to Mike, "I represent Chris Mills."

"What do you mean you represent him?" Mike asked. "What happened?"

"Mike, the kid wants to go to UNLV, and you can get him at the right price, $25,000."

"First of all, Tark is not going to go for $25, let alone $25,000. He ain't buying any players. The NCAA's on him. If he does anything, they'll get him."

So now it didn't look good with Chris Mills.

That summer the Millses came to my office in Vegas. He didn't visit any other schools. But Mr. Mills asked for a convertible, and then we could have his son.

"You can't do that; you're going to ruin this kid," I said.

But the dad had a plan—he even had all of these names to put the car under so the NCAA would never find out. I just said no again. I was real paranoid then.

Mike Toney was at the meeting also and he told Mr. Mills, "Man's ambition got to be small, so write his name on the shithouse wall. But a man's ambition is smaller still, to sell his ass for a five-dollar bill. And that's what you're doing."

The craziest thing was he kept coming back to us. Chris really wanted to come to UNLV. His high school team played in a tournament during the summer, and they were staying at the Dunes. We set up a lunch at the casino, but you could tell by Chris's face that he wasn't coming to UNLV, even though he wanted to. I told Mike to get the scoop, and I went to the bathroom.

Mike said to Chris, "Now tell me the truth. You're my buddy. I don't care what school you go to. I've known you for four years now, and I'm going to be here. I don't care what school you go to as long as you're happy. So tell me the truth. What school you going to?"

"Kentucky."

Kentucky? Damn, the kid is from Los Angeles, and he is going to go to school in Lexington?

"How did you get to Kentucky?"

Chris just shrugged.

Of course, it all blew up when an Emery overnight envelope from the University of Kentucky addressed to Chris Mills was opened by accident and $1,500 in cash fell out. The NCAA found out and busted Kentucky. It cost Eddie Sutton his job there. And it finished Chris and UK. He still wanted to come to UNLV, but I wasn't that dumb. I wouldn't touch him with a 10-foot pole. He wound up at Arizona, and that year we played Arizona at our place. Chris was sitting out that season, but he drove up to the game. After the game, he hung around and said, "God, I should have come here."

Then there was Lloyd Daniels, who turned out to be my most famous mistake.

Lloyd was a playground legend from Queens, New York. He was a six-foot-seven smooth-as-could-be point guard who had incredible scoring ability. The word on him was he was Magic Johnson with a jump shot. Back in New York, they called him "Swee' Pea." The first time I saw Lloyd was when he came to Vegas to play in a summer tournament when he was a freshman in high school. Bernie Fine, who was a Syracuse assistant, told me that this was the best freshman in the country. They played right in our campus gym, so I watched him. And he was great. He was incredible. Then he came out again after his sophomore year, and I was even more in love. I was famously quoted as saying, "When they write the final chapter on guards, they'll start with Jerry West, Oscar Robertson, Magic Johnson, and Lloyd Daniels." At the time, I believed it.

By that point, a lot of the black kids liked me. And we had had Sid Green, Ricky Sobers, and Richie Adams from New York, so we were in on Lloyd. The problem with Lloyd was he had a lot of problems. He hung out on the streets a lot, and he was into drugs, which we didn't know. He was completely unreliable and a bad student. On the plus side, in one year at Andrew Jackson High School, he averaged 31.2 points, 12.3 rebounds, and 10 assists a game. That is the kind of talent that makes coaches overlook the negatives. And deep down, Lloyd was a likeable kid.

We were close to Ron Naclerio, a high school coach in New York. He told us Lloyd was not going to finish high school. He would not have a diploma or a GED. He was going to have to go to junior college. Naclerio called us and asked if we would be interested.

"Yeah, we'd like to put him in junior college."

We figured that if we put him in junior college, we were going to get him. When I say, "Put him in junior college," I mean we were going to pick the junior college for him. People did that all of the time in those days. If I put a guy at a junior college, I was helping out the juco coach by getting him a great player. As a sign of thanks, the coach was going to help me get the player back and keep other recruiters away. It was a back-and-forth deal. That was how those juco coaches operated. They all had college coaches they worked with. In those days, California jucos were free, and you didn't even need a GED. You just had to be 18. So, obviously, you could get anyone into a juco, including Lloyd Daniels.

One thing about my recruits throughout the years is that no one can ever say we fixed SAT scores or high school transcripts like you always hear about. None of my players ever came from those "fly-by-night" prep schools. My guys always had to either sit out as nonqualifiers or go to juco.

What it came down to was Syracuse, Kansas, St. John's, and us. We all recruited Lloyd to put him in junior college. St. John's was in strong because it was the local school, and Louie Carnesecca had just done a similar deal with Walter Berry, who was a great forward from Brooklyn but didn't have a high school diploma. Louie sent him to San Jacinto in Texas and got him back; Walter led St. John's to the 1985 Final Four. He had a proven route for Lloyd to take. But Lloyd picked us. So we put him at Mount SAC, which is officially Mount San Antonio College near Los Angeles, where one of my good friends was coaching. I figured he'd play there, get eligible, and then come to our school after two years.

But he goofed up. He wasn't going to class. He was a disaster; he played only two games at Mount SAC before the coach kicked him off the team.

"Tark, I don't even want this kid," the coach said.

What I should have done is let him go. But I didn't. He was so talented, and I thought I could make it work. I was blinded by those soft passes he could throw.

Back then Nevada had this law: If you passed six college credits in either Nevada or California, you could be admitted to UNLV. That was all it took. Lloyd had managed to get his credits at Mount SAC, and he was admitted to UNLV. We got a lot of heat for that, but there was no way we could have denied admission. It was the law. So he was admitted even though he couldn't play or practice with our team. He wasn't on scholarship. He wasn't officially in our program. He had to pass some classes at UNLV to get eligible to join the team and get a scholarship.

To survive, he got a job in town. I wasn't supposed to get him a job, but he worked at an advertising company where he was a runner. Lloyd's name had been in the newspapers as this big, talented player, so it was easy for him to get a job. Everyone in Vegas wanted to help him out. Then, in an effort to get him straightened out, we had Mark Warkentein become Lloyd's legal guardian. That seemed like a good idea at the time. But we got killed by the press for that one, too.

When he first came out, we had Anthony Jones, who was an All-American as a senior. There was a health club in Vegas called the Sporting House, which had a gym, and a lot of the players liked to play there in the offseason. They had a game where Lloyd went against Anthony, and all of the players came back and told me that Lloyd had destroyed him. Then I sent my son Danny over to play with him, and he came back with all of these stories. So then I watched him a few times, and I was really impressed. It was his court vision more than anything else. He could just play the game. He was born to play the game. I got blinded by that.

That February, we were playing Pacific in Stockton, California, and we had just clinched the league championship. Our next stop was Fresno. I was in a bar in Stockton celebrating when I got a phone call: Lloyd Daniels was just arrested. It was on TV. The local news had film. He was at a crack house buying drugs.

Right away, I got a hold of Lloyd.

"Coach, it isn't true, I was buying concert tickets."

He was giving me all of that. We went and played Fresno State and then came home. As soon as we got home on Monday, I went and met with the college president and suspended Lloyd totally from the team, even though he wasn't even officially on the team. Then I said I wanted to look into all of the details and perform my own investigation. I found out he was lying. He wasn't buying concert tickets. It was right on television.

Lloyd has turned around his life lately. Later when I coached the San Antonio Spurs, I signed him to a contract. I always stayed in touch with him. When I coached at Fresno State, Lloyd even helped me when I tried to recruit Lamar Odom, who was also from Queens. Those two were

tight. Lloyd was never a bad guy; he was never violent; he just had
troubles with drugs. These days he lives on the Jersey Shore with his two
children and coaches youth teams that are all called the Runnin' Rebels.
He calls me regularly to tell me about the teams and his life. He actually
is a great story.

But at that time, his story was all negative. The media just killed us.
Two days after his arrest, we had a press conference and said he would
never play for UNLV. I thought we handled it as well as we could. But we
got crushed on it in the press anyway. Even after all of that, even after the
arrest, Larry Brown was at Kansas, and he came out in the papers and said
they were still interested in "helping" Lloyd. He still wanted to recruit
him. But no one ever killed Larry for that. It was always me. I'm not sure
we ever lived down Lloyd Daniels.

23

Recruiting the Champs

" Perry got me Anderson Hunt because I ate chicken wings and drank beer with him one night in Grand Rapids. *"*

—JERRY TARKANIAN

T he biggest coaching fallacy of all is that recruiting is so tough. A lot of coaches repeat that, so I guess it stuck, because I've had so many people say, "Boy, I bet the toughest part of the job is recruiting."

But really, how tough is it? It was tough when I was at Long Beach State, because we didn't have any money for travel. But at a major school, it's easy, especially now that recruiting and scouting are so organized. In July, they hold these big AAU tournaments in Las Vegas, with all-star teams coming in from all over the country. You go, watch four or five games during the day, stay in a nice hotel, afterward go out and get a nice steak and some wine, and maybe go out after that with your coaching friends. Then you go back and tell your boosters how tough it is. And they fall for it.

The only time recruiting is actually tough is if you don't like being around people. But I enjoyed people, and if you like that, hell, recruiting is fun. You get to meet all sorts of different, interesting people from all over the country whom you normally would never have met. You meet the moms and dads, the high school coaches. All sorts of characters. I even enjoyed home visits until I got to Fresno, and then I got a little older and didn't want to travel.

The guys who really recruit for you are your players. I used to tell the parents, "Wherever you go, every coach is going to give you his best side. You're going to see the best side of campus. The best side of town." Coaches get so detail oriented that when a recruit comes in on a visit, the route they are driven from the airport to the campus is determined so they only see the nicest streets. I always said, "The only way to really know what a program is about is to talk to the players in the program. And it's even better if you talk to players who have graduated from the program. They're going to tell you the truth."

If your players are happy, then you can win a lot of recruiting battles. Fortunately for me, when it came time to assemble what would turn out to be the 1990 national championship team, I had happy players and a hot program. Everything was set for us to make a major breakthrough, and we did. Here's how I recruited that team.

Stacey Augmon

Stacey Augmon was an athletic six-foot-seven forward from Pasadena, California, my hometown. UCLA and USC did not recruit Stacey in part because he was not going to be eligible academically. Kansas recruited him, but not real hard. Some other lesser schools were after him, but we could beat them out. I knew how good Stacey could be, and he was my hometown kid. I have a lot of friends there: My brother was coaching at Pasadena City College; the football coach, Harvey Hyde, was one of my best friends. I had the entire city wired with years and years of friends and contacts. So I got everyone together, and we got Stacey Augmon. There was no way I wasn't getting him.

Anderson Hunt

At some point in the early 1980s, I spoke at a coaching clinic in Grand Rapids, Michigan. I was the last speaker of the night, and afterward some high school coaches came up and asked questions. A lot of college coaches like to skip out as soon as possible, but I always enjoyed talking with high school coaches. I was a high school coach once. I was a no-name junior college coach. So I know the position those guys are in. They're just eager for information on how to get their teams better.

At this clinic, a bunch of black coaches from Detroit came up and talked to me. We discussed strategy and practice drills, things like that. I stayed for a long, long time, going over some of the stuff we do.

"Hey Coach," one of them asked, "we are going to get some chicken wings and beer, you want to go with us?"

"Yeah, I'll go with you guys."

So we went to some little place in Grand Rapids that had chicken wings and beer. Not a fancy place, just a little place. It was great.

"Tark, you are the first major coach to ever go out with us," one of them explained. "Usually when we ask, they say they have a flight to catch."

Then another coach said, "You know no one has ever done this with us before, and when I get a great player, I'm going to send him to you."

"Hey," I said, "that's great, I appreciate it."

I don't remember names well, but I wrote that guy's name down and kept it with me.

It turned out to be Perry Watson, now head coach at the University of Detroit, but at the time he was coach at Detroit Southwestern High School, where he had a real powerhouse going. He reached seven state championship games with his teams in nine years, an incredible feat in a state as big and full of talent as Michigan. About two years later, I was reading in a basketball recruiting magazine that there was a six-foot-seven kid from Detroit Southwestern going to Iowa. So I called Perry up.

"Hey Perry, remember you said you were going to send me a guy when you got one, and I see this guy is going to Iowa. What's up?"

"Tark, he's good, but he's not great. You've got players like him in L.A. When I get the great one, a difference maker, I'll call you. I haven't forgotten you."

I figured nothing would ever come of it, but a few years later Perry called and told me about this guard he had, Anderson Hunt. He said if I wanted Anderson, it was done. I checked it out, and Anderson was a hell of a player. I thought he could make a great off guard for us. Even though he wasn't going to be eligible academically, Ohio State and DePaul were also after him. But when Perry offered, I took him. He signed with us without ever visiting our campus; he didn't take an official visit until after he had signed. And that was it. Perry got me Anderson Hunt because I ate chicken wings and drank beer with him one night in Grand Rapids.

Greg Anthony

Greg Anthony was a local Vegas kid, a pretty good guard whom we recruited out of high school. But he was a shooting guard who wasn't a good shooter. He was a great athlete, though. I loved his quickness and toughness, but I thought he needed to play point guard. But he kept saying he wanted to get out of town, so we said fine. He went up to University of Portland and had a good year; he scored like 12 points a game as a freshman.

One day that summer, he walked into our office and said he wanted to come back home to be closer to his family; he wanted to transfer to UNLV.

"Great, we'll take you, I'd love to have you back."

"But," Greg said, "I'll be honest with you, I'm going to go visit USC."

"Screw you. You're a Vegas kid, you left to go to Portland, and now you're going to tell me you're going to visit USC? Just go to USC. Get out of here."

"No, no, Coach."

"Look, if you're going to visit other places, then you can't come here."

"I want to come here."

And that was that. He didn't visit USC or anywhere else. But when we got him, we had to make a point guard out of him because he couldn't shoot the ball well enough. He redshirted that first year, and we just really worked on him hard to be a point guard. And he was one of the few guys who made the transfer from shooting guard to point. He learned the position, and then when he got to the NBA, he became a great shooter.

David Butler and Moses Scurry

David Butler and Moses Scurry were from San Jacinto Junior College just outside Houston. We had a good relationship with the coach down there because we had gotten a kid named Spoon James a few years before. Butler committed after visiting us; he really liked our style of play. I knew he would be pretty good. Then I became very interested in Moses Scurry, who was only six foot five but was a hell of a great rebounder. He only played inside because he couldn't shoot a lick.

Moses was a funny guy. He was from Brooklyn and one of the toughest guys I ever coached. He used to play high school ball against Lloyd "Swee' Pea" Daniels. I offered him a scholarship and a chance to come out to visit. He said he'd think about it. Then he watched us one day on television, called me up after, and committed, just like that. He signed without even visiting our campus; it was one of the easiest recruitments I ever had. What had happened was on television they showed our pregame introductions, which included a light show, fireworks, and all of that stuff. Moses liked the light show. And that was it. He even told the newspapers that story.

For all of the time and effort a coach puts into recruiting, sometimes you just never know. You wind up with a key player on a national championship team because of a light show.

Larry Johnson

We never recruited Larry out of high school because I never thought we had a shot with him. Larry attended Dallas's Skyline High School, and I had never had much success getting big-time high school stars out of Texas. That was when the Southwest Conference was still going, and it was tough to beat those schools for a recruit. When it came to cheating, those boys wrote the book. You just knew it was going to get very nasty. So we sat that one out.

Larry signed with Southern Methodist University in Dallas. He was one of the most important recruits in SMU history, but then the school disallowed his standardized test score. It claimed there was something wrong with it, so he was denied admission. Larry decided to go to Odessa Junior College out in West Texas.

When I heard that, I thought, "Hey, any kid who goes to junior college, we've got a shot at. We're popular with junior college players." I knew how good Larry, a six-foot-six forward, was, so I wanted to get in there and get involved with him. Even though Larry would have to play two years at Odessa before we could get him, I didn't waste any time getting in on the recruiting process. The problem was I didn't know any of Larry's peripheral people, the people around him. Because I didn't like recruiting against Southwest Conference or SEC schools, I didn't know a lot of people in the South. It wasn't like Los Angeles, New York, or Detroit.

Right away I called Ron Meyer, who was the football coach at SMU. He had been the coach at UNLV before that, and Ron and I were great friends, real close.

"Ron, I'm going to recruit this kid out of Dallas. We've not talked to him yet, and I know you know some Dallas people. Who can I contact back there who can help me with the kid? I just want to get an in with the kid."

Ron asked around and then called me back a couple hours later.

"Larry's guy is named Sherwood Blount. He was an All-America football player at SMU."

After retiring from football, Sherwood had become a successful lawyer and real estate developer in Dallas. He even owned a country club. And he took Larry Johnson under his wing at an early age. Larry's mother had worked for him at the country club since Larry was in the eighth grade.

Ron got me in contact with Sherwood, and I flew down to Dallas to meet with him at his law office. This was before I ever called Larry. Sherwood was an SMU grad and the reason Larry had been headed there. I started a relationship with Sherwood right then. We even went by the country club, and sure enough, Larry's mother worked there.

Larry had a great freshman season at Odessa, and that summer he played on a USA Basketball team. His roommate turned out to be Stacey Augmon, who had just finished his freshman season at UNLV. He and Stacey got to be real close. I could call Stacey, and he'd hand the phone over to Larry. I kept telling Larry that they should play together. I thought we had a good chance because we now had the in with Stacey, and I had the in with Sherwood. But Larry was so good, everyone wanted him. In the end it came down to UNLV, Kansas, Oklahoma, and Georgetown.

I thought we were going to lose him to Georgetown. They really worried me. John Thompson had won a national title and been to three Final Fours, and he was an icon then to blacks. He was cleaning up in recruiting. Mothers couldn't say no to John Thompson. If John Thompson got into a mother's living room, that was all she wrote. So I thought, "Oh no, here comes John Thompson, and he's going to get Larry right out from underneath me."

But Larry and his mother told me John Thompson was supposed to call them on two or three occasions. They were excited to talk to him. The Georgetown assistants set up the time, and Larry and his mother waited by the phone for John to call them, but he never did. They rescheduled, and the same thing happened. Not one time did John call them. They got upset at him for that and eliminated Georgetown. Larry Brown was at Kansas, and they were in pretty strong, too. I thought they were going to beat us for Larry, but then at the end, just before signing day Larry Brown left KU to become head coach of the San Antonio Spurs. So they were out. In the end, it was just Oklahoma, who was really good then under Billy Tubbs, and us.

But then Sherwood and I had a talk.

"Tark," he said, "Larry's mom has worked for me since Larry was in the eighth grade, and I have looked after them for all these years. Larry is my guy. I love that kid. He is going to help you more off the court than on the court. But I want to be sure that if he goes to Vegas, nobody gets close to Larry but me. If Larry has a problem, he calls me."

"Hey, no problem."

All he wanted me to do was follow NCAA rules, to keep boosters and agents away from Larry. (Usually when you have a "talk," someone wants you to break the rules, not follow them.) I figured out that Sherwood wanted to represent Larry as his agent once Larry graduated and went on to the NBA. Sherwood wasn't an agent yet, but he saw Larry as his chance to get into that business. All I knew was I was getting Larry Johnson.

So the whole time Larry was at UNLV, I made sure he never associated with or got involved with any boosters. I protected him. I told them to stay away from Larry. The only time Larry ever asked for anything was when we played at Arkansas, and he asked for two tickets for his high school coach and even said the coach would pay for them. When agents came into town, I made extra sure Larry stayed clear of them. It was simple. I just loved Larry as a kid and a player.

And then when it came time for Larry to go pro, everyone tried to sign him, but Larry stayed loyal to Sherwood. Sherwood was his guy. He signed with Sherwood and was drafted second by the Charlotte Hornets, where he got an $84-million rookie contract and a huge shoe deal with Nike. So Sherwood made out in the end.

And it worked out pretty well for UNLV. He was the greatest player we ever had, and I swear we never gave him a single nickel. Not one single nickel.

24

On the Verge

" Greg, you can' t play with that muzzle on. "

—*JERRY TARKANIAN*

n 1989, Greg Anthony and Stacey Augmon were sophomores. Anderson Hunt was a freshman. They were just young kids. Moses Scurry and David Butler had just arrived from San Jacinto. Larry Johnson didn't come in until the following year, and that was when we started blowing people away.

But the groundwork for the national championship was laid during the 1988-1989 season. The key was getting Greg Anthony straightened out. In one of Greg's first games at UNLV, we played DePaul in the Maui Classic, and he had 28 points. It was an incredible game, and he was the hero, the new local guy made good. The fans patted him on the back, and the media hyped him up. We were in the locker room afterward, and he was really excited. I went up to him.

"That was one of the best performances I've ever seen, Greg, but don't ever score like that again."

"What?"

"We can't be a good team if you're scoring. Your job is to distribute the ball and play defense."

I didn't like my point guards to be big scorers. I always liked my two guards to be good shooters. Even if they were not good shooters, we talked them into believing they were good shooters. My point guard needed to be a passer. The best ones I had had were Danny Tarkanian and Mark Wade; both were UNLV assist record holders but not big scorers. Mark Wade almost never shot. One year he shot 63 times in 37 games. I needed Greg to be that.

It was funny, but the best thing that ever happened to Greg was when, in a game against Fresno State, he fell down and broke his jaw. The doctors wired it shut, and he couldn't talk for two weeks. Greg now works for ESPN, where he's an NBA analyst. I think he's the best analyst they have because he's so smart. The fact he makes his living talking is not a surprise. The guy always talked. But with a wired jaw, he had to sit there and listen for once. And he learned something. That was what made our season. That was what made Greg.

Greg was not real consistent as a player, but he was such a bright guy. He was into politics, debating issues, things like that. He said he wanted to be the first black Republican governor of Nevada. He had a lot of interests outside of basketball that the other guys didn't, so he wasn't that close with the rest of the team, they weren't sold on him.

So Greg still had something to prove to the guys when he broke his jaw. And one key in sports is to have everyone on the team believe in each other. If you don't have that, it can really hurt you. The players knew Greg wasn't milking a broken jaw; they knew it really hurt.

After he broke it, we had to play New Mexico State, which had a good team, and then Arizona on national TV. I was just sick about it, because I figured he might be out for the year, and we needed him to win those games. We were at practice when Greg arrived from the doctor. He was all wired up, but he had been fitted for a muzzle over his face. It looked crazy. But he grabbed a ball and started shooting on his own.

"Coach, I'm going to play."

"Greg, you can't play with that muzzle on."

"I can play."

So we talked to the doctor. He said Greg could play but probably only about 12 to 15 minutes a game, because he would not be able to breathe well through that muzzle. We had to have a doctor sit on our bench, and during a timeout he cut the wire on Greg's muzzle to get some oxygen in there so Greg could breathe. Then he rewired it, and Greg played some more.

And even though the doctors told him to stay out of the lineup, Greg went out and played 32 to 34 minutes for us every game. His broken jaw wasn't even four days old when we played Arizona. During the game, he took a charge and just got knocked over completely without regard for the pain of his broken jaw. Oh, the team loved him that day. After that, everybody loved him. That was a real bonding moment for us. Greg wasn't really well respected by his teammates until he broke his jaw.

At the 1990 Final Four, the press asked him, "Greg, was it painful to play with a wired jaw?"

"Yes, but it would have been a lot more painful if I had to sit on the bench and watch."

The other players loved that, too. Everything changed with that.

The thing that got me most excited about that 1988-1989 team was our defensive ability. We had guys who could really just shut people down. Stacey was incredible. We played a game that year against Pepperdine, where my old recruit Tommy Lewis had transferred. I told Stacey before the game that Tommy had committed to us and then backed out and gone originally to USC. I told Stacey that Tommy had lied to the Runnin' Rebels and he needed to make him pay. "It's a matter of Rebel Pride," I said. He went out there, and Tommy didn't score a single point. We won by 32. That's how good we were defensively.

We had a big rivalry back then with the University of Arizona. We were the two best teams in the West then, and we fought on the recruiting trail a lot. The only time recruiting is tough is when a kid is committed to you, he said he's coming, and then you lose him at the last minute. Anytime you lose a guy at the last minute, probably 75 to 80 percent of the time, it's because someone came in and did something or gave him something. You don't recruit a kid all year round, have him committed, and then the night before, have him go someplace else.

Lute Olson did that all the time. You'd go to bed, and a recruit was coming with you. You'd wake up, and he was going to Arizona. I gave him the nickname "Midnight Lute" because he got so many players right at the end, right at midnight. So many times. One of my former assistants and great friends was George McQuarn, and he was head coach at Cal State–Fullerton. During Lute's first year at Arizona, he got two kids

George McQuarn had had at the last minute. Before I coached there, Fresno State had Boyd Grant as head coach. He had a kid from Bakersfield committed to him, and on the last day, Lute got him. I don't think Lute was cheating, because I don't think Lute got into that, but he got them all at the last minute. I don't know how.

The one that got me was the guy who's on TV now, Tom Tolbert. He had committed to us; he was coming. He was at Cerritos Junior College in Southern California, and he came up for his visit and loved it. Then in the very last minute, Lute got him. The kid told us the reason he went to Arizona was because they kept telling him, "Who do you want to be your friends, Steve Kerr and Sean Elliott or some of their guys?" But our guys were good guys.

The thing that bothered me about Arizona was their assistant coaches were always badmouthing us. One time, I recruited this big, six-foot-10 white kid from San Diego to UNLV. One thing I always did when I recruited a kid was tell the parents: "You know I had a son who was a great athlete, and I coached in junior college and had a lot of great athletes, so I've sat in on a lot of recruiting visits. I know what you are going through.

"The one thing I want to tell you is that through my years, I've found out you shouldn't let your son go to any school that comes in and badmouths other schools. Because if they do that, they're going to badmouth your son if he gets hurt or if he doesn't play as well as they think he can play. They are just that kind of people."

And I always said that primarily because I knew Arizona had already badmouthed us. So I threw it out just to get them.

So I was in the home with this kid from San Diego, and Arizona was recruiting him. The dad went to every one of his son's games and every practice. The dad just loved this kid like you wouldn't believe. The dad started asking what I thought of different schools.

"What do you think of Arizona?"

"Oh, they have a great program."

And he pounds the table. "You're saying nice things about them?"

"Yeah."

"Well, Coach, let me tell you, all they do is badmouth you. In fact, one of their assistants sends us every negative article that is written against UNLV."

So the dad went out of the room and came back with a file of all of the negative articles from all over the country written on UNLV. Arizona had sent them all.

But I had said nothing but praise for Arizona. So the dad loved me.

"You know," I told him, "as much as I'd love to have your son, I think he should go to San Diego State."

"What?"

"You love this kid so much, you go to every practice. That kid should stay right here and go to San Diego State."

The kid wound up going to San Diego State, left there, and went and played at Long Beach. But his dad told people how straight I was.

In 1991, the first two rounds of the NCAA Tournament were in Tucson. The games were on the campus of the University of Arizona, and we were assigned the U of A locker room. Arizona had a great big basketball in their locker room, and on the way out before a game, all of the Wildcat players put their hands on the ball. It was a big tradition for them. It was supposed to fire them up, I guess. I wasn't sure. I just knew it was a big sacred thing. We were going to play Georgetown in the second round, and I came into the locker room before the game. Out of the corner of my eye, I saw some writing on the U of A ball. I hadn't noticed it before, so I looked to see what was on there, and I found out all of my players had signed the damn thing. They had ruined their sacred ball. Oh, man, did Arizona hate us then. After that, Arizona wouldn't play UNLV, but I thought signing the ball was pretty damn funny.

That 1988-1989 season, though, Arizona had been No. 1 in the country. They had gone to the Final Four in 1988, and they had Sean Elliott as their All-American. They beat us during the regular season down in Tucson. Now we were in the NCAA Tournament and set to play them in the Sweet 16 in Denver. Indiana was playing Seton Hall in the other game.

We went out and beat them 68-67 in a great game. That was the happiest I have ever been in coaching, except for winning the national championship. They were big favorites, and we beat them. They were such big rivals for us; it just felt good. We wound up losing to Seton Hall in the Elite Eight, but that wasn't a surprise. My guys were so tired. We were young. Seton Hall was better. We had not really been a great team during the season, but we were pretty good at the end of the year. But that set up the 1989-1990 season, where we had all five starters back, and we had signed Larry Johnson, and we knew he was better than anyone we had. We knew the big year was here.

25

Sweet Success

❝ I didn' t hit the coach. I didn' t hit anybody with a tie on. I made sure I didn' t hit anybody with a tie on. ❞

—*Moses Scurry*

We had a hell of a team going into the 1989-1990 season, and everyone knew it. Unfortunately, that included the NCAA, which did not want us to win the national championship. I had been fighting with them since the early 1970s, and they could never stop us. We had gone through all of that, and we were even stronger, with a team that could win the national championship. That's why we knew they were going to do their darnedest to stop us.

What they did was investigate us at a level no program could withstand. They were all over us. Even before the season started, David Butler and Moses Scurry were suspended because they each had an incomplete in the same class. All they had to do was finish a paper, and they were back. They finished it, but it got dragged out. It was big news in Vegas, and the professor was on television every night, making statements, "We're going through the papers now." Or, "We'll have a final grade soon." The guy got so much publicity; he loved it. We wound up losing them, both our centers, for the first eight games. We had loaded up the schedule, so that cost us in losses to Kansas and at Oklahoma.

The NCAA's big thing was not telling us they were going to suspend a player until the last possible minute, when we couldn't make any adjustments to the game plan. We were scheduled to play a great Temple team in Philadelphia on a Saturday afternoon. At 11 p.m. Friday, I was in a lounge with my athletic director. The NCAA called and said Anderson Hunt was ineligible. As a freshman, he was a Prop 48 academic nonqualifier and couldn't be on scholarship. To pay his tuition, he had taken out a student loan. The woman who had run the program had been transferred, so Anderson hadn't been sent a reminder. So he hadn't paid. The NCAA found out he was behind on the loan and thus claimed he was getting an "extra benefit." I had never heard of such a thing. But there was no arguing with them. Anderson was done until he made payment. At that point, all of the way in Philadelphia, after the banks closed, there was no way he could do it. If they had told us a day earlier before we flew to Philly, Anderson would have made the loan payment and played. That was how they operated.

We had a team breakfast the next morning, and I told them what the NCAA had done and told them Anderson was out.

"There's no doubt they are after us. There's no doubt the NCAA is going to do everything it can to stop us this season. They're going to try to suspend all of you. If the game is close, the refs will not give us a break. It's us against them. There's no use crying about it. There's only one thing we can do about it: Kick everyone's ass. They can't stop that."

The next day, we went out and beat Temple at Temple 82-76. And I thought right then, "We can win this thing."

But that didn't stop the NCAA. A month later, we were about to fly to Louisiana to play LSU, which starred Shaquille O'Neal, when we got word at the airport that Stacey and Chris Jeter were suspended for making long-distance calls from a hotel room on a previous trip. They owed like $11. The school paid the hotel room bill, but per NCAA rules, the players had to pay UNLV the $11. The NCAA called that "extra benefits," and they were out. We found out so late that we had to pull their luggage off the plane and leave them in Vegas. We wound up losing 107-105 to LSU.

We were in Hawaii when some surfboards at our hotel were stolen. The hotel just said some black guys stole it, and the NCAA decided to suspend a couple of my players one game for supposedly stealing the surfboards. But Anderson Hunt told me, "Coach, we don't even swim. You think any of us were going to take a surfboard out into that deep ocean?"

Probably the most ridiculous thing was when we lost Travis Bice for a game when it was discovered he had taken a bag of peanuts from the minibar in a hotel room during an away game. He had not repaid the school. The NCAA ruled it an "extra benefit." A bag of peanuts? His entire bill was $7.51. It was comical. He was a great shooter, a great guy, and a great student. No one in his right mind would think we were paying Travis. But that is how hard the NCAA was after us. They even investigated the room bills of our bench guys. By the end of the year, only three of my players hadn't been suspended for at least one game by the NCAA. You don't think they were out to get me?

But we just kept getting better and better. What the NCAA didn't count on was that the adversity made us stronger and made us closer. It was like every time they did something to us, we just got better and tougher. The other guys learned to step up. I had an incredibly tight team. We showed it during a January game against Utah State. We had become big rivals with them because they had this stupid coach, Kohn Smith. One time Smith told the newspapers that when we last visited Logan to play them, our guys had all of these beautiful clothes, fancy suits, and things. He acted like we were cheating.

"Shit," I said, "everybody knocks me in Las Vegas because my guys wear jogging suits to every game."

That was all they would wear—sweats. We didn't wear suits and ties like Duke. One thing we didn't have was fancy clothes. So I thought, "Now this guy's saying that we have all these fancy clothes, like we are wearing designer suits or something. Who in the hell has he been watching, you know?" I was upset. And he knocked us on some other stuff, too. So now we had a rivalry going.

Utah State came down to Vegas, and we were beating them by about 40 points. We just killed them. The game was almost over, and one of my players, Chris Jeter, who is six foot eight and the toughest kid we had in the entire school, head-butted a Utah State kid. It was Chris's fault. He had no business doing it. After it happened, I called timeout—there was only about 30 seconds left—and took Chris out of the game and yelled at him. So the game ended, and we were walking off the court. But we had to walk right by the Utah State bench. Utah State had this six-foot-four guard, and he stopped Chris.

"Hey mother-so-and-so, you think you're so tough. Why don't you hit me?"

So Chris hit him. Damn, you don't have to ask a guy like that twice. I could have told the Utah State kid that much.

So a big fight broke out and people were fighting all over the place. And that's when Moses Scurry punched Kohn Smith, the Utah State coach. It became a big deal, of course. It was all over newspapers across the country—"UNLV player punches Utah State coach."

After everything got settled down, I said, "Moses, why did you hit the coach?"

"I didn't hit the coach," he insisted. "I didn't hit anybody with a tie on. I made sure I didn't hit anybody with a tie on."

And that's what he told the newspapers. The problem was Kohn Smith had been an assistant under Bob Knight, who never wore ties. So Smith didn't wear ties.

"If the coach had worn a tie, I would never have hit him," Moses said. "But he didn't have a tie on."

Our very next game was against North Carolina State, where my friend Jimmy Valvano coached. We had suspended Moses for punching the Utah State coach, but he was allowed to sit on our bench in street clothes. Before the game, Valvano came over to the bench, went up to Moses, and began pulling on his tie.

"See, Moses, I've got a tie on. Don't hit me."

It was funny.

We had to go to Utah State for our last game of the regular season. In all of my years I never lost to Utah State, 19-0. They had some good teams, but we always beat them. They had the craziest fans, though. There was one time they threw these little tinfoil spitballs at the players while they were shooting foul shots. Another time up there, they put some kind of water bubble behind our bench and had it rigged to my seat. When I sat down, the thing blew up. It splattered all over; it was like a shock. People were going crazy and everything, but I just started laughing. I thought it was funny. Another time we got to the game and the students all had these Jerry Tarkanian masks. I told my assistants to get me one of those things.

The game in 1990 was going to be a big thing and really wild. Everything was played up. The commissioner of the league came and met with our team. He said he was afraid there was going to be a riot up there. Chris and Moses were suspended; they couldn't even make the trip. Our president sent a proclamation out that our students shouldn't go up because he feared for their safety. They thought it was going to be a really ugly scene. We didn't even get into Logan until the day of the game. We had a police escort and everything.

Our team took the court, and the sellout crowd was crazier than hell. Our guys warmed up and then came into the locker room. We had the toughest group of players ever, but I could sense some of them were a little uptight. So I made a speech.

"Hey, now look, I know there's a lot of shit that's been going on about this game. Don't let those people intimidate you down there."

And David Butler said, "Coach, are you kidding? If they want to fight, we'll knock the shit out of all 15,000 of them."

I don't think David was kidding. That's how tough that team was. We won, of course, and they wanted to get us out of town as soon as the game was over, so they said they were going to have the bus with the motor running right outside the arena and we were told quick showers only.

But nothing fazed my guys. Nothing. Not the NCAA, not the media, not the fans. Nothing. That's why going into the NCAA Tournament, I thought we had as good of a chance as anyone. We were a great defensive team. On offense, we led the nation in field-goal percentage because of our defense. We didn't have great shooters, but we got good shots, a lot of layups and dunks off of turnovers. We were just great defensively.

We rolled through the first two rounds of the NCAA Tournament. We got the winner of the Louisville–Ball State game in the Sweet 16, and we thought we would be playing Louisville, but Ball State upset them. That was the worst thing that could have happened to us. We watched the game at the arena and then went to catch a flight, and all the way back to Las Vegas, our guys talked about the upset. I think our guys thought it would be easy now. They hadn't heard of Ball State. But I had coached at Long Beach State, and I knew that lesser name teams could be great. I knew how tough it would be. I couldn't convince my guys, though, and Ball State had a shot to beat us at the end, but they turned it over. We barely survived.

Up next was the winner of the Loyola Marymount–Alabama game. Loyola Marymount had become everyone's favorite team in the NCAA Tournament. Early on they had beaten Michigan 149-115. Michigan had been the defending national champion, and Marymount had just killed them. The way they played was fun; they averaged 122.4 points a game that year. My assistants did not want to play Loyola, but I did. Alabama had a great team led by Robert Horry. I thought they were the tougher matchup. Marymount loved to run the ball. They would full-court press you and try for steals and layups. Alabama would not run against them. They would get through the press and have a 3-on-2 or a 3-on-1, and their coach, Wimp Sanderson, would yell, "Hold the ball." Loyola beat them by two points anyway, 62-60.

That was fine with me. I don't know if I have ever been as confident going into a game. Usually I was a nervous wreck; I worried about everything.

But I told my wife before the game, "We're going to kill Loyola."

"Don't talk like that. You never talk like that."

She thought I would jinx us. But I was convinced.

Loyola was real confident they could outrun us. They had a center who said, "UNLV thinks it knows about running, but they don't know what real running is." He compared Larry Johnson to a boxer. He said boxers can go four or five rounds, but by round six, they run out of gas. He said Larry would run out of gas in the game. The press went and asked Larry about that and he said, "Yeah, but nobody lasts more than one or two rounds with me."

The other reason everyone was pulling for Loyola was they had Bo Kimble and Hank Gathers that year, the Philly kids who Stan Morrison had originally brought out to USC. They had transferred to Loyola Marymount, and then Gathers died of heart failure just before the NCAA Tournament. Even though Gathers was their best player, the team rallied, played on emotion, and sprung some upsets. Gathers was a lefty, and in honor of him, Bo Kimble would shoot his first free throw of the game as a lefty. He made each one of them. It was incredible. All of America rooted for them.

Loyola's motto was "Living the Dream." On the way to the game, our bus drove past their hotel. I never allowed talking on the bus. I wanted silence. I wanted the guys to think about the game. So no one ever spoke on the bus. But as we passed the Loyola hotel, there was the banner, "Living the Dream." Greg Anthony said out loud, "We're going to wake Loyola up tonight."

And we did. I knew all we had to do was beat the press and we would wipe them out. What we did was have Larry Johnson inbound the ball. He threw a high pass to David Butler, so we made the first pass safe. David hit Greg running up the middle. Then we had Anderson and Stacey running the lanes. It was like a layup drill; both of those guys had more than 30 points in that game. Anderson had 13 assists, too. We shot 62 percent in the first half and were up 20 at the half. We won 131-101.

The Final Four that year was in Denver. We played a real good Georgia Tech team that included Kenny Anderson in the semifinals. We knew it would be a tough game, and we were very concerned about the officials. We truly believed the NCAA would do what it could to stop us from winning the title. We knew if it were close, we would get no calls. After what the NCAA had put us through that year, and now being so close, we had good reason to think that. So we had as our mindset that we had to win games decisively. In the Tech game, Larry and David got in foul trouble, but Moses came in and got every single rebound. He was a man possessed. He just elevated his game.

Tech led at the half, but we turned on the defensive pressure in the second half and won 80-71. When we played defense like that, we were just about unbeatable. One of the great things was after we beat Georgia Tech and Duke beat Arkansas. All of the Tech fans started chanting, "A-C-C! A-C-C!", because Duke had won and they were siding with the other ACC school. So then the UNLV fans started chanting, "Big West. Big West." I started laughing. I said, "Can you believe, 'Big West'?"

After all we had been through that year, we were getting painted as the bad guys of college basketball. To make things tougher, in the finals we played the Blue Devils, who were considered the good guys.

I didn't realize it was such a media slant until after the Georgia Tech game. I was headed to the pressroom for the postgame press conference. Dick Vitale grabbed me.

"Now Tark, after you finish your interviews, you've got to go on ESPN. They want you real bad."

Dick wasn't even the guy who was going to conduct the interview, someone else would, but he tried to get it set up.

"Dick, I want to go back to the hotel with my team."

The Vegas guys party, and I wanted to get back with my team and enjoy it.

"You have to do this for me, Coach. We'll have a limo to take you and Lois back to the hotel. Consider this a personal favor to me."

"OK, Dick, I'll do it for you."

So I went over there and sat down, and I didn't even want to be there.

The first thing the ESPN interviewer said was, "Coach, they are already saying this is a game of the good versus the bad."

"Boy," I said, "that really upsets me, because I don't think that is fair at all. I got to know some of those Duke kids, and they are good kids once you get to know them."

The guy almost died.

That was the focus, though. They asked my players about it in the press conferences, what it was like playing an academic school like Duke. It was tough on them, but Greg Anthony had the best answer. He said, "God bless schools like UNLV. Our country is so much better because we have universities that educate everybody, not just the elite."

Going in, I thought it was going to be a tossup. Duke was a little young, but they were young with Christian Laettner and Bobby Hurley. They had Alaa Abdelnaby, Phil Henderson, Thomas Hill, and some really good players. They were stacked. Mike Krzyzewski was one of the best coaches in the country. And this was no upstart team. Duke used to go to the Final Four every year; they just hadn't won it all yet, so they were good and hungry. I knew how good we were, but I thought to win we would have to play some of our best basketball of the season. That was how much I respected Duke.

I was so nervous. Before the game, my athletic director, Brad Rothermel, called me. He said Walter Payton had called and wanted to know if he could come and talk to the team in the locker room.

"God, that'd be great. I'd love to have him for the Duke game."

So he came in with his son. My team just loved him. He and his son loved us and never missed a game. He not only knew our starters, but knew all of our substitutes. It was obvious that he had watched them a lot. He sat down and talked to each one of them. He made a great speech. He told the guys that they didn't know the impact that they had had on people like him around the country. He said we were his team and how much he cared about our team. We couldn't believe it. Then at the end he said, "This is a special opportunity you have—go out and enjoy—have fun playing the game tonight, but make it count."

Then my team all got up and hugged him. That was one of the greatest locker room speeches I had ever heard. Walter Payton. My players couldn't have been more fired up. It was great.

And then we kicked them. It was incredible. Everything went right for us and bad for Duke. We just got on a roll. The game was close most of the first half, but we forced 14 turnovers and went into the locker room up 47-35. I told the guys that Duke was good enough to come back, so treat the game like it was tied. We had a saying that year, "Tighten the vise." When we got teams down, we wanted to tighten the vise so they couldn't escape. We wanted to play even harder. And we did.

We switched our defense, and we played the Amoeba zone some, and Duke had a lot of trouble with Amoeba. The Amoeba was a defense that was basically an aggressive zone with man-to-man principles, and because of that game, it became famous. Everybody kept talking about our Amoeba defense, but hell, we only played it two percent of the season. But everyone thought that is what we used all of the time. But we played man-to-man most of the time.

We went on an 18-0 run early the second half, and I just figured we couldn't blow it now. Duke just gave up at that point. Anderson got hot, and everything went right from there. We just hit everything. The ball bounced right. At one point in the second half, we had Duke down by 39. It is almost impossible to do that to a good team. They were literally done. We could have beaten them by 50. I mean it, it was pick-the-score time. But I didn't want to run it up on them. I just respected Krzyzewski so much, and their kids didn't deserve that. So I pulled my guys out. Krzyzewski recognized that afterward. He knew we worked to keep it to a 30-pointer. Even so, it was the largest victory ever in a championship game.

For me, winning that championship felt more like a relief than joy. I had worked my entire life for that moment, but after all we had been through with the NCAA and the media, all of the adversity, it just felt like a relief. The media asked me if it was sweet revenge considering I had been fighting with the NCAA all of these years. But I said it wasn't sweet revenge; it was just sweet. It was sweet for our players, our school, our fans, and the people of Las Vegas, Nevada, who deserved a championship team of their own.

As for the NCAA, I didn't even want to take the trophy from the NCAA. I wanted our athletic director to do it, but they said I had to grab it. So I did. When we eventually hung our championship banner in the Thomas & Mack, it didn't say we were "NCAA Champions." It read "National Champions." It didn't even mention the NCAA.

26

Chasing Perfection

" We lose to Duke, a team with three lottery picks and a great coach that goes on to win consecutive national titles, and people questioned whether we threw the game? **"**

—JERRY TARKANIAN

After we won the national title, I thought my No. 1 problem would be keeping my team intact. The big question was whether Larry Johnson and Stacey Augmon, both juniors, would turn pro on us. Their stock was really high. Larry would have gone No. 2 in the draft that year, behind Derrick Coleman. Even some of our close boosters were telling Larry to turn pro. The key was Larry. If Larry went, Stacey probably would go pro, too. But if he stayed, I thought Stacey would stay, too. Larry asked me what I thought.

"Larry, nobody can make that decision but you and your mom."

After we won the title, we got to go to Washington and meet the President of the United States, George H.W. Bush. The players were telling the president that they were going repeat as national champs and be back at the White House the next year, too.

So President Bush asked Larry, "If you're coming back here after your senior year, will you get a degree?"

"Yeah, if I go to summer school, I can get a degree."

"Well, do that. Get your degree."

Larry was like, "Yeah, OK, I'm going to do it."

Then the president mentioned it in his Rose Garden speech.

When we got back to Vegas, I wasn't sure what Larry was going to do. There was all of this speculation. I called him into my office.

"Coach, I'm not going to jump, I promised President Bush I wasn't jumping. So I'm not jumping. I'll be here next year."

He couldn't break that promise to George Bush. The President of the United States got me one more year out of Larry Johnson.

I had always been a George Bush supporter, but after that, I would have voted three or four times for him.

Larry was the greatest human being I ever met. Just the classiest guy. He changed our program. Because of Larry we started getting some really good kids, some really good students. I thought we had turned the corner. We had Ed O'Bannon out of Los Angeles committed, who was a terrific person and player. We had both Shon Tarver and H. Waldman, two kids who also had visited Stanford, committed. They saw that UNLV was for kids like them. Everything was changing.

I remember one time after Larry became a pro, he was in Japan for something. My friend, Mike Toney, whom Larry loved, had a small part in a movie. It was called *Deadly Vet*, and Mike played a collector, which if you know Mike isn't much of a stretch. Well, the movie got distributed worldwide, but they dubbed the words, so in Japan, obviously, the actors spoke in Japanese. So one morning, about 4 a.m., Mike said he got a call from Larry.

"Mike, this is Larry Johnson. What's up?"

Mike figured something was wrong, but Larry said, "I'm in Japan. We're watching a movie, and I told these guys I know you. You're in this movie."

Mike explained that he had done a little acting.

So Larry said, "These guys don't believe I know you. Tell them I know you."

So he handed the phone over, and Mike said he knew Larry Johnson and all that.

And then Larry got back on the phone and said, "Mike, one thing, you didn't tell me you could talk Japanese."

Anyway, with my team all coming back, my real No. 1 problem returned: the NCAA. If you thought they were after us before we won it all, you should have seen them after. The NCAA had tried to get me suspended from coaching at UNLV in 1977 for what they determined were recruiting violations from the early 1970s, but federal courts had blocked that because it infringed on my rights. However, on July 20, 1990, with the court case resolved in my favor, the NCAA was pissed that I had never received formal punishment from the original case. Because they hadn't been able to suspend me in 1977, they decided the penalty should now be to suspend my current team from the 1991 NCAA Tournament. They were not going to allow us to defend our championship even though we returned four starters and had a club that we thought could go undefeated.

I offered to step aside. I knew the NCAA wasn't after Larry or Stacey, they were after me. I didn't want to deny those kids the chance to repeat as national champions. It wasn't fair to them. The NCAA case was about things that happened when they were five or six years old. I had our president offer that deal to the NCAA. We tried to keep it quiet, but it got out in the public, and when that happened, my team said that they wouldn't play without me. They said if I was going to sit out, they were going to sit out. Greg told the newspapers that we would just go 30-0 in the regular season, destroy everyone, then sit out the Tournament, and make the entire thing a farce.

The NCAA then said that because we were banned from the Tournament, it was only fair that our seniors be allowed to transfer to another school and be eligible to play immediately. Normally when a player transfers, he has to sit out a season. The NCAA was willing to waive that of course, making it more appealing for the players to leave. Larry, Stacey, and Greg all got tons of calls from other schools, but they decided they weren't going anywhere. They weren't going to let the NCAA break them up. My players were just so loyal to me it was incredible.

Fortunately, the media saw through the NCAA's act. The NCAA was so corrupt back then, that I swear the mob had stronger morals. And everyone could see that. The media defended the players; they ripped the NCAA for taking a personal battle against me and trying to hurt the players. They agreed the NCAA Tournament would be a farce. They defended us on this one because we were so right. The entire thing was just so ridiculous. The NCAA couldn't stand it. In September, they allowed us to make some counter-penalty offers. On November 19, they decided for the 1991-1992 season we would sit out the NCAA Tournament and be banned from appearing on national television.

I hated it. I didn't think we deserved any of that, but at least we could play the 1990-1991 season and defend our title. So I agreed to it. I shouldn't have, but I just wanted to save the season.

Not that it got the NCAA off our back. In our second game, we beat Nevada–Reno by 50 points. Some of the Reno players had made some comments in the newspaper before the game that they would beat us. It fired us up. After the game, I told the press that when we saw the Reno quotes, in an effort to motivate our team, "We went out and bought a bunch of newspapers and passed them out." I got a memo a couple days later saying that handing out 25-cent newspapers to the players was an "extra benefit."

Not that it mattered. There was no stopping us that year. We had set the goal in the preseason to be the greatest defensive team of all time. After we had won the championship with such great defense, we thought about extending it to the full court. We had the athletes and the depth, and we thought if we pressed full court, we could just overwhelm teams; no one would get the ball across halfcourt. We were going to do it, but then at the end, I decided against it. I thought if we spent practice reemphasizing everything we taught the year before, footwork, closeouts, assignments, and stuck to the halfcourt, we could be the greatest defensive team of all time.

And we might have been. Technique-wise, no one was like us. Great coaches such as Pete Newell came to our practice and just marveled at it. We just pounded people that season. Our defense was incredible. We held Princeton to 34 points. We beat Michigan State by 20, Florida State by 32, Rutgers by 42, Fresno State by 49, Long Beach by 51, and on and on. We were 19-0, ranked No. 1, and our average margin of victory was 31.6.

The NCAA record was UCLA's 30.3 back in 1972. And we did it while sitting my starters almost the entire second half. I did not want to run up the score on anyone, and we tried our best not to. I used to say that was the year my towel never got any use because I was never nervous. I sat on the bench sometimes, watched us play, and said to Tim Grgurich, "Could we be this good?"

Even though we had beaten some good teams, there was a question just how good were we. So the matchup February 10 in Fayetteville against second-ranked Arkansas became the biggest regular-season game in years. Sportswriters came from all over the country to be there, there was just such anticipation for that game. It was like a Final Four atmosphere. It became this big showdown game, No. 1 versus No. 2. They had Todd Day, Lee Mayberry, and Oliver Miller, all future NBA guys. This was going to be a challenge.

Our problem was Frank Broyles, the Arkansas athletic director, really screwed us. We had a deal that the visiting team got 10 percent of the tickets. When they came to Thomas & Mack the year before, we gave them like 1,900 tickets. We went down there, and their place only sat 9,600. We thought we were going to get about 1,000 tickets. They gave us like 47 tickets, and they were bad seats. We had all of these boosters, all of these fans, celebrities, pro athletes, everyone wanted to come to the game. They were calling me because they couldn't get a ticket. We couldn't get them any. That's all Arkansas would give us. They said that the rest were all season tickets.

"Nothing we can do about it," they said.

So, we go down there, and before practice, my friend Irwin Molasky, who founded Lorimar Productions in Hollywood, paid off CBS to put a row of seats behind our bench. We got another 22 seats with locker room passes. That wasn't enough, but it was something. The problem was we had a new athletic director, this goofball Dennis Finfrock, who was probably the worst athletic director in the history of college sports. We went from Brad Rothermel, who in my opinion was one of the two or three best ever, to one of the very worst in one year. If they had decided to pay a guy to come in and destroy a program overnight, they couldn't have found a better person. From the beginning he would say or do anything to try to tank our program. He wasn't an AD, he was an assassin. He didn't like it when he was stuck up in the bad seats Arkansas gave us, and Irwin, Mike Toney, Freddie Glusman, and a bunch of other big boosters were right behind our bench and had locker room passes. Finfrock couldn't get into our locker room. That wound up hurting me with Finfrock, but it was funny at the time.

Broyles wouldn't help us one bit until Walter Payton called and said he and his son wanted to come to the game. Broyles was an old football coach, so we told him about Walter, and he sent a limo to the airport to pick him up. I think Frank thought he'd get to sit with Walter, but Walter came right to our locker room and gave another pep talk.

That was one of the wildest games ever. The crowd in Fayetteville was crazy. Arkansas led at the half, but we played great in the second half and kicked them. We were incredible. We led by 23 at one point, and I pulled back and we won easily 112-105. No one was questioning us at that point; they started wondering if we were the best team of all time.

We were 30-0 by the time we reached the NCAA Tournament, and we had never been challenged. We just blew everyone out. The NCAA stacked the field against us and tried to make it as tough as possible by giving us Georgetown, which had two great centers, Alonzo Mourning and Dikembe Mutombo, in the second round. Our one weakness was outside shooting, and these were two of the greatest shot blockers of all time. But we won that one 62-54. The Sweet 16 was in Seattle that year, and we beat Utah by 17, but we still hadn't played very well in the Tournament. I thought we were coasting too much. Our guys were just so confident that they could turn on the defense and get a big run going that they hardly paid attention to whom we were playing. Our fans started getting nervous, but we played great in beating Seton Hall in the Elite Eight to push our record to 34-0 and to advance to the Final Four in Indianapolis. We needed two more victories, and we would have a perfect season and back-to-back national titles.

Waiting for us in the semifinals was Duke, and Duke was the worst matchup possible for us. I was so nervous the week before that game. Duke was really good. They had 30 wins when we met them. They had Bobby Hurley and Christian Laettner back and a freshman named Grant Hill, who was as good as anybody. That's not just three future NBA lottery picks, that's three guys all picked in the top seven the year they came out. We had three top 12 picks (Larry, Stacey, and Greg). People look back on that game like Duke was the Sisters of the Poor. But that was a heck of a team.

The problem was our guys had just crushed them the year before to win the national title. That was a game where everything went right for us and everything went wrong for them. Duke wasn't as bad in 1990 as they had played in our game. And they were a lot tougher. They quit in that title game, but I knew they wouldn't do that again.

Duke had spent the entire offseason hearing about how they got embarrassed in the national championship game. That motivated them. I am sure they wanted us in the worst possible way. I told my guys Duke had a huge psychological advantage over us. It wasn't even close. I knew they would play harder than any team had ever played against us. They were motivated out of revenge and were every bit as talented as we were. Duke had the best things you could have going for you.

So now a team, which was better than my guys thought a year ago, was even better this year, and I couldn't convince anyone of that. I had spent the entire season trying to warn my guys that some opponent was really good and then they'd go out and beat them by 32 or something. They were sick of hearing it from me. They didn't believe it anymore. To them, Duke would just roll over like the year before. There is no question we were overconfident. We had been screwing around the entire Tournament, and now we had to face the best team we had played in two years.

Duke had one other big advantage on us—Laettner. I was so scared of Laettner because he could play all over the floor, and our center, George Ackles, couldn't guard him. That was a huge advantage. Other teams tried to play their center out on the perimeter and make the offense run through him, but no one had a player as good Laettner. I knew he could kill us.

And he did. Duke was so fired up to start the game that they put together a 15-6 run. No one had played us like that all year. We came back and made it 43-41 at the half, and I think everyone thought we would bust out a 20-something run on them, just like last year. But Duke was too good for that. They shot 52 percent against us, and we were a good defensive team. And with 3:51 left, Greg fouled out on a tough charging call. That hurt. He was the one who made everything work. We also couldn't stop Laettner. He wound up with 28 points and seven rebounds. With the game tied 77-77 and 12.7 seconds left, he hit two free throws. It was our ball, down two.

We had won 45 consecutive games, but we hadn't played in a really close one since we beat Ball State in the 1990 Sweet 16. That was 37 games and 53 weeks before. We got it to Larry, but he was guarded and passed to Anderson, who missed a jumper. That was it. Duke won, and we lost. They went on to win the next two NCAA titles.

The worst part of the loss was nobody let us just lose. After 45 games, it happens. We didn't play well, and a great team did. I thought Duke deserved all of the credit. Mike Krzyzewski and those kids had done a great job. But people wouldn't let it rest. The NCAA Tournament has all of these upsets every year, but we couldn't just get "upset" by a team with three lottery picks and one of the greatest coaches of all time.

That's when our AD Dennis Finfrock started the rumor that we were point shaving, and it got out of hand and we couldn't come back and win the game. That was so sick. That just shows you how sick Finfrock was. He would do anything to hurt me. Suddenly there were all of these theories about why we "really" lost the game. Do I think we were point shaving in the Duke game? If you know how competitive my team was or how bad they felt after, you would know that was ridiculous. No one would have said that if our school hadn't been from Las Vegas. It was unbelievable. Like the mob isn't capable of getting to a player at a school in another town.

Every March there are upsets, Bucknell over Kansas, Princeton over UCLA, Hampton over Iowa State. Small schools over big ones, upsets that should never reasonably happen, but when it occurs, no one says Kansas or UCLA or Iowa State had thrown the game. They just say, "That's March Madness." We lost to Duke, a team with three lottery picks and a great coach that goes on to win consecutive national titles, and people questioned whether we threw the game?

The idea that our guys threw the game for money is unbelievable. Larry, Stacey, and Greg all became millionaires the second the season ended. All of them were NBA lottery picks. They didn't need any money. My God, they had all of the money they could ever spend after the season ended. It just doesn't make financial sense that a guy who would make millions over the next year would throw a Final Four game for a few thousand. Stacey only shot three-for-10 from the floor that night, and that cost him money in the NBA, more than it would have been worth. I think as people got to know Greg, Stacey, and Larry in the NBA, they knew what kind of quality people they were.

I was sick over the entire thing. I was so angry. For anyone to say something like that just really hurt me and hurt the players. It had already been a tough way to end a great run.

27

Leaving Las Vegas

" In the early 1990s as the casinos were bought out by corporations, the owner of the casino was no longer a local guy, a fan of ours. 'He' was a group of businessmen back East. **"**

—*JERRY TARKANIAN*

T he hot tub. The most famous hot tub in college basketball history was the one that eventually ended my time at UNLV. On Sunday, May 26, 1991, the *Las Vegas Review-Journal* ran a photo on the front page of Moses Scurry, Anderson Hunt, and David Butler, drinking beer in a hot tub with a man known as Richie "The Fixer" Perry. I was at our family condominium in San Diego when UNLV president Robert Maxson called and told me about it. I flew back to Vegas immediately.

Moses knew Perry from New York, where Perry had coached Moses's AAU basketball team. Also on that team had been three players who had helped Seton Hall reach the 1989 championship game. Perry knew Lloyd Daniels, too. He was a real big-time AAU coach and a big recruiting contact in New York. Every college coach in America knew him. But he didn't go by the name Richie—he was called "Sam Perry." That is how we knew him, and even then we didn't know his background. Not even Moses knew. He got the name Richie "The Fixer," because he had been convicted of fixing harness races in New York for the Lucchese crime family and pled guilty to being involved in the 1981 point-shaving scandal at Boston College. He even served time in prison. He was a bad guy; he worked with Henry Hill, about whom they made the movie *Goodfellas*.

Perry was involved in the recruitment of Lloyd Daniels; they were real tight. He came to some of our games under the name of "Sam Perry." But we didn't know about his criminal past until April 1989 when *Time* magazine ran an article about him. I immediately banned my players from having any contact with him and made sure we stopped leaving him game tickets. I couldn't believe what I had read. If I had known his background sooner, I would have banned my players from talking to him then. People act as though I had approved of it. The idea that I would want a guy like that around my players is ridiculous. Why would I want that?

No one knows when that hot tub picture was taken. It was at least two years old; we know that. Perry moved to Vegas in the late 1980s when Lloyd was at UNLV. Moses came to UNLV in 1988, and Perry reconnected with him. At the time, Moses just thought it was his old AAU coach from New York, a familiar face. So he went over to his house, and one time Anderson and David went along. And that was when the picture was taken. Moses swore it was sometime in 1988, before we had learned who Perry was. Moses said Perry never did anything wrong with him, never suggested fixing a game. Moses said all Perry ever tried to do was get him to do well in school.

But it didn't matter. Once the photo was printed in the newspaper, people started thinking our players were hanging around with convicted game fixers. They thought the photo was taken the night before the 1990 national championship game or our 1991 Final Four loss to Duke. Everyone thought our games must have been fixed. It just got ridiculous. Everyone assumed everything. It was a bad picture.

Our athletic director, Dennis Finfrock, and our president, Robert Maxson, were already trying to get rid of me. At that point, I didn't believe they really could have fired me. I was a full professor with tenure at UNLV. It's very difficult to fire someone with tenure. But the newspaper kept running that picture of the guys in the hot tub. They ran it every day. And it got rerun in newspapers around the country. They kept coming up with all kinds of insinuations about violations with Lloyd and this and that. But that stuff had come out earlier.

"Hey, if there's one major violation, any major violation gets me or my coaches, I'll resign," I told them. "We'll all resign. Where's the violation?"

And they didn't have one. If I wanted to fight it, I could have fought it. Except the papers kept running that photo of the hot tub, and there was just no way I could continue. Our reputation was crushed. It was a disaster. It was over.

I made up my mind and said this was bullshit. I didn't want to quit, because I had a good group of kids coming back who were counting on me, and I wanted to fight through the NCAA probation and bring the program back. But I was 62, so I thought that was about time to quit. So I went and told the president and the regents that I wanted to finish out with these kids and then I would step down. I wanted to coach the 1991-1992 season, and that was it.

The hardest part for me was letting Maxson and Finfrock get me. Finfrock had come in during the 1990-1991 season and was just terrible. He destroyed our program in one year, just totally destroyed it. He created havoc within the city. He worked against me with boosters. He leaked unflattering stories to the media. It was unbelievable. All with Maxson's approval. Then Maxson wrote these incredible letters praising me and complimenting me on the things I had done. If you read the letters, you would have thought he loved me. But the whole time he was sabotaging me.

One time we were all at a fundraiser held by Jimmy Newman, who ran the Las Vegas Hilton. Jimmy had donated $360,000 worth of stock to our basketball academic program.

We were sitting there when out of the clear blue sky, Finfrock said in front of everyone, "Isn't it a shame that the president of the university doesn't make as much as the basketball coach?"

And the Hilton people looked at me. It was embarrassing. The media asked me what I thought of that statement.

"Oh, I hope he makes more than I do. I hope he gets a big raise as long as they don't take any from me. I don't care what he makes."

I didn't care if he made more money than me; in fact, I wish he had. That was the last thing I wanted to get into. It wasn't like I was the only basketball coach making more than the president of the school. The head basketball and football coach of every major program in the country is paid more than the school president. That's the business of college sports. I didn't create it. I didn't get into coaching to get rich. I started as a high school coach in Fresno. Because of my tenure deal, I wasn't even making the kind of money from UNLV that I probably could have. So, sure, I made more than the school president, but no one who was a big-time athletic director would have been troubled by it. They would have expected it.

That was when people around Vegas started coming up to me and saying Finfrock was a snake and was out to get me. And he was. You couldn't believe some of the things that happened here. It was embarrassing.

They had the university attorney, Brad Booke, try to find violations against us. He investigated everything but couldn't find one. So they hired students whose work-study job was to follow players and find a violation. But the students didn't come up with anything.

One time Finfrock and Booke accused my friend, Mike Toney, who was a greeter at the Dunes, of buying car insurance for the kids. Booke was pointing his finger right in Mike's face, and Mike went nuts on him. Mike is a big, tough guy from Canton, Ohio, and I thought he was going bite that finger right off. Mike grabbed Booke by the throat; it was like he going to whack him.

"I'm going tell you something, you motherfucker," Mike said. "You better tell me who's telling you I'm paying these guys."

But Brad wouldn't tell Mike.

"You ain't going to tell me? Well, you'll tell me, or I'm going to beat the fuck out of you right now."

Mike threw him up against a wall, and I had to get in there and break it up. I think if I hadn't, Mike might have killed him. And Finfrock sat there the whole time and didn't say a thing. He didn't even move.

That's how contentious it got. It was really bad.

Finfrock was obsessed with catching us. He thought that Tim Grgurich was holding an illegal workout. It was the summer, so the players couldn't participate in supervised practices. Finfrock called the television stations and local sportswriters and told them to meet him outside the gym. Tim always locked the doors when he was working guys out so strangers couldn't come in. He was just that way. He didn't like anyone in the gym whom he didn't know. Finfrock got a key, and with the TV cameras rolling he opened the door, and everyone barged in. Tim was in there, but he was working out some of our former players— Armon Gilliam, Mark Wade, and a few others. Those guys always came back to Vegas in the summer because Tim was such a good coach. There were no current players so there were no violations because the NCAA doesn't care if an assistant coach is working out NBA players in his spare time. It embarrassed the shit out of Finfrock. The media that he had assembled to jump on us jumped all over him.

That didn't stop him, though. He installed a hidden camera in the rafters of our practice gym because we had set up a conditioning class with the team, which was legal, but Finfrock thought it was actually an offseason practice. They filmed Tim working out with the team, but there was no basketball. Tim knew the rules, and it stated that as long as no basketball is present, you could do various drills without a ball. Tim got a little carried away and rolled up a towel, and they passed that back and forth like a ball. But it was still NCAA legal. Finfrock didn't realize it was a towel on the film; he thought it was a basketball. He thought he got us. But he didn't. It was all just so ridiculous. It was no way to run a program.

The guy was unbelievable. He was just so petty. I dislike him more than I do Maxson. Maxson had a purpose in what he was doing. Finfrock was a nobody. He had been in charge of booking acts into the Thomas & Mack, and he used to have me speak to all of these different people when they would come to town. And I always did. I always did whatever he asked me to do. He'd always act like I was his friend. But he wanted the athletic director position so badly that he was willing to sell me and everybody else out. He was willing to kill the program. I have no respect for him. Ego is the one thing that brought us down.

Not that there aren't all sorts of theories as to why things changed. I had complete support in Las Vegas for 18 years, and then that last one, it changed. One of our state senators at the time swore we were done in by the casinos. We were the only school in the NCAA you couldn't bet on at a Las Vegas sports book. You could bet Maine versus New Hampshire but not a UNLV game. We were off of the board. I liked that because it helped me. The media always brought up gambling.

I always said, "Hey, you can't bet on UNLV games in sports books. But you can bet on UCLA and Duke and Arizona. Go talk to them about gambling."

The problem with us being so good was we were costing the sports books a lot of action. As long as we were in the NCAA Tournament, the entire NCAA Tournament was off the board—every game in the Tournament; not just UNLV games. At the time, the sports books didn't worry about the first couple rounds. But, boy, when you got to the Elite Eight and the Final Four, it was really big money. UNLV being good was costing the casinos. In the early 1990s as the casinos were bought out by corporations, the owner of the casino was no longer a local guy, a fan of ours. "He" was a group of businessmen back East.

These days, the first weekend of the NCAA Tournament is one of the biggest times of the year in Vegas. The casinos are packed. To get a seat at a sports book, you have to get there at the crack of dawn. Everybody sits, bets, and watches the upsets. It's a huge profit time for sports books, and when we were going to the Final Four, it wasn't there. I don't know if I believe that the casinos did me in or not, but it's interesting. Maybe it isn't a coincidence that UNLV has not won a single NCAA Tournament game since I left. And there's no question things turned on me in Vegas.

That's why when the hot tub photo ran, I knew it was time to give up. I knew that even if I could win and even if I could survive, it wasn't worth the fight. Things had changed in Vegas. The deal I made was to let me coach one final season, which I wanted to do because I really liked the kids we had. Then I would give up my tenure. We weren't eligible for the NCAA Tournament, but in 1991-1992, with five new starters we went 26-2. We lost at Missouri on December 14 and never lost again. My last two and a half months at UNLV, I didn't lose a single game. We ended the season on a 23-game win streak.

UNLV hasn't won more than seven consecutive games since.

28

The Pro Ranks

" That' s bad karma, and it' s going to bring you bad luck. "

—LOIS TARKANIAN

I never really dreamed of coaching in the NBA. It wasn't something that I really wanted to do. I wasn't against it, I used to listen when NBA teams called me, but I just wasn't obsessed with it. I loved the college game. I loved building a team, watching it grow together, and teaching the kids how to play. I loved practice. I never loved games. Games always had so much pressure, but practice was fun. I thought the NBA had too many games and too little practice. But then I got done in at UNLV, and I was so sick of the NCAA that I started thinking differently.

I got to be really good friends with the owner of the Philadelphia 76ers, Harold Katz. He used to come to Vegas a lot and stay at Caesar's Palace. I had been friends with Billy Cunningham, the 76ers great, and we'd always all go to dinner and go out for the night, stuff like that.

During the 1991-1992 season at UNLV, it was obvious I was not going to survive. Harold got a hold of me and asked if I ever thought about going to work for the 76ers as head coach?

"Yeah Harold, I'd love to come work for you."

We talked it over, and we had it all done. I was going to be the coach of the 76ers in 1992-1993, but we didn't tell anybody. I went to the Final Four in Minneapolis and thought I was going to Philadelphia. In fact, I talked to a lot of guys about what Philadelphia was like. I didn't tell them I was about to become the coach, I just asked about the players, the media, and the town. Then all of a sudden, I was in my hotel room with Freddie Glusman, my friend who owned Piero's, when Red McCombs, the owner of the San Antonio Spurs, called. He wanted to know if I'd be interested in the San Antonio job after the NBA season.

"Yeah, I'd like to talk to you about it."

The Spurs were playing the Lakers in Los Angeles a few days later, so he flew me, my son Danny, and Freddie to the game.

Afterward we went and had a bite to eat at the Marriott in Marina del Ray. I just thought we were going to talk about the job, you know, what kind of team they had, what my thoughts on coaching in the NBA were, and what his expectations were. But McCombs offered me the job on the spot. I had never even met the general manager. I started thinking, "You know, God, this is better than Philadelphia." The Spurs had David Robinson. They had Rod Strickland, who was a great point guard whom I really loved. And they had Sean Elliott, who was a great player. It was out West, and I thought that was better for me. So I accepted the job right then and there. I didn't hesitate.

Then I called Harold and told him I had taken the San Antonio job instead of Philadelphia. He wouldn't even speak to me. To this day, Harold won't speak to me, and I've tried to talk to him several times. It's one of my big regrets of my life, because I loved Harold. We had a great relationship, and I wish I had handled that situation differently or just gone to Philadelphia as I had agreed to. Lois was all over me for that.

"Jerry, that's not right. You gave your word to him. That's bad karma, and it's going to bring you bad luck."

I had no idea how right she was. Lois was convinced it would end badly. She didn't even move down from Vegas to San Antonio. She would come to visit for a while, but she wouldn't move. The whole time I was there, I lived in a hotel, the Marriott Riverwalk.

I went to San Antonio, and almost immediately things broke badly. What really blows my mind is the karma thing. During the summer Terry Cummings, who was the starting power forward, tore up his knee in a pickup game back in Chicago, and he was lost for the year. Willie Anderson, who was their starting two man, had surgery, but the doctors did it wrong, and they had to do it again, so he was out the whole year. Right off the bat, I lost Willie Anderson and Terry Cummings. That's bad karma.

I had never met the general manager, Bob Bass, when Red McCombs hired me. That was a mistake. You see, Bass was the interim coach because the Spurs had fired Larry Brown in the middle of the season. Well, Bass was a real fraud. He was the general manager, and he had never met me, so I don't think he liked that I had been hired. While he was the interim coach, he and Rod Strickland got into an argument and Rod challenged him to a fistfight in Denver in the locker room. He hated Rod Strickland.

When I had been hired, Red had said to me, "The most important thing to the team next to David Robinson is Rod Strickland. Rod's a New York City kid, and I hear that you do real well with New York City kids." That was one of the things he liked most about me. He thought I could handle Rod. So Red said, "I want you to get close to Rod."

The regular season had ended, and the Spurs were going to the playoffs. But it was already announced, press conference and everything, that I was the coach the next season. They just didn't want to throw me in at the end, so Bass continued to coach. The playoff series was in Phoenix, so I went with the team and I stayed in the team hotel.

The owner had told me to get close to Rod. So the whole time we were in Phoenix, I ate lunch with Rod Strickland; I laid by the pool with him; I sat next to him. Whatever. It was the playoffs, and Rod and I hit it off great. Rod called his college coach at DePaul, Joey Meyer, and told him how excited he was about me coming because we were going to run now, and he was going to have the ball. And I loved Rod. I thought he was a great player. He could get anywhere on the court he wanted. I began feeling good about the next season.

I was new to the NBA, though, so I was a little concerned. They had a summer league in Utah, like a developmental league. I wanted to get our team in there so I could coach because the rules are a little bit different, and I thought it would be great for me to call timeout and things like that. But Bass turned that down because he claimed we didn't have the money.

It only got worse from there. Strickland was making $1.2 million, and for the Spurs to re-sign him, they needed to make an offer of $1.6 million by July 1. But they didn't offer him a contract, which made Rod a free agent. I couldn't believe it. I had no idea that this would happen. I went right into Red's office and raised hell.

"You told me the most important guy on the team, other than David Robinson, was Rod Strickland, and now we don't sign him?"

"Jerry, Bob Bass says you can't win with Rod, that he's got a bad attitude," he replied. "I don't think anybody's going to touch him anyway."

They figured no one would take him because the word had leaked out he had tried to fight Bass. The Spurs thought they could get him back for cheap. But shit, the very first day, Portland signed him for $2 million. The very first day.

When I lost Rod, I was sick. I raised more hell with the owner.

"Don't worry, we have a $1.2 million to spend, we'll get you a point guard," he said.

I couldn't imagine getting one better than Rod, but I was still new, so I waited. They got me Vinny Del Negro, who had played shooting guard for Jim Valvano at N.C. State. The previous season, he had played in Italy. At the press conference, Bass introduced him as the best point guard the Spurs had ever had. I was thinking to myself, "Vinny Del Negro? I know he's a great shooter, but he's slow." I couldn't believe I had lost Rod Strickland for Vinny Del Negro.

Larry Brown called me the next day.

"Jerry, he's not a point guard. He's a two guard."

Then Al Menendez, who was a scout with Indianapolis at the time, called and said the same thing. So I went storming into Red's office again.

"Red, he's not even a point guard." I told him that Larry Brown had called me.

"Jerry, first thing you got to understand is Larry Brown may be your friend, but he doesn't want you to win here. Larry failed here. He doesn't want you to win. You've got to understand how the NBA works."

But Larry and I had been good friends for a long time, so I didn't think that was true. Then I told Red about Al Menendez.

"What does Al know? He's just a scout out there in Indianapolis. Look, you're going to have training camp, and if you're not happy with

him, we'll get you a point guard. I give you my word; we're going to get
you a point guard."

So I went along with it. We started camp, and I wanted to play
pressure defense because that was how I coached. I wanted to play hard
with pressure defense. But I had Vinny Del Negro and Dale Ellis as my
two guards. They were both good guys, but you couldn't get two slower
guards. I wanted fast guards, and I had two shooting guards who were
slow. It wasn't perfect, but we played okay. We went 6-2 in exhibition
games.

Our very first regular-season game was at Sacramento. One of the guys
on the team I loved was Antoine Carr, with whom I had a close
relationship. He was playing his ass off for me, but then he
hyperextended his knee in the first game. He missed nine games because
of the injury and was slowed for a long time after that. That really hurt.
We lost the game, too. My final 10 seasons UNLV we averaged a 31-4
record, and I agonized over every one of those losses, because they were
so rare. After we lost the opener, I was devastated. Then Sean Elliott
grabbed me.

"Coach, this is going to be a long season. You're going to have a lot of
these losses. You better get used to them."

That was the big difference between the NBA and college basketball.
The pressure to win and the team chemistry was so different. The one
thing I liked more about the NBA than college was that in the NBA I
took a nap every day.

When I went on the road with a college team, we always ate together,
breakfast or a pregame meal. You spent a lot of time together. In the
NBA, you get on a charter plane, you land at the airport, they have a bus
pick you up, they take your luggage, they check you into the hotel, and
they give you room keys. You go to your room; they bring the luggage
there. You don't see anybody. The only time I saw the players was when
we got ready to go to practice or shootaround, or for the game. We never
ate together. I didn't even see them. I used to go down to the lobby
because I figured I would run into somebody. But I never saw anybody.
They were all in their rooms. So I just started taking naps. Which was
nice, too, that kind of felt good, but it didn't feel like a team.

When we did have practice, especially after a loss, I would really want
to get everything figured out. I'd want to really work hard. But the first

thing David Robinson or somebody would say, "Don't forget, we play tomorrow. Don't forget we've got a game tomorrow." That was their favorite saying. In college, you got three or four days between games, so you could really get after it. That was the difference. I liked the NBA fine. I really feel that I could have adjusted to it. But it *was* an adjustment.

Red did do one thing for me. He got me J.R. Reed after Antoine Carr hurt his knee. I had been playing Sidney Green, who was still my guy all of these years later, and Larry Smith at the forward positions. But Larry Smith had just come off of knee surgery, so he was about half speed. We had David Robinson as the center, of course.

When we got J.R. Reed, I called Red and sent him a nice letter.

"Now that we've got J.R. Reed, if you get me a good point guard, we could play with anybody in this league," I said.

Then Vinny Del Negro broke his nose, and he had to play with some headgear on. But he couldn't see real well laterally. I loved Vinny, but he couldn't have too many setbacks, because he was a shooting guard, not a point.

I tried to get a point guard because I wanted Vinny to play the two and Dale Ellis to be his backup. I wanted to get a quick point guard who could guard the ball. The problem was I wasn't the general manager, and the general manager did not want me to win. I had a deal worked out for Bimbo Coles, but Bass killed it. I had a deal for Mookie Blaylock in exchange for a first-round pick, but Bass killed that. He said, "Well, we can't give that much up for Mookie."

I brought in Lloyd Daniels to be a backup for us, and he played pretty well in exhibition games. He cost us a game at Portland when he missed a layup with about 20 seconds to go. But other than that, he was pretty good. I thought he could have been very good, but he wasn't as good as I had once envisioned because he had been so heavily into drugs. After he left Vegas, he really had hit rock bottom. He had even been shot three times, once in the neck. He was clean by the time he came to the Spurs, but you know it wasn't the same once he had been through what he went through. He had put all of those drugs in his body. It shows how good a player he was that even after all of that he could still play in the NBA. But he wasn't the answer.

Maybe my biggest mistake was we had signed Avery Johnson about 15 games into the season. Avery had the quickness I liked, but Bass told me that he couldn't guard anybody. He said that people went around him all of the time, and I wanted a guy who could guard the ball. So I listened to what Bass said and didn't pay much attention to Avery. But in practice, I loved the way he played. We were about to go on a four-game road trip, and I was going to play him and see how he did in the game. But his mother grew extremely ill, and Avery couldn't go on the trip. If I had had him from day one, I probably would have liked him, because if you look at all of my college teams, they were always best when I had a point guard who didn't shoot a lot. So I blame myself, because I should have taken a better look at Avery from the start. I should have realized the point guard I was looking for was right there.

I tried to get Gary Grant, whom nobody in the league wanted. I was the only guy who wanted him, because I had tried to recruit him out of high school, and I had followed his career in Michigan. He was a great defensive guard. He was quicker than hell. But Bass killed that, and Gary Grant wasn't even that good. That's how bad it got. And that's when I got fired.

I was so frustrated with Bass that I went to Red.

"Hey, man, every time I try to do something, Bob Bass is killing it."

"Let's have a meeting tomorrow," Red suggested.

So I went to the meeting, and I thought we were going to work something out.

"Jerry, do you think we can win with what we have?" Red asked.

Our record was 9-11, but we were in every game. We got beat by Houston twice in the last seconds. Twice Sean Elliott missed wide-open shots that he could have made. Sean was in a shooting slump that I knew wouldn't last because he was such an incredible shooter. I mean it was just like we were snake-bit.

"No, I don't think we can win. I have got to have a point guard."

"If you don't think we can win with what we have, I'm going to have to replace you," he responded.

I thought he was calling my bluff, I mean, we were 9-11 with a ton of injuries.

"Look, if you're not getting me a point guard, I'll be glad to have you relieve me. I'll be glad." I thought this would show Red how serious I was about needing a point guard and because of it we would get one.

But sure enough, Red looked at me and said, "OK."

And then he fired me.

He paid me off; I had a three-year deal, but to a guy like Red, that was not that much money. I never thought he'd do it because he and I had a good relationship. I liked him. He said in the press release that he never questioned my ability to coach in the league. He said that if I didn't believe that I could win with the players that we had, then there was no way that we could win.

I would have liked another shot at coaching in the NBA, because I always felt that I never had a chance to do what I could do. I have always envisioned that you could win if you could get a team to play hard and play good pressure halfcourt defense. I believe that in the NBA the two things you've got to do is defend the pick-and-roll and rotate out of the double team. I would have had half my practice time allotted to those two things. I think that I could have done something in the NBA. But I never really had a chance to do it.

It really frustrates me when they talk about college coaches struggling in the NBA and they include me. I thought, considering the circumstances, we were doing a hell of a job. I thought if we had kept Rod Strickland, we would have played the Chicago Bulls for the NBA championship.

Lois was correct, though. It was bad karma. If I had gone to Philly, at least I would have had a whole year. Jimmy Lynam had just gotten fired as coach, but they had made him the general manager there. He and I were real close from all of our old Nike trips. Jimmy would have been good with me. Bass had never met me; he never wanted me. I was forced on him. He had nothing to do with hiring me. I sealed my fate before I even started.

29

Beating the System

« Jerry, I never in my life dreamed that there could be an organization this crooked existing in this country. »

—*JERRY TARKANIAN'S ATTORNEY*

n 1998 the NCAA had to pay me $2.5 million for violating my
rights. If you want to know why, all you need to know is this story:
The NCAA was investigating us at UNLV in 1977. I didn't trust
them because they had made up a bunch of stuff about my program at
Long Beach State. Now they were back trying to get me, and they decided
to interview Rodney Parker, who was a playground coach in New York.

Rodney was a great guy. I first met him when we tried to recruit a six-
foot-nine forward named Rudy Jackson from Brooklyn. We recruited
Rudy hard, but he went to Wichita State. He made a visit to UNLV,
though, and the NCAA claimed we did some illegal things with Rudy.
But Rudy and Rodney Parker denied it. The problem was Rodney Parker
had been featured in Rick Telander's book *Heaven Is a Playground*, which
was about a lot of New York playground legends. In the book, Rodney

was portrayed as a middleman who matched up kids and schools. He probably put 40 or 50 guys in schools, people such as Fly Williams and Lloyd Free. That's how recruiting was back then, because scouting was primitive, and you didn't have things like the ABCD All-America camp. Both players and coaches relied on people like Rodney to match them up.

I thought Rodney was great to help all of those city kids get college scholarships. But because of the attention he received in *Heaven Is a Playground*, I guess the NCAA thought he was a bad guy.

And so they were convinced we had done something with Rodney to get Rudy Jackson—even though we didn't even get him. UNLV had an internal investigation and asked Rodney all sorts of questions, and he denied anything against the rules had gone down.

The NCAA wasn't satisfied, so they sent one of their investigators, David Berst, to interview Rodney. Berst had it out for me. Once he called me a "rug merchant" because of my Armenian heritage. That's the kind of guys the NCAA hired. I let that go, but his investigation was unbelievable. He questioned Rodney for an hour, but he didn't tape the interview and he didn't take notes. He came out and reported Rodney had said the UNLV internal investigators asked questions in a "general manner" so that he wouldn't reveal any violations. Berst then accused us of covering up the truth and paying for Rodney to attend the Dapper Dan Roundball Classic in Pittsburgh, both major violations.

But what Berst didn't know was that Rodney secretly tape-recorded the conversation. On the tape, Rodney never said UNLV asked questions in a "general manner," never said we tried to cover up the truth, and said he went to the Roundball every year and paid his own way. Rodney said we did nothing wrong. On the tape, Berst even complimented UNLV for trying to dig and get the truth. What Berst had reported was said in the interview was the exact opposite of what the tape revealed.

In the middle of the 1977 NCAA Tournament, my attorney and I flew to NCAA headquarters in Kansas City. We requested a supplemental hearing because we wanted to play this tape to show Berst was lying, not us. The NCAA granted us the meeting.

"Boy, we got them now, there's no way they can deny it," I said. "I mean it's all on the tape."

We went to that meeting, and my attorney said he wanted to play the tape. The NCAA hadn't expected this and didn't know what to say. They sent us out of the room so they could discuss it.

When they called us back, they said, "You can't play the tape because David Berst is not on trial, UNLV is."

They refused to listen to the tape or read the transcript of the tape. My attorney tried to argue, but they wouldn't have it.

"You are going to take David Berst's word for it when we have proof that he's lying?" my attorney asked.

And they just kept saying that David Berst wasn't on trial.

We were about to be found guilty of violations because of what Berst had lied about. But we couldn't defend ourselves with the truth. That tape would have eliminated the entire case against us. We would have been cleared of all charges. But they didn't care. They wouldn't let us play it.

I was crushed. My attorney said, "Jerry, I never in my life dreamed that there could be an organization this crooked existing in this country." I was really depressed, but he said we would eventually just kill them in court. He said UNLV would be found guilty of the charges by the NCAA because the investigation was a fix. But once we got into a real court, no one in the country would allow this. And he was right. Eventually, we did kill them in court, because everything they did back then was against the law. The NCAA thought it was above the law.

All you need to know about the NCAA is Berst got promoted after our deal.

It was always like that with them, though. We had another charge that was hard to believe. In 1973 we had a player named David Vaughn, who had transferred in from Oral Roberts and was sitting out a year as a redshirt. Hale McMenamin, who was as bad as Berst, was the NCAA investigator. He reported a UNLV professor told him that he gave David Vaughn a B in a class that Vaughn rarely attended because I told him to do it. McMenamin claimed the professor said that because I was one of the most powerful figures in town, the professor thought if he didn't give him the B, he could lose his job. Well, first of all, what professor would admit he did such thing, even if he did it? That's about the surest way to lose your job if you are a tenured professor.

When the professor found out that was what the NCAA reported, he went nuts. He contacted the NCAA committee, but they wouldn't even listen to him. So he went and hired his own attorney and gave a sworn affidavit that he had never told McMenamin anything of the sort, and in fact had said the opposite, that David Vaughn earned his B. His attorney contacted a dozen or so students in the class, and all of them said David Vaughn regularly attended class. They said they were positive of this, because he was seven feet tall and difficult to miss. Then we found out that while Vaughn got a B in the class, the average grade in the class was an A-minus. The professor was an easy grader, so a B was one of the lower grades. Most of the kids in the class got an A. The professor then took a polygraph, repeated everything, and said McMenamin had made the entire thing up. The professor passed. Then he took a voice analysis test, which was a new technology then, said all of the same things again, and passed.

We took all of that information to the NCAA appeals committee, and they voted against us anyway. They said McMenamin was telling the truth, not the professor or the students, no matter what the polygraph said.

We had lots of other examples just like this. It was crazy. How in the hell are you supposed to fight this stuff? The investigator makes up charges that didn't happen, supports it with testimony the witnesses refute, and the NCAA won't let you find out what you're accused of, by whom you are accused, or why until they rule you're guilty. Then, when you prove everything is a lie in the appeals process, they say it's all true anyway. It was like dealing with the Gestapo.

Those NCAA investigators were so corrupt it wasn't even funny. Actually, it was occasionally funny, because they were easy to mess with. The first time McMenamin came out to Vegas I had an assistant coach named Lynn Archibald. Lynn happened to be at the airport when he spotted McMenamin and wondered why he was in Vegas. So Lynn followed him. The first place McMenamin, this supposedly honest and forthright NCAA investigator, went to was one of these porno movie theaters. That was Hale McMenamin for you.

After he started investigating us, Lynn decided to screw with him and sent McMenamin a little letter saying that the movie theater was going to have some new films coming in and he thought McMenamin might want to know so he could stop in there on his next visit to Las Vegas. We wanted to let McMenamin know we knew where in the hell he had been.

Looking back, that probably didn't help our cause or make us any additional friends at the NCAA. But it was pretty funny at the time.

I admit I also smiled on April 2, 1998, when the NCAA agreed to pay me $2.5 million for violating my rights during a 26-year battle. They admitted they had made findings against me without any evidence and that I never received a fair hearing. They had to admit it was wrong and they were wrong about me. They cut me this big check and had NCAA president Cedric Dempsey issue the following statement:

"The NCAA regrets the 26-year ongoing dispute with Jerry Tarkanian and looks forward to putting this matter to rest. Obviously, Jerry Tarkanian has proven himself to be an excellent college basketball coach, and we wish him and his family continued success for the remainder of his career. We know that this dispute has caused distress for all concerned. We sincerely hope that by resolving this conflict, wounds can begin to heal.

"The issues raised by the case brought by [C]oach Tarkanian have contributed in a positive way to changes in the NCAA enforcement procedures. and we are pleased that we can all move forward with a clean slate."

To me this was total vindication. It couldn't have gone better. It wasn't even about the money. I was the coach at Fresno State then, so Lois and I donated $100,000 to the Fresno State library. It was about being proven correct. The NCAA had to revamp its investigative techniques. They started tape-recording their interviews so the investigators couldn't just make stuff up. They allowed more due process. They were more forthcoming with evidence. They changed a lot of things. I believe that was my greatest contribution to college basketball. The sport is a better place because of that.

What pissed me off was we had taken all of this heat and bad press through the years from what the NCAA had lied about us. The press killed me for decades, and I said all along that I would be proven correct. But then when I was, they just ran these little stories buried inside the paper. We didn't get all of these front-page stories when we won the lawsuit. It was incredible to me how little attention it got in the media. The NCAA investigated us for seven years, and they didn't come up with one single major violation. Not one. After all that time. They had to pay me $2.5 million. They had to admit they were wrong. The president of the NCAA had to issue that statement. And it barely got any attention at all.

30

Not-So-Perfect Homecoming

"**As soon as the NCAA could find any chance of getting in, they came in. That chance at Fresno State turned out to be a $3.40 bowl of rice.**"

—JERRY TARKANIAN

A fter everything that went down at UNLV and in San Antonio, I had no intention of coaching again. I had retired and was very content with my life. I spent time with my family, which I had never been able to do as a coach, because a coach is always busy—always recruiting or speaking somewhere. I did color commentary on USC games on TV. I did a few Clippers games, too. I judged the Miss Hawaiian Tropic Pageant twice a year. I had a lot of fun at those. I had a radio show in Vegas that was getting really big. During the basketball season, I went and sat in on practices of other coaches and offered advice. I did a lot of speaking engagements around the country. I was very happy.

I had a speaking engagement set up in Fresno for late March 1995. It had been scheduled eight months earlier and was set for a Monday. The Wednesday before, Fresno State fired its coach, Gary Colson. A reporter from Stockton, California, called and asked if I would be interested in the job.

"You know, I never thought I'd coach again," I said, "but that's one job I might be interested in."

The story ran, and I started getting all sorts of calls from alumni, community leaders, and friends of mine. It just steamrolled. The whole Fresno community started pushing for me. I had always loved Fresno State and Fresno. It was my alma mater. It gave me a chance when I was just a kid from Pasadena who probably didn't deserve one. When I went there as a student, the whole town was small, but I had a great time; I loved it. Then right out of college, I got my first job at San Joaquin Memorial High School. I always returned for fundraisers. I always felt like I owed them. As it turned out, a lot of the kids I coached during my two years there had become community and business leaders in town.

On Friday, the people at San Joaquin called and asked if I could come up Sunday, a day early, to help with a fundraiser. When I got there, all of the talk was about me becoming the next coach at Fresno State. The next day at the speaking engagement, I drew the luncheon's biggest crowd ever. More people came to hear me than had come to hear President Ronald Reagan speak a few years before.

Even though I was very happy not coaching, I got caught up in all of the excitement. Lois kind of liked it, because she was a Fresno State graduate and her parents still lived in Kerman, a small farming community outside the city. Danny was a practicing attorney, but he wanted to get into coaching. At first I was against it, because I knew how tough the business was. But then I thought he could be my assistant at Fresno State, and it would be a good way for him to get into it. I thought we could win enough that he could succeed me as head coach.

There was also just something about the people in Fresno. In Vegas, people made money in real estate and they made money in gaming. There's nothing wrong with that, but it's different in Fresno. People there worked like hell for their money. They were farmers. They were blue-collar people. They were really solid. There's nothing flashy about them; there's nothing flashy about Fresno. The city is about a four-hour drive from both Los Angeles and San Francisco, out in the San Joaquin Valley. It's in California, but it feels more like the Midwest. I just felt at home there. And that attracted me.

Fresno State had gotten into the Big West during the final eight years I had been at UNLV. Whenever we went up there to play, the people lined up all night to get tickets. It was a big event. I looked at Fresno a little like I once had looked at Las Vegas. I knew we could be the professional team in town. We would be the town's team and get a lot of support. And we did. The fans chartered a plane to all of our away games because so many of them took off work to go to the game. I don't know any school in the West that did that. I was kind of excited about going up there. I thought we could win. I decided I wanted to coach again.

The reaction was incredible. Fresno State is a school that survives off of the community. People were so down on Gary Colson that the athletic department was expecting a $2 million budget shortfall. When I got there, not only did they *not* have a $2 million shortfall, they had a $1 million surplus. We saved a bunch of the Olympic sports from getting cut.

The reaction around the country was positive, too. I thought recruiting would take some work, but right away, we started getting calls from players who wanted to play for us. I had accepted the Fresno job and was at the Final Four when I ran into my old friend, Perry Watson, who is now head coach at the University of Detroit.

"Who's still out there in the Detroit area we can recruit?" I asked him.

He told me about Terrance Roberson, a top-25 recruit and a swingman from Saginaw, Michigan. He said he didn't think Michigan or Michigan State was going to take him. Terrance had been great as a sophomore, but his junior and senior years he had had some hassles with his coach. He also would have to sit out one year because he didn't have great grades. Perry wanted him at Detroit, but he didn't think he could get him. He said Terrance was probably going to go to UMass, which had just been to the Final Four, or Florida State.

Perry gave me Terrance's phone number, and I called him right then, with Perry standing next to me. This was the first time I talked to him, but Terrance was excited.

"You know, Coach," he said, "when I was a kid, I was watching a UNLV game and I pointed at you on TV and told my grandfather I am going to play for that man one day."

He visited us right after visiting UMass, and he committed. Just like that we had a top-25 recruit.

One of our local writers asked him, "What is it you like about Fresno?"

"I don't like anything about Fresno. I didn't even know there was a Fresno. I just want to play for Coach Tark."

At the same time, I got a call from Chris Herren, who had been a McDonald's All-America point guard from Fall River, Massachusetts. Chris was a tough kid, and he had gone to Boston College out of high school but got hurt and got in some trouble. He was looking to transfer. It took about two phone calls and one visit, and he committed to Fresno State. It was unbelievable. He had to sit out a year because he was a transfer, but he was a heck of a player. Within a couple weeks, we had two top recruits signed up.

Recruiting was so easy, it turned out to be fool's gold.

I had always been a very hard recruiter; I got to know everyone around a player, his parents, coaches, friends, and girlfriends. I got to know them real well. I could judge their character. But at Fresno, good players just called us up and wanted to come. It was so easy; I just got lazy. I was older, and I didn't like to travel the way I used to. So I started signing players I barely knew. As a result, I took some kids I never should have taken. I thought they would all turn out to be good kids, but they didn't.

That first year at Fresno, 1995-1996, was one of the best years I ever had in coaching. I had Terrance and Chris sitting out, and I brought in two other guys who weren't that good. I inherited a team that had really struggled the season before, but it did have one really good player, Dominick Young, a five-foot-nine guard out of Chicago.

The previous staff told me to get rid of Dominick because he wouldn't be eligible. Then my athletic director, Gary Cunningham, told me I had to worry about Dominick and that Dominick was doing this and that. Everyone was down on Dominick. I didn't know what to think, so I finally went to the player, because I wanted to hear his side.

"Dominick, Gary Cunningham told me all of this stuff."

"Coach, I'm sick of Gary Cunningham. Tell Gary Cunningham to stop saying things about me, or I'm going on ESPN and telling that the previous coaching staff got me 52 junior college credits in one year to be eligible here."

I went and told Gary that, and his face changed colors.

We wound up having a great year. We beat Michigan State. We beat Utah twice, including up there when they were ranked No. 8 in the county. We beat Oregon. It wasn't a very talented group, but they played hard. Dominick Young won about five games for us at the buzzer. He was incredible. He was always on the borderline of causing us trouble, but he was great that year. We lost in the Elite Eight of the NIT to Nebraska, who went on to win the tournament. Every game was a sellout. I just loved that year. I thought I would continue to enjoy it.

That was when the road got rocky. One difficulty we had was rival recruiters using my age against me. Obviously I wasn't going to coach forever, so people told recruits I was about to retire. Actually, they said stuff a lot worse than that. In 1996 we recruited a six-foot-11 center named Souleymane Wane who was originally from Senegal but was attending a prep school in Troy, New York. It got down to Connecticut and us.

That is when an administrator at the school told us that one of the UConn coaching staff had said I was dying of cancer and Souleymane shouldn't sign with Fresno. It was unbelievable, I wasn't sick at all, but UConn said that to get the kid away from us. *The Fresno Bee* even did a story on it—talked to people at the school and everything.

The cancer story worked, too, because Souleymane signed with UConn. Now that was a pretty tough way to lose a recruit. I had seen some stuff in my career, I had been in some battles, but I had never even heard of something like that. But I really like UConn coach Jim Calhoun; he is a great guy. Things just get out of hand sometimes. All I can say is they must take that Coaches versus Cancer thing seriously back East.

Even without Souleymane, in 1996-1997, we had Terrance, Chris, and a juco kid, Damon Forney. I thought we were really going to be great. But then Dominick, who had won all of those games for us the year before, lost his focus and really hurt us a lot. He didn't play well.

We played the greatest schedule in school history. I stuck with my thing at UNLV: We'll play anybody, anytime, anywhere. We wound up having 13 consecutive road games. Only an idiot would play 13 consecutive road games, but I thought it was a good idea at the time. We had some great wins—we beat UMass by 20 back East—but we were up and down. At home, though, we had the place rocking. Toward the end of the season, we were playing very well. We beat Wyoming at our place,

but late in that game, Dominick was at the free-throw line and shot an
air ball.

The Fresno Bee picked up on it and said there was point shaving.
Supposedly, Dominick was point shaving. But they held the story until
the morning of our first-round WAC tournament game. If we had won
that game, we would have gotten a NCAA Tournament bid. We had
really been on a roll, but when that broke, it really demoralized the whole
team. At shootaround before the game, everyone was reading the
newspaper instead of practicing. We weren't mentally into it, got upset by
TCU, and wound up back in the NIT.

The Fresno Bee never let up on the point shaving. The FBI and a
federal grand jury investigated the allegations, but no charges were ever
filed. I knew several people who ran the sports books back in Vegas, and
they called me and said there was no point shaving going on with our
games. They said the sports books were the first people to know about
point shaving, because if a game is getting fixed, the line shifts. If a team
is supposed to fail to beat the spread, people will bet that way, and the
sports books will notice. This was when Arizona State had been caught in
a point-shaving scheme, and the sports books said it was obvious, because
all of the money came in on one side. But they said with us, there was no
increase in betting.

So then The Fresno Bee said it was point shaving but for a small
amount of money. That was ridiculous. Why would anyone go through
the trouble of fixing a game if you weren't going to make any money off
of it? I guess guys were throwing games for a grilled cheese sandwich or
something.

That was when everything got difficult for me. After I had beaten the
NCAA in 1998 and they were forced to cut me a check for $2.5 million
and got humiliated nationally, I thought they would never come after me
again. But I was naïve. With the NCAA, every time I beat them, they just
got madder and madder. Not even a federal judge or a $2.5 million check
would stop them.

As soon as they could find any chance of getting in, they came in.
That chance at Fresno State turned out to be a $3.40 bowl of rice. The
father of a Fresno State softball player had a restaurant in town, and he
fed the softball team, football players, and all sorts of athletes. Many
athletes could go in there and get a free bowl of rice. No one really cared;

it was just some kids getting lunch. Then the NCAA heard a couple of my players had had some rice, and in they came to investigate. Everything went downhill from there.

The NCAA came in and interviewed 12 of our 15 players, many of them repeatedly and often for hour after hour. They would just keep asking them questions over and over, trying to catch them in lies. We complained about the way they questioned these kids and the tactics used. It was crazy. It was all over a bowl of rice that no one denied had been eaten.

Fresno State's president was John Welty, who was basically a good guy. He had me over to his house, and we had a good relationship. But when the NCAA came in, he thought if he was nice to them, they'd be nice to him. But that never happens. When the NCAA questioned a kid, the school made him ineligible until the investigation was over. That was terrible, because even when the kid was cleared, he had already been forced to sit out for nothing. They suspended everyone for all sorts of little things. For a few years there, we had to lead the country in suspensions.

In 1998, I thought we'd have a great, great team. I still had Terrance and Chris, and I had brought in Tremaine Fowlkes, who was a good forward from the University of California, and Rafer Alston, a playground legend from New York who went by the nickname "Skip-to-my-Lou" because of the way he dribbled. I thought we would be like my UNLV teams. But then Chris tested positive for drugs, and that really hurt us. We put him in rehab, but I still thought I had enough players to win.

I had agreed to let Fox Sports Net follow my team around all year for a documentary. I thought it would be a good idea, because the players knew cameras were on them. But several of our players screwed up anyway. I had four guys test positive for marijuana that year. It really hurt us. We looked bad. What made it worse was that Fox Sports Net was supposed to show the documentary once the next year. But the NBA went on strike, and Fox Sports Net had nothing to show. So instead of NBA games, it kept replaying our documentary all over the country. It was terrible. That was a mistake.

I supported the marijuana suspensions because I thought it would set the tone that if you smoke, don't come to Fresno. The problem was no other athletes were getting suspended. My players were saying they were getting the marijuana from the football players, but they were the only ones getting suspended. They kept saying it was unfair.

I was in favor of the suspensions, but I didn't want it in *The Fresno Bee;* I wanted to just say a player was suspended for "violating team rules." That way no one got hurt.

But when I was hired there was a real battle going on between the women's teams and the men's teams over gender equality. The men and the women in the department were fighting nonstop.

(I had wanted to get along with both sides. I said right off the bat that we were going to go out of our way to get along with the women's basketball program. And we did. We had a great relationship with them. Any time there was a conflict over gym time—say we both wanted to practice at the same time—I would take my team somewhere else. We'd practice at high schools around town, junior highs, anywhere. Once we even practiced at the Armenian Church. We were in the top 20 and practicing in junior high facilities. But we wanted a good relationship with the women.)

But then came the marijuana suspensions. And every time we had a meeting our AD Al Bohl would say, "OK, I don't want this getting out to the press and hurting the kid." Then the next morning it would be in *The Fresno Bee.* Every time. We started suspecting people in the women's athletic department were leaking it, but it turned out that was wrong. It was a guy named Scott Johnson, who was the assistant athletic director. That really turned us sour on him. Then Bohl who was a good guy, left for Kansas, and they promoted Scott Johnson. I knew we were in trouble then, because he was such a miss-fit for the job.

Maybe my biggest mistake at Fresno State was taking a player named Avondre Jones. Avondre was a real talented six-foot-11 center from Artesia High School in California, which is where the O'Bannon brothers went. He was going to have come to UNLV if I had stayed there, but because I was gone, he had gone to USC after a real heavy recruitment. He didn't pan out at USC, though, and they got rid of him. Then he played a year for my son George, who was coaching Chaffee Junior College at the time. He wasn't very consistent, but a lot of schools recruited him again—and he wound up going back to USC. Then they dropped him again.

I should have known right then not to take him; I mean USC let him go twice. But Avondre was from a good family, and I liked them a lot. His mother called me and said I was the only one who could get all that talent out of him. So I took him and redshirted him. He was going to play one season for us, but he was just a problem from day one. In 1998, after we beat Memphis in the NIT, he got into an argument with a friend of his, and he pulled out a samurai sword. The cops arrested him, and because it was such a wild story, it made national headlines, "Fresno Player Uses Samurai Sword." Eventually Avondre was found innocent of all of the assault charges, but he was found guilty of a weapons possession charge. Avondre always said he and his friend were just playing, but the damage was done. It really hurt us. If there was something I could do over again, I wish I had never recruited Avondre Jones.

Even with all of the off-court stuff and the NCAA hounding us at Fresno, we had things going pretty well. We reached the NCAA Tournament in 1999-2000 and were led by Courtney Alexander, who led the nation in scoring. Then in 2000-2001, we had our best team. I had Tito Maddox, a really good point guard from Compton; Chris Jefferies, who was a six-foot-eight kid from Fresno and had transferred from Arkansas; and Melvin Ely, a six-foot-nine big man from outside Chicago, who was our best player. We went 26-7, but we drew defending national champion Michigan State in the second round of the Tournament, and that was one team we could not handle.

The next year we had almost everyone back, and we had added some other good players, so I thought my 2001-2002 team would be my best. I told my friends that I thought we were a potential Final Four team. But the NCAA did not want that to happen. They screwed with us nonstop.

We lost Tito Maddox right off the bat. Tito had put his name in for the NBA draft before taking it out because he wasn't going to be picked high enough. But while he was in the draft, a friend bought him a plane ticket to go to El Paso to see his girlfriend. When he took his name out of the draft, he didn't repay the friend. The NCAA ruled that an "extra benefit," and he was hit with an automatic six-game suspension. I didn't have a problem with that. That was the rule, and he broke it. But the university was trying to get on the good side of the NCAA, so it decided to dismiss Tito from the team for violating the rule. There was nothing I could do about that.

I still thought we could be good because I signed a point guard from Brooklyn named Chris Sandy. I just loved that kid; however, the NCAA made him ineligible because his family minister back in Brooklyn had paid for one of his correspondence courses. The minister had done that for hundreds of kids, but Chris was suspended anyway. The NCAA screwed with that kid nonstop. He had been suspended, then returned, then played his best game when we beat nationally ranked Oklahoma State and he scored 23, only to be suspended again the following Monday. He played only 16 games for us.

We still started the season well. We made the preseason NIT Final Four and beat USC and Michigan State; we were a pretty strong team. But then everyone started getting suspended. The one I felt worst about was Melvin Ely, who was such a great kid and just a really good person. But from the day he got to Fresno, the NCAA hounded him. They interviewed him on seven different occasions for more than 30 hours, looking for anything they could to suspend him. They just dug and dug.

Melvin was the best player we ever had at Fresno State, and he never had a car. He was there five years, and he rode a bike; a six-foot-nine guy on a bike. He must have been the only All-American in the country without a car. He played on a summer team that went to China with all of these other college stars, and he came back and said everyone had money and cars. Melvin didn't have anything. Then he came back, and the NCAA was asking about everything, and he told them to go look at some other schools. The poor kid could never get on track. They finally suspended him for eight games, because without his knowledge, a friend of his got a free hotel room in Las Vegas. Melvin didn't even stay in the room. And his friend stayed in the Budget Suites; it wasn't like he was at the Bellagio. My son Danny, who's a lawyer, was my assistant coach then and researched it, and it was the only time in NCAA history a guy was suspended because of something one of his friends did.

It was just an awful season. The NCAA ruined all of the fun. You can't build a team when guys are always getting six- or eight-game suspensions. You can't build continuity. I never felt we were a well-coached team. I didn't enjoy watching us play except for that first year. Plus that was the year Scott Johnson became the athletic director. He wasn't ready for the job. He never returned calls. He leaked stuff to the newspaper. He was always lying. He really didn't know how to tell the truth. It was the damnedest thing. You had a meeting and came out not knowing what to believe. You knew he was lying when his lips were moving. If he ever took a polygraph, he would have gotten electrocuted. If he said good morning, you turned your car lights on.

I usually got along with my athletic directors, but he was just a misfit. It was difficult enough beating our opponents. But we were having more trouble within our own school. He told us to do one thing, then we did it, and then he said we shouldn't have done that. So what I thought would have been one of my best years turned out to be my most miserable. We finished 19-15, only my second season as a college coach when I didn't win 20 games. It was also my last year in coaching. I was so glad to get out at that point because I wasn't having any fun.

My time at Fresno State was the most difficult coaching time of my life, because I got so frustrated with the distractions. I honestly do not think I had a chance to be successful. You can't win unless the players have pride in the program. And because of all of the suspensions, we couldn't develop that pride. I went there as the winningest coach in college basketball history and came out about fifth.

The one thing we did get accomplished at Fresno State was getting the Save Mart Center built. Even John Welty said that never would have happened without me. If I could have just gone there, built them an arena, and not even coached, it would have been better for me. But the Save Mart Center, a brand new 16,000-seat on-campus arena that is as nice as anything in the country, is incredible. It is really great that Fresno State and the city of Fresno have it. And I'm proud that I helped get it built.

I just wish I could have put better teams in it.

Afterword

I n life we are given choices that will determine our path, we are never sure of the outcome of those choices or whether that path will lead us to accomplish our goals. But if given the proper advice and guidance combined with a work ethic and desire, at least one has the possibility of fulfilling those goals and ultimately making something productive with one's existence.

When I was asked to write the afterword for this book, I really struggled to come up with what to say about Coach Tarkanian. He has meant so much to me and to so many others that it would seem obvious why he is revered by all of us who played for him. However it's not just that simple.

There are a lot of coaches who can coach the game of basketball, but this is not about the game it's about *you* and your journey through life and where so many who have played for him (myself included) have had to come from. The hardships of being poor, dealing with racism, coming from broken homes—these are real and a lot of us have this story to tell.

This is the life we've lived and who we are. It's not the path we chose, it is the one we were given. Now we are all trying to take these negative experiences and use them as fuel to take us places that we've only dreamed of going.

I asked myself why, why do we love him so much? Why are we so loyal to him? Yes, we've become a part of his family, but it goes beyond that.

The real reason is so many of us identify with Coach is because we are very much like him! It doesn't matter if you're black or white, Muslim or Christian, American or Armenian. The majority of us who played for him were never the best at what we did, but we still believed that we could be.

Coach was just like us. He had to earn his respect and do more with what others perceived to be less ability. His life was a constant struggle with adversity and hardship and what we respected is he never gave in to it or accepted someone else's path for him. I mean here's a man who never gave up.

When you think of what a coach looks like or the kind of background he is supposed to come from, Jerry Tarkanian does not come to mind. He just doesn't look like a guy who understands athletics even if he understands it better than almost everyone. He wasn't a famous player. He never tried to overdress or be anything that he wasn't. As a result people have taken one look at him and decided he must not be a great coach. They don't understand or appreciate what kind of coach he is. I played 11 seasons in the NBA, I know great coaching, and Jerry Tarkanian is a great coach. The fact he isn't in the Hall of Fame is a joke.

When he was at UNLV, he dealt constantly with NCAA interference and not getting fair shake with media. It was like an extra opponent his teams had to deal with. But all of these were issues he always overcame. That constant struggle he went through was recognized by his players, many of us who were minorities, came from difficult backgrounds, or were not highly recruited because we didn't fit the traditional definition of a player.

That is a powerful example to set for a young man who has to face his own demons in a society where oftentimes people have made up their minds about who you are and where you're going before they ever get to know you. Coach was a role model for us and that gave a young man two of the most important assets he could ever have—hope and opportunity.

Coach was never prejudiced when so many others were. He saw beyond race and background and even past actions to try to see the good in a young person. That is rare. America is supposed to be the land of opportunity, but a lot of young people, because of the environment they grew up in, do not have the same opportunity as others, mainly because of the educational system. Those kids start at a disadvantage. You would think our country would be more apt to a give second chance to a young person, but instead it is the exact opposite.

When so many others wrote those guys off, Coach was willing to give them an opportunity to turn their lives around.

Sometimes it didn't pan out. But for many, myself included, it did. Thank God Coach did not allow some failures to stop him from seeing the good in kids and give them a chance to make something of their lives. Society needs those kinds of people because a lot of us wouldn't be where we are if he hadn't gone against the grain and accepted the adversity and criticism that came from it.

When you think of coaching on the collegiate level, it's really the last opportunity for a coach to have a profound impact on young people's lives. A coach at this level can give guidance that will give young people an opportunity to achieve the goals that they've set for themselves. He can give them confidence that can stay with them forever.

This is what Jerry Tarkanian did for me and the countless others who have played for him throughout the years. So often it's about the lessons that we learn and the examples that are set; for so many of us who played for Coach he was as much an influence as anyone else in our lives.

That is a powerful statement to make, but when you grow up without a father, as so many of his players did, and you can identify with someone who has traveled a similar path and overcome the odds and defied the critics, it makes you proud and it gives you a foundation to maybe one day influence others the way you've been influenced and make a difference in someone's life.

Jerry Tarkanian is a man in every sense of the word.

Coach, I just want to say thank you for all you've given to me. I am forever grateful for the lessons you've taught me and continue to teach. You are a winner and I'm proud to call you a friend.

—Greg Anthony
September 6, 2005
Miami Beach, Florida

Epilogue

I've been asked to reflect on what basketball has meant to me and what place it now holds in my life. It seems that even today the things that I enjoy most, other than my family, pertain to basketball. A lot has happened in basketball since this book was first written: the NCAA has made some positive changes: "mega" conferences are being formed; the tournament itself has changed; and more and more players are leaving college after only one year.

And much has remained the same, including: the importance of making more money off of the sport (obvious in some of the decisions made by those in control). Also, investigative inequities still exist. But that's not to say the NCAA isn't trying. March Madness and college basketball are more popular than ever, and I greatly enjoy the athleticism on display and the pure love and enthusiasm of the fans and players.

Because of my interactions with the NCAA, as horrible as they were to live through, some very good changes have been made in the NCAA investigative procedures. Do they need to make more changes? Yes. But at least they are moving in the right direction. In fact, this very year, NCAA president Mark Emmert stated that the organization is going to review the rules and regulations because they are "simply far too complex." And he's supporting a package of sweeping rules changes to address these issues. He is going after what he calls a "common sense" approach. This is what I've been hoping for and talking about since the 1970's.

I've been told the NCAA is making changes for stricter guidelines on academics for athletes. In general, this sounds good, but it makes me think that we have to be careful in how far it goes. I remember the old Prop 48 rules, which set minimum grades and standardized test scores that student-athletes needed to meet in order to be eligible to compete in college athletics. Walter Byers, head of the NCAA at the time, stated many times that if a player could not meet qualifications and fell into the Prop 48 area, he could never graduate. Byers felt very strongly about that. Well, many Prop 48 players did go on to graduate from many different colleges. Two of my Prop 48 players from two different teams graduated and went on to eventually coach and teach at Division I universities. We cannot take the opportunity to go to college away from young men and women whose incentive may be playing the game, but who use that interest to matriculate with a degree. This is true particularly for a lot of kids from lower socio-economic families who may not have any other opportunity to go to college, to move themselves up in the world, to become successful. And why should sports scholarship holders have to meet higher requirements than those who receive other types of scholarships?

Schools are changing conferences, losing some great rivalries. I don't like the idea of so many schools in one conference. I like the idea of competition and rivalry in each conference. In addition, in a time of economic concerns, I don't see the reason why we would have teams in competition with schools across the country on a league basis. For preseason tournaments—that is, once-in-a-while—ok. But for league competition there is too much time lost for the student traveling and too much money that perhaps could be spent more wisely somewhere else. It comes down to money, without the best interests of the kids, taking precedence.

The caliber of college players has changed. The really great ones leave early for the NBA. I have been asked my thoughts about these 'one and done' players, and personally, I do not like it. I understand each player has to make a decision based on his or her particular situation, but I still don't like it. Kids should enjoy the total college experience. They need time to mature as a person and as a ball player. These kids have so much pressure on them, and not necessarily only from their coach, but also from their families and friends who are all relying on the player to take care of them. The problem is, so few players actually make it big in the NBA.

A lot of mid-major schools are making deep runs in the tournament each year. There are great players and great coaches at every level. I think it is good to mix it up and not have the same perennial powerhouse schools in the Final Four year after year. It adds excitement, people root for the underdog. Yet adding even more schools to the tournament will not improve it, but is just another revenue source for the NCAA and the networks. Never has the "64th" ranked team beaten the number 1 ranked team—yet quite possibly the winner of the NIT might.

They have great high school tournaments in Las Vegas, especially in the summer, bringing a lot of college coaches to scout the players. I will go to the games and meet up with some of my coaching buddies to watch the games and then we all go out to dinner. We spend the night rehashing old stories and telling some new ones. It is really special to continue this coaching fraternity. It warms my heart when some of the coaching greats and the up-and-coming coaches come tell me how I have been an inspiration to them in some way or another. Some even ask for coaching tips. It is great to see the coaches who were young and just starting out when I still was coaching and how successful they have become.

This year, a new Las Vegas high school basketball tournament, The Jerry Tarkanian Classic, was inaugurated. This is a big honor to have a tournament named after me. I am proud and excited. They had some of the top high school teams in the country attend. It was really well-planned and presented at Bishop Gorman High School. I'll be looking forward to see how it grows. I'm told they are already getting calls from top high school teams that want to play in it next year.

This year is the 75th anniversary of the NCAA tournament. March Madness has become big all over the world. Great to see! The Final Four is in Atlanta this year. Atlanta was the site of my first final four. I have some great memories of that time, but also some painful ones. We almost beat North Carolina, losing by one point. North Carolina went on to win the championship. We were ahead until the end of the game when our center, Larry Moffet, had his nose broken and had to leave the game. Tony Smith shot a 3-pointer to bring us within one, but we lost. To this day the remaining members of that team cannot forget that one-point loss. We were so in awe of the Final Four, just so pleased to be there, that it didn't hit us until years later how much the lost opportunity really meant. We were so new on the scene, mostly all junior college kids. We were the only team at the Final Four without a band. Our school was less than 20 years old. It did show the country, however, that UNLV was a school to be reckoned with. It was an amazing experience not just for me and my team, but also so much so for the fans that traveled with us. You work so hard just to get to a Final Four. I don't think people realize how hard it really is to get there. I'm extremely grateful for having been there as often as I was and for all the team members and coaching staffs that got us there. Their hard work and motivation were unmatched.

I am extremely proud to see UNLV back in the national spotlight with my former players coaching. Dave Rice has done a great job with the team; recruiting outstanding players and handling all the pressure very well. He brought Stacey Augmon in as an assistant. Stacey was so good on defense as a player that you can see his influence on the team. He added Kreigh Warkentien (she is the daughter of Mark Warkentien, who was one of my assistants) as director of operations. We're still a close bunch. It's good to see many other familiar faces that are still with UNLV today.

These past few years, I've had several opportunities to meet again with my former players. I'm so proud of them all. My first college group at Riverside City College is still close. It's hard to believe that some of the kids who came by bus from Detroit to Riverside with only ten dollars in their pockets and worked cleaning dirty dishes while playing ball are now strong and proud professionals whose children have attended and graduated from schools such as California at Berkeley, USC, Colorado, and Air Force. When those children tell me how much I meant to their dads, it puts everything into a very positive perspective. And I can say the same thing about Pasadena, Long Beach and UNLV.

I have loved basketball my entire life and it is still in the forefront of things I enjoy today. Even though I no longer coach the game, I enjoy it greatly. I don't miss the games, but I do miss the practices, the strategizing, the camaraderie, the companionship, and the love and determination among us all. It's an experience rare to find.

There were great highs and deep lows at times, but it's worth it to not rank, as Theodore Roosevelt said, among those timid souls that know neither victory nor defeat.

Appendix

Career Breakdown

Overall (38 years)	988-228 (.813)
Major College (31 years)	778-202 (.794)
Junior College (7 years)	210-26 (.891)

Individual Schools

Fresno State (7 years)	153-80 (.657)
UNLV (19 years)	509-105 (.829)
Long Beach State (5 years)	116-17 (.872)
Pasadena City College (2 years)	67-4 (.944)
Riverside City College (5 years)	143-22 (.868)

Year-by-Year Records

FRESNO STATE

2001-2002	19-15	(NIT First Round)
2000-2001	26-7	(NCAA Second Round)
1999-2000	24-10	(NCAA First Round)
1998-1999	21-12	(NIT First Round)
1997-1998	21-13	(NIT Semifinals)
1996-1997	20-12	(NIT First Round)
1995-1996	22-11	(NIT Quarterfinals)

UNLV

1991-1992	26-2	
1990-1991	34-1	(NCAA Final Four)
1989-1990	35-5	(NCAA Champion)
1988-1989	29-8	(NCAA Elite Eight)
1987-1988	28-6	(NCAA Second Round)
1986-1987	37-2	(NCAA Final Four)
1985-1986	33-5	(NCAA Sweet 16)

1984-1985	28-4	(NCAA Second Round)
1983-1984	29-6	(NCAA Sweet 16)
1982-1983	28-3	(NCAA Second Round)
1981-1982	20-10	(NIT Second Round)
1980-1981	16-12	
1979-1980	23-9	(NIT Fourth Place)
1978-1979	21-8	
1977-1978	20-8	
1976-1977	29-3	(NCAA Final Four)
1975-1976	29-2	(NCAA Sweet 16)
1974-1975	24-5	(NCAA Sweet 16)
1973-1974	20-6	

LONG BEACH STATE

1972-1973	24-2	(NCAA Sweet 16)
1971-1972	23-3	(NCAA Elite Eight)
1970-1971	22-4	(NCAA Elite Eight)
1969-1970	24-5	(NCAA Sweet 16)
1968-1969	23-3	

PASADENA CITY COLLEGE

1967-1968	32-3	
1966-1967	35-1	(California Junior College Champion)

RIVERSIDE CITY COLLEGE

1965-1966	31-1	(California Junior College Champion)
1964-1965	31-5	(California Junior College Champion)
1963-1964	35-0	(California Junior College Champion)
1962-1963	32-3	
1961-1962	14-13